The Business Marketing Course

The Business Marketing Course
Managing in Complex Networks

David Ford

Pierre Berthon
Stephen Brown
Lars-Erik Gadde
Håkan Håkansson
Peter Naudé
Thomas Ritter
Ivan Snehota

JOHN WILEY & SONS, LTD

Chichester • New York • Weinheim • Brisbane • Singapore • Toronto

Other Wiley Editorial Offices

John Wiley & Sons, Inc., 605 Third Avenue,
New York, NY 10158-0012, USA

WILEY-VCH GmbH, Pappelallee 3,
D-69469 Weinheim, Germany

John Wiley & Sons Australia, 33 Park Road, Milton,
Queensland 4064, Australia

John Wiley & Sons (Asia) Pte Ltd, 2 Clementi Loop #02-01,
Jin Xing Distripark, Singapore 129809

John Wiley & Sons (Canada) Ltd, 22 Worcester Road,
Rexdale, Ontario M9W 1L1, Canada

Library of Congress Cataloging-in-Publication Data

Ford, David, professor.
    The business marketing course : managing in complex networks / David Ford
       p. cm.
    Includes bibliographical references and index.
    ISBN 0-471-87722-0
    1. Marketing. 2. Marketing–Management. 3. Business networks–Management. I.
Berthon, Pierre. II. Title.

    HF5415 .F566 2002
    658 8–dc21

                                    2001056905

British Library Cataloguing in Publication Data

A catalogue record for this book is available from the British Library

ISBN 0-471-87722-0

Typeset by Mathematical Composition Setters Limited, Salisbury, Wiltshire.
Printed and bound in Great Britain by Biddles Ltd, Guildford and King's Lynn.
This book is printed on acid-free paper responsibly manufactured from sustainable forestry,
in which at least two trees are planted for each one used for paper production.

The IMP (Industrial Marketing and Purchasing) Group was formed in 1976 by researchers from five European countries. The group's first work was a large-scale comparative study of industrial marketing and purchasing across Europe. Results from this study were published by John Wiley in 1982, edited by Håkan Håkansson, under the title *International Industrial Marketing and Purchasing: An Interaction Approach*. The group's "interaction approach" is based on the importance for both researchers and managers of understanding the *interaction* between *active* buyers and sellers in continuing business *relationships*. The group has since carried out a large number of studies into business relationships and the wider networks in which they operate. This work is published in numerous books and articles. A selection of this work can be seen in *Understanding Business Marketing and Purchasing* (Third Edition), edited by David Ford, International Thomson, 2001. *Managing Business Relationships*, also by David Ford and a team of IMP authors, was published in 1998 by John Wiley & Sons, Ltd. This book encapsulates the teaching, research, consulting and writing experience of the IMP Group. The group hosts an international conference in September of each year which attracts a large number of researchers working in the areas of business marketing, purchasing and inter-company networks.

CONTENTS

Notes on the Authors

David Ford is Professor of Marketing at the University of Bath in the UK.

Pierre Berthon is Professor of Marketing at Bentley College, Boston, USA.

Stephen Brown is Professor of Operations at the University of Bath, School of Management.

Lars-Erik Gadde is Professor of Industrial Marketing at the Chalmers University of Technology, Gothenburg, Sweden.

Håkan Håkansson is Professor of Industrial Marketing at BI, the Nordic School of Management, Oslo, Norway.

Peter Naudé is Professor of Marketing at the University of Bath, School of Management.

Thomas Ritter is Associate Professor of Marketing at Copenhagen Business School, Denmark.

Ivan Snehota is Associate Professor at the Stockholm School of Economics.

PREFACE

This book is intended to provide the basis for a course on business marketing for students on undergraduate or MBA courses. We also hope that it will be useful for managers wishing to understand what happens in business markets and to improve their skills in analysis and strategy development.

The book is firmly based on the ideas of the IMP (Industrial Marketing and Purchasing) Group. The group is an informal network of researchers who have spent many years trying to understand what happens in business markets. The group has carried out a wide range of studies over the past twenty-five years into business marketing and purchasing and this research has formed the basis for countless courses, management seminars and consulting projects.

However, this book is different from most others in the area in at least two ways: first, we did not want to produce a long, heavy, expensive "textbook" that students taking a relatively short option in business marketing would be unlikely to buy. Or if they did buy it, they would be unlikely to read it. Therefore, the book consists of just ten chapters that deal with what we believe are the critical issues that students need to understand. These chapters correspond approximately to the ten or twelve sessions of a typical option.

Second, and more importantly, we have tried to write a book for students based on our view of the reality of business marketing. We believe that business marketing is not just something that a supplier does *to* its customers. It is something that happens *between* a supplier and each of its customers, as they search for and find each other, meet and negotiate, assess each other, make deals, develop offerings, deliver them, monitor their use, develop them further, and so on.

Both supplier and customer are actively involved in this *interaction*. Both of them have problems that they try to solve by dealing with each other. This interaction takes place in a *relationship* between the customer and supplier that may last for many years. Some of these relationships will be vital to either or both of the companies involved. Others will be just one of many hundreds or thousands that make up the company's *portfolio*. But whatever their size or importance, each of these customers has to be understood and each of these relationships has to be *managed*.

We believe that managing customer relationships is the critical task of the business marketer and this book concentrates on describing this task. The book begins by describing what happens in business marketing and helps readers to understand how it is different from what they may have been taught on an introductory marketing course. We then introduce two aspects that distinguish business marketing and provide major challenges for marketers. The first is that it is not enough for marketers just to try to understand and work with their customers. Instead they must understand what happens in the wider *network* that surrounds them and both constrains their operations and provides opportunities for growth. Second, business marketing is based on the skills or technologies of the supplier (and of the customer). Chapter 3 shows how a marketer can make sense of the skills and technologies of his or her own company and of customers, as the basis for developing an offering to solve customers' problems. In Chapter 4 we look at the problems of customers in more detail and show how these lead to the strategy that different customers are likely to adopt in their supplier relationships.

Armed with this understanding of technologies, networks and customers, Chapter 5 is intended to show students how to manage customer relationships. A business supplier solves its customers' problems through a complex *offering* consisting of a number of elements such as product, service, adaptation, advice and logistics. Getting the offering right is critical to business success and Chapter 6 deals with this question. But a supplier's offering is little more than a promise to solve a customer's problem and this is of no use to the customer, unless the promise is actually fulfilled. How a company can fulfil its promises accurately and on time is the subject of Chapter 7. Marketers often make promises to their customers, but their actual fulfilment depends on many other people working in the supplier's operations. Marketers must understand these operations if they are not to make the wrong promises and if their promises are to be fulfilled.

Business marketing is about making profits and, in order to achieve this, marketers have to understand the costs of their own operations and those of their customers and the value to the customer of their offerings and their relationship. Chapter 8 reveals this knowledge and enables the reader to develop a pricing strategy for their offerings and their relationships.

The final two chapters in the book take a somewhat wider perspective. Chapter 9 looks at how the nature of business marketing and customer relationships are changing as customer requirements shift and information technology alters the way they operate. Chapter 10 then tries to bring together many of the ideas in the book to show how marketers can develop a strategic focus to their work.

At the last count there were eight co-authors associated with this book. This reflects the fact that no-one can ever really claim ideas as their own. Because many of us have worked with each other for so long, then what little we do know is largely held in common, rather than being ours alone. We are also very grateful for the research and ideas of many others, including our students, who have also contributed greatly to this book and to the continuing work of the IMP Group.

Writing a book together is a pleasant social process and a good way to learn from each other, even though it is dramatically inefficient in terms of time. I hope that my co-authors have also enjoyed this process. We all hope that readers will also gain as much from it as we have.

Note on the text

We have varied the use of he and she throughout the text when discussing the business marketer as, obviously, business marketers can be female as well as male.

UNDERSTANDING BUSINESS MARKETING AND PURCHASING

Aims of this Chapter

- To point out the particular characteristics of business markets and business customers and to explain the similarities and differences between consumer and business markets.
- To explain the *problems* and *uncertainties* that business customers face, the *solutions* that they seek and why they choose the *offerings* of particular suppliers.
- To highlight the critical task of the business marketing company as the management of its *relationships* with customers and others and to make a first examination of these relationships.
- To explain how each business relationship is part of a complex *network* of relationships.

The first three chapters in this book discuss ways for the business marketer to understand the complex world in which he has to operate. This understanding will then form the basis for later chapters in which we deal with the tasks facing a marketer. This first chapter will introduce many of the key terms and concepts that we will use throughout this course.

Introduction

We all know the efforts of companies that try to encourage us to shop in their stores, eat in their restaurants or buy their brands of chocolate bars, insurance policies or cars. We are familiar with the way that these companies package together a combination of product and service in the hope that they will meet our requirements. We spend time reading their brochures or looking in their shop windows. We compare prices and try to judge the relative value of offerings from different companies, before parting with our money. We see their advertising, designed to excite our curiosity or make us identify with the people and lifestyle that they portray. We talk to our friends about the marketing skill of these companies. We are all "experts" in consumer marketing!

But each purchase that we make is the culmination of a vast array of business activities that are not so easy to see and are carried out by many companies, often unknown to us. It is through these activities that products and services are developed, designed, produced, bought, sold, delivered and combined to make up the offerings that are finally marketed to us. This book is about those activities and, in particular, about how marketing takes place *between* these companies. This is business marketing and it has many similarities to consumer marketing:

- Both consumer and business marketing are profits-oriented.
- Both are parts of a single process that leads to a purchase by a final consumer.
- Both require companies to develop and tailor their skills and resources to satisfy customers' requirements.
- Both involve attempts by companies to influence the behaviour of customers.
- Both must be based on an understanding of customers' problems and motivations.

However, we will see in this book that business marketing is also different from consumer marketing in a number of ways. These differences are because of the particular problems of business customers and the ways in which they try to solve them. Most students of marketing take up jobs in business marketing and therefore need to understand its special characteristics. Business marketing is more complex than consumer marketing in many ways and thus it can be more challenging for those who work in or study it. But an understanding of business marketing can also help students to a better appreciation of the realities of market behaviour and marketing in general.

The main task of this chapter is to provide a foundation for understanding business marketing. We will not attempt to do this by looking at what happens *inside* a marketing company and examining its problems and the ways it can plan and operate. Instead, like all good marketers, we will start by looking *outside* the company at the reality of the surrounding world and the network of companies on which it depends for its success. This analysis will give us an idea of the scale and complexity of business markets. It will also help us to avoid the common marketing problems that follow from looking at the world solely as a set of people that might be persuaded to buy the products that we are selling. Such an approach leads to a very distorted view of those people and their real problems and requirements and ultimately is less likely to be successful.

In this analysis we will also see that business marketing is not just a set of easily learned techniques that can be applied in a mechanical fashion. Instead, it is a complex process of understanding the network of companies around us and working *with* customers, suppliers and sometimes even with competitors, but also sometimes working *against* them, *through* them or *in spite of* them.

The Nature of Business Markets

Let us start our analysis with the example of a single company that is thinking of buying a major software package. This potential customer will try to evaluate the offerings of a number of potential suppliers. Each is likely to be different from the others. Even if the functionality of their software is similar, each may offer a different level of service, or more immediate availability. These differences in offerings will occur because the suppliers have different abilities, or want different types of customers, or want to gain different things from each sale that they make. The customer will also evaluate the suppliers themselves, as well as their offerings, to find out if they will tailor their offering to its particular requirements, or if they just provide the same to everyone. Because the purchase is important, the customer will also want to check if the suppliers are likely to be a source of future development and whether each supplier is likely to "stand behind" its offer and sort out any problems that may arise.

Similarities and differences between business and consumer purchases

There are some clear similarities between the way that this customer company buys and the way that individual consumers make purchases:

- Both the company and consumers will be affected by their previous experience with different suppliers and both will bear in mind the possibility of any future purchases of similar products.
- Both will need reassurance if there are aspects of the purchase that they cannot assess for themselves. Both will seek advice from specialists, colleagues or friends if the purchase is difficult or complex.
- Both will agonize over some issues they think are important and over some that are unimportant and both will disregard some of each.
- Both will make some of these issues explicit, but others will be only implicit and hence much harder for a marketer to see.
- Both will also make many simple, repetitive purchases with little or no evaluation.
- Both will make purchases when their main concern is to minimize the amount of time that is involved.

But if we look closer, there also seem to be some differences between this business purchase and many consumer purchases. For example:

- **A number of people are likely to be involved in a business purchase:** These may be from different levels in the customer's hierarchy and from a number of functions, such as operations, finance, marketing or purchasing. Each individual will have their own concerns about a purchase, about such things as how reliable the software will be in use, how it will add to the performance of the company's own products or how expensive it will be to buy. Some of these people may provide information to others about possible suppliers, some may evaluate different offerings or suppliers, others may fix the maximum price that the company is prepared to pay. Some may advise on what should be bought, while others take decisions based on that advice. The business marketer must identify who is involved in the purchase, where they are located, what are their interests and how he can reach and influence them.[1]

The number of people involved means that business purchases are often much more complex than those by consumers. But we should also remember that many important consumer purchases, such as a new car, or even a pair of shoes that are apparently made by only a single person are often influenced by others, such as friends or family.

- **The people involved in a business purchase are professional:** Trained individuals with the job title of "buyer" are often involved in making business purchases, sometimes alone and sometimes with others. But in a major software purchase, the potential users of the software may be most involved and most concerned with what is bought and from whom. In this case the professional buyer may simply be the person who places the order after these others have decided what they want. In some cases there may be a formal procedure for making purchases, but in other cases the process may be quite informal and it will be difficult for a marketer to see what is happening or who is involved.

  However, the difference between the skill and "professionalism" of business and consumer purchasers is not clear-cut. In the software case, the company may be making a major purchase of software for the first time and those involved may be rather intimidated by the process. They will be far less self-confident or "expert" than those consumer buyers who are experienced buyers of products that are important to them, such as when a keen cyclist buys a new bike.[2]

- **A business purchase may take a long time from the moment when the issue is first raised till final delivery:** How long a business purchase takes will depend on many factors, such as the complexity of the customer's requirements; the importance or value of the purchase; the number of different interest groups involved in the purchase and the level of their knowledge and the help and advice that previous suppliers can provide.[3]

  All these factors would be important when buying a major business operating software, just as they would be in the purchase of a gas-fired power station by a company that had previously only used coal or when an airline was thinking of outsourcing its aircraft maintenance to a contractor. In contrast, many other business purchases for low-value, high-use products or services, such as printing paper or car

[1] Attempts to model both the process of business buyer behaviour and the involvement of different individuals and functions can be found in FE Webster and Y Wind, A General Model of Organisational Buying Behaviour, *Journal of Marketing*, vol. 36, no. 2, 1972, pp. 12–19 and Wesley Johnston and Thomas V Bonoma, The Buying Center: Structure and Interaction Patterns, *Journal of Marketing*, vol. 45, no. 2, 1981, pp. 143–56.

[2] For a discussion of the different buying motives of business buyers, see Jagdish Sheth, A Model of Industrial Buying Behaviour, *Journal of Marketing*, vol. 37, October 1973, pp. 50–6.

[3] For a model of the stages in the business buying process and how they vary in different circumstances, see Partick Robinson, Charles Faris and Yoram Wind, *Industrial Buying and Creative Marketing*, Boston, Allyn and Bacon, 1967 and Richard N Cardozo, Modelling Organisational Buying Behaviour as a Sequence of Decisions, *Industrial Marketing Management*, vol. 12, February 1983, pp. 75–81.

rental are made instantly by a computer from the previous supplier when stocks reach a certain low point, or the item is needed.

Consumer purchases can also take a long time, such as when someone changes their car. It may be a couple of years from when the consumer first thinks that their current car is getting past its best to the time when they actually purchase a new one.

- **In many cases each business customer is individually important to a supplier and responsible for a significant proportion of its total sales. Similarly, each supplier can be individually important to a customer:** If the customer in our example of the software purchase was a large corporation, then the loss of the account would be a disaster to the supplier. It would be a similar disaster for a customer to lose a software supplier on which it had relied for handling all its operations. An even more extreme case of dependence occurs in commercial aviation, where there are only two main suppliers of airliners and only a few dozen major customers.

In contrast, other businesses have many *individually* unimportant customers. For example, Federal Express provides deliveries for thousands of small businesses. Many business marketers face both situations simultaneously. They have a small number of large customers and a large number of small ones. For example, the major multinational engineering company, ABB has 100 customers that represent 60 per cent of its total sales and 39 000 that account for the remaining 40 per cent.

In the consumer case, each customer is usually relatively unimportant to a supplier, but a single supplier can be very important to a particular customer. Many people buy almost all of their food from a single supermarket or completely furnish their house from Ikea.

- **A business purchase or sale is not an isolated event**: Every purchase will be affected by the previous experience of both customer and supplier, with each other and with others. Each transaction will also affect the future dealings between the companies. Because of this we say that business purchases occur as part of a *relationship* between customer and supplier. Many business relationships are complex. There is often frequent interaction and information exchange between the two companies, involving a number of people from different functional areas on both sides. Business relationships are often long-term and require both customer and supplier to adapt a number of aspects of their activities.

Consumers also have continuing relationships with supermarkets, fashion stores and producers of everything from cars to coffee. When they need to make a particular purchase they are likely to go to the supplier with whom they have a good relationship. Consumer marketers try to cultivate these relationships using the techniques of "Relationship Marketing".[4] However, the interactions between consumers and their

---

[4] For a description of ideas on Relationship Marketing see Kristian Moller and Aino Halinen-Kaila, Relationship Marketing, Its Roots and Direction, *Journal of Marketing Management*, vol. 16, nos 1–3, 2000, pp. 29–54; JN Sheth and A Parvatiyar, Relationship Marketing in Consumer Markets: Antecedents and Consequences, *Journal of the Academy of Marketing Science*, vol. 23, no. 4, pp. 255–71. Francis Buttle, *Relationship Marketing: Theory and Practice*, London, Paul Chapman, 1996, and E Gummesson, *Total Relationship Marketing*, Oxford, Butterworth-Heinemann, 1999.

suppliers are likely to be *one-way*, from supplier to customer by impersonal media such as mail-shots. Consumer marketers are also much less likely to make adaptations to suit particular consumers. Although recently many of them have tried to develop the idea of "mass customization" to more closely tailor their offerings to customer requirements.

A Definition of Business Marketing

These similarities and differences lead us to the definition of business marketing that will form the basis of this book:

> Business marketing is the task of selecting, developing and *managing* customer relationships for the advantage of both customer and supplier, with regard to their respective skills, resources, technologies, strategies and objectives.

Each business relationship has to be managed by a marketing company:

- whether it is individually critical to the company's survival;
- whether it represents a major part of the company's total sales or purchases or whether it is only one of thousands of similar relationships;
- whether it is friendly or antagonistic, close or distant, complex or simple.

This definition has a number of implications for the way that we think about business marketing and purchasing:

- The unit of analysis for the business marketing manager cannot be a single purchase or sale, or project or deal, or sales territory or market, but each relationship that forms part of his total *portfolio of relationships*.
- It is not possible to make sense of a single business purchase or sale by looking at it in isolation, but only within the context of the relationship of which it forms part. Each transaction both affects and is affected by that relationship.
- Business relationships are a company's primary assets. Without them it cannot buy, sell, produce or deliver products or services. The development of relationships requires investment of time, money and resources and the marketer's task is to maximize his company's benefits from those relationship investments.
- Business relationships develop, integrate and exploit the skills, resources and technologies of both the supplier and the customer. Relationships link the activities of the companies, tie their resources to each other and form bonds between individuals from each company.
- Business marketing involves many relationships, each having different actual and potential benefits to the supplier to each customer. Some relationships may be highly profitable, others generate a high volume of business. Some may lead to new technological developments or provide access to other companies, others are individually unimportant, but together are a useful source of business. Together they constitute the company's relationship portfolio and we will examine the tasks of portfolio management in some detail in Chapter 5.

- Business purchasing is a very similar activity to business marketing. Business buyers have to choose suppliers on the basis of their own resources and skills. They often have to persuade them that they are a "good" customer. They have to develop their relationship with them, often they have to train them. They have to manage and exploit them on the basis of their own interests and those of their suppliers.
- The similarities between business marketing and purchasing emphasize a critical difference between much of business marketing and consumer marketing. Consumer marketing is a relatively one-sided activity carried out by active selling, seeking a reaction from a passive buyer. But business marketing is a process of *interaction* between two active parties.

Box 1.1 on pp. 15–16 shows a letter from a customer to a supplier who has failed to appreciate the importance of good relationship management.

Are Close Relationships Always a Good Idea?

It is important to emphasize at the start of this book that a company should not aspire to having close, complex or long-term relationships with all of its customers or suppliers. The issues involved in this choice are as follows.

The case for close relationships

Close relationships between customers and suppliers enable them to learn about each other and to adapt to each other's requirements and to benefit fully from each other's skills and resources. These relationships involve the investment of both time and money. It is unlikely that companies will be able to benefit from dealing with each other, or make a return on their investments *in just one transaction*. Therefore the two companies are likely to invest in a long-term relationship. A company in a close relationship may also have fewer uncertainties because it can plan on the basis of its knowledge of the supplier's good and bad characteristics. It also avoids the risks and costs of constantly having to deal with new counterparts – "better the devil you know".

The case against close relationships

Learning and adapting often take a long time and are expensive. In many cases neither customer nor supplier would gain great benefits from this investment. Instead they may benefit more from being able to "shop around" for their requirements as they arise. In this case a customer may choose to deal with suppliers only as and when necessary, in a series of discrete transactions. Similarly, a supplier may sell to a series of customers without investing in a relationship with any of them or in adapting its offering. Limiting its investment in a relationship means that a customer is less dependent on that relationship and thus avoids the risks of tailoring its operations to a particular supplier's way of thinking. It also maximizes its freedom to deal with other companies.

For example, well-developed, long-term relationships benefited Japanese industry in the 1980s. But it has been suggested that these close relationships prevented the rapid restructuring in Japan that was such a feature of the high-growth performance of US industry in the 1990s. In the USA, more open, competitive supplier links are the norm.

Throughout this book we will argue that business marketers and their customers must constantly re-assess their relationships and manage each one according to its individual benefits and in line with their overall aims, rather than using any standard approach or formula. We will also see in Chapter 9 that changes in business marketing and specifically the growth of the Internet are introducing new types of companies into networks and fostering innovative relationships, thus encouraging this diversity of approach.[5]

Relationships, Markets and Networks

We have already described how the things that consumers buy are the end products of a vast range of business activities. These activities are carried out in the relationships between many companies. But none of these relationships exist in isolation; each of them is intimately linked to others in a network. Any one purchase can both affect and be affected by these other relationships. Understanding what happens in a business network is essential for success in business marketing and we can start to develop this understanding by returning to our example of the company that is considering making a software purchase. Figure 1.1 shows this customer enmeshed in a network of relationships.

The software customer will not evaluate competing suppliers of software and their offerings in isolation. Its views will also be affected by its relationships with other companies as well. These other companies may include equipment, component and services suppliers, advisers, financiers, distributors, customers and development partners.

Suppose the company buying the software is a producer of hospital equipment. It will use a large number of components and materials from a range of suppliers in its production. The customer may discuss the software purchase with its main component suppliers so that the new software will be compatible and enable them to co-ordinate deliveries and reduce inventories. In turn, these component suppliers' relationships with their other customers may well be affected by the new ways of working that they develop with the equipment maker.

Business networks are not neatly structured lines of companies, designed and managed by a customer into "supply chains". Instead, they consist of a very wide range of companies, each of which simultaneously has numerous relationships with many suppliers

[5] For a discussion of the problems of close relationships, see H Håkansson and I Snehota, The Burden of Relationships, in Peter Naudé and Peter Turnbull, *Network Dynamics in International Marketing*, Oxford, Elsevier Science, 1998.

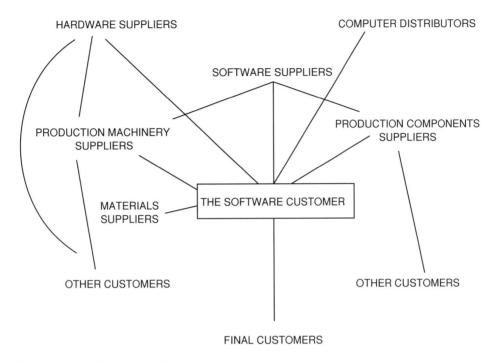

Figure 1.1 A simple network.

and customers. Nor can business networks be divided into neat categories of "manufacturers" who sell to "distributors" who, in turn, sell to "retailers", etc. Instead, any one customer in the network is able to choose between a wide variety of suppliers that operate in a variety of ways and offer different benefits to the customer. These different relationships and the benefits and obligations that arise from them together constitute a company's *network position*.[6] For example, our software customer may have a well-developed relationship with a computer distributor that it uses for the supply of its personal computers. This supplier may offer a standardized package that is much cheaper than the offering from a software house that can be tailored more closely to the customer's requirements. The customer may also have worked closely with a computer hardware company in the past and this company may offer the customer a solution that it previously developed for one of its other customers. The software purchase may have been suggested by some of the customer's own customers that have been concerned about its lack of flexibility in meeting their individual equipment requirements or delivery schedules. The need to "rescue" these relationships may be an important factor in the customer's software purchase. The software customer will also have relationships with

[6] An interesting study of network position is provided by Barbara Henders, Positions in Industrial Networks, unpublished doctoral thesis, University of Uppsala, 1992. See also G Easton, Industrial Networks, A Review, in B Axelsson and G Easton (eds), *Industrial Networks: A New View of Reality*, London, Routledge, 1992, pp. 1–27.

suppliers of other types of equipment. It may need to take these into account when making its purchase.

This example indicates the complexity of business networks. A network consists of a number of individual markets, such as the market for components, the market for operating equipment, the market for the customer's own products and of course the market for the software itself. Business marketers cannot restrict their attention to the immediate market for their offerings. Instead, they must understand what is happening in the wider network and how this will affect their own operations and those of their customers. We will explore the analysis of business networks in Chapter 2.

What (and Why) Do Companies Buy?

The answer to the question of *what* companies do buy is that they buy lots of things. Some of these are similar to those bought by consumers and some are different. For example, they buy cars, components, raw materials, nights in hotels, machinery, delivery and cleaning services, advertising, advice, accounting, insurance and toilet rolls.

But if we ask a manager *why* he has chosen a certain supplier for a particular purchase, then we may get a wide variety of answers. A first response may be, "I want the best quality". If we probe deeper then the manager may say that he has chosen the "most trusted supplier", or the "most versatile service", "the highest performance", "highest specification", "longest lasting", "most up-to-date", "most consistent", or that he wants "best value", "highest technology" or simply "reassurance".

A manager may say that he always buys from the same supplier, because this particular purchase is important to him and he dare not risk a change. But another manager may use the same supplier each time because that particular purchase is not important to her and she does not want to take time to think about it. Another might say that what really counts is not how good a product is, but how convenient it is to get hold of it.

This variety of answers tells us quite a lot about business marketing:

- Different customers can buy the same physical product or service for quite different reasons.
- "Quality" can mean many different things to different customers in different circumstances and the term is meaningless unless carefully defined in each context. We will return to the problem of managing quality in Chapters 6–8.
- We cannot make sense of the reasons for a customer's purchase by describing the physical properties of what it bought, or even by asking the customer why it made the purchase.

But we do need to make sense of why companies really buy if we are to be able to develop and provide something to satisfy their requirements. To do this we have to look behind what customers obviously buy and what they say that they are seeking. In doing this we will introduce some more of the language that we will use throughout this book. The terms we will use are illustrated in Figure 1.2.

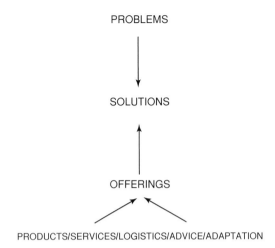

Figure 1.2   **What do companies buy?**

Problems

A customer's problems are the starting point for its purchases and so are at the heart of business marketing. These problems can arise for many reasons, but they all relate to two basic activities of customers:

- **Rationalization:** This concerns the customer's need to carry out its day-to-day operations as efficiently and economically as possible. If a customer has a problem in its operations it may consider changing the type of offering that it buys, or the way that it is produced or delivered. Examples of this type of customer problem include such things as an unacceptable failure rate in the components on the customer's production line, or a customer that faces poor utilization of the time of its staff who are working in contract-cleaning, or a customer that faces escalating costs in operating a distribution depot.
- **Development:** Problems can also arise for positive reasons, such as when a company wishes to develop its operations and its offerings. Suppliers have become more important in development problems as companies have come to rely more on them as an important source of ideas and information. An example of a development problem would be when a company planned to introduce an innovative domestic appliance and needed to fit a sophisticated control system that it was unable to develop for itself. Another would be if a company planned to extend its personal loan business to a different country but did not have the skills to set up and manage a call centre in that country.

Different people in a company will each have their own problems. For example, the operations department may have the problem of operating with a shortage of skilled labour, while the marketing department may have the problem of poor customer data. Customers will be aware of some of their problems, but there may be others that they will not recognize. They will only be able to address some problems and they will simply ignore others or have to live with them. Often it is a supplier that leads a customer to recognize a problem and address it. Solutions to many problems are found within customer–supplier relationships. Each customer can solve a single problem in a wide variety of ways. For example:

- A producer of consumer-durables may have the problem of increasing production costs. It can try to obtain a solution to this rationalization problem by buying new production equipment; employing a consultant to advise it on its production methods; contracting out the production to a specialist company or using the services of a design house, to change its products so that they are simpler to assemble.
- An accounting company may have a rationalization problem in meeting the more demanding requirements of its audit customers. It can try to solve this by hiring new staff. Alternatively, it could establish a relationship with a company with strong auditing resources and agree to transfer audit work to them in return for taking on some of the other company's financial consulting business.
- A construction company may have the development problem that its growth is restricted because of inadequate capital. It could try to solve this by building a strong relationship over several years with a venture capital supplier, in return for an equity stake in the business. Alternatively, it could take out a conventional interest-bearing loan, or it could reduce its capital requirements by selling and leasing back some of its facilities.

This means that successful business marketing must be based on an understanding both of the problems that each customer faces and the range of possible solutions that are available to it through its network of relationships.

Products and services

Managers are naturally preoccupied with how their products and services compare with those of their competitors. But a concentration on products and services is a poor starting point for successful business marketing. This is for the following reasons.

Products and services are simply part of what a marketing company supplies. *Customers are not interested in products or services themselves.* They are only interested in what products and services will actually *do* for them and the problems that they will solve. A business marketer must look behind his products or services to see the real problems of his customers and what the marketer actually can do to solve them. For example, only approximately 30 per cent of the lifetime costs of operating a fork-lift truck are associated with the vehicle itself. Some 70 per cent of costs are associated with the driver. So the main rationalization problems for a warehouse operator are likely to concern its staff costs, damage to products in the warehouse, faulty selection of items and safety. One fork-truck producer has become aware of this and offers assessment and training schemes for truck operators and company managers as a way of solving their problems. It is also looking at innovative ways of charging customers for the improvements it can make in their efficiency, rather than simply fixing a price for its trucks. However, the company has difficulties with its own sales force which still sees its task as to sell the company's products, based on their technical specification.

Second, products and services are difficult to separate. Almost all "products" have some service elements associated with them, such as installation or after-sales service. In fact, in some cases, service performance is more important than the specification of the physical product. For example, a customer may say to a supplier of software, "Your software is no use to me, unless I get on-site help if things go wrong." Similarly, almost all "services" have some physical products associated with them. The services of a freight-forwarder include provision of physical containers and space in a ship or aircraft. Some intangible services can be associated with considerable physical equipment. For example, when we have a car serviced we are not only buying a mechanic's time, but we are gaining the benefit of the garage's specialized tuning equipment. In contrast, some large-scale service providers, such as merchant banks or management consultants use little equipment and little physical product is associated with their activities.

Third, products and services are often interchangeable in the mind of a customer. For example, a firm of lawyers faced with the problem of how to keep its offices clean could decide to clean them itself by buying the necessary products, in this case vacuum cleaners. Alternatively, the firm could buy the services of a contract cleaning organization. On a much larger scale, an airline can buy the engines (products) for a new fleet of airliners or it can rent "power-by-the-hour" from the engine manufacturer, who would be responsible for the maintenance of the engines (service).

Finally, products and services are only part of what is required for successful business marketing. It is important for a marketer to understand that if he is to solve a customer's problem, he will have to provide a complete *offering*.

Offerings

A supplier's offering can be defined as follows:

> A supplier's offering is a *package* consisting of different proportions of the elements of physical product, service, advice, adaptation and logistics and the costs that it involves.

The multiple elements of an offering strongly affect business marketing, as follows:

- A marketer may provide a different offering for each customer, even if all the offerings include the same physical product or service.
- A marketer's offering only has value or "quality" in terms of how effective it is as a solution to the problems of a specific customer.
- A business marketer can successfully compete, even if the product or service elements of his offering are identical to those of others, as in so-called commodity markets. He

can do this by differentiating any of the other elements of his offering to better solve customers' problems, rather than simply cutting his price. For example, the marketer's offering may have better delivery, or advice on how to use the product more efficiently. He may also adapt one or more elements of the offering to the particular situation of the customer.

- Business marketers must appreciate that in many cases neither the physical product nor service nor logistical content of their offering is the most important element for a customer. Often it is their *advice* on what type of offering the customer should choose, or on how it can use the offering that is a vital part of customer choice. Other times it is the supplier's ability or willingness to adapt to suit a customer's particular situation that is important. A marketer's skills in providing, managing and controlling the costs of this adaptation and advice are often critical to business success.

- Buying a supplier's offering will involve a range of costs for the customer, only one of which will be the purchase price they pay. The customer may also face the costs of adapting itself, or training its staff to use the new offering. It also faces the costs of losing its relationships with the suppliers it is not buying from and the benefits of their offerings. It is just as important for the marketer to understand and manage these customer costs as it is to assemble his offering. We will examine the management of costs and prices in Chapter 8.

- The marketer must appreciate that a supplier's offering is never produced in isolation. It will be developed, produced and delivered to the customer by the company and by many others in the network. A supplier will always need to use the resources of these other companies in the surrounding network and combine them with its own skills and resources to produce an offering. In many cases around 70–80 per cent of the costs of the supplier's offering is accounted for by what it buys from others. These purchases can include everything from electricity from a utility company, to logistic services or critical components for its equipment.

- Similarly, a supplier's offering is not developed in isolation from its customers, but *interactively* in the relationship between them. The supplier's offering is *the outcome of the relationship between them*.

This means that an important aspect of business marketing is for the marketer to build productive relationships with many others in the surrounding network, both customers and suppliers, in order to be able to provide an offering and enable the customer to solve its problems.

Box 1.1 shows a letter from an unhappy customer to a supplier. This is a real letter, only the names have been changed to protect the guilty! This illustrates what can happen if a supplier does not carefully manage its interactions with each customer. The company in this case has a particular problem of managing its purchasing of thousands of small items at eighteen different locations. But the supplier has failed to adapt its offering to cope with the customer's problem and the relationship is in crisis. We will examine how the marketer can manage relationships with customers in Chapter 5.

Box 1.1 How Not to Manage a Business Relationship

JENNINGS CONSTRUCTION

James Carmichael,
Swift Supplies,
Baylis Road,
London
SE22 7PB

Dear James

I have worked in purchasing for fifteen years or so and I have always held Swift Supplies in high regard as a reliable supplier. To this end, when I joined Jennings as Purchasing Manager in 1997, I was keen to establish a formal purchasing agreement between our group of companies and your organization.

This initial agreement was reached with your Peter Smith and both parties soon began to reap the benefits of the deal. Peter subsequently moved on and Alan Coles took over as our account manager. During Alan's time looking after our account, we established good communications with regular quarterly review meetings. Unfortunately, following further reorganization at your company, Alan, like Peter, was moved on.

Our next account manager was David Jones, and it was from this point that we started experiencing problems and by the end of the year I was ready to prohibit any of our locations from using you. This was due mainly to David's threat to terminate our retrospective rebate agreement as he felt you were obtaining no additional business by providing this incentive. Having explained at length to David the structure of our business and the approach I suggested you should take, he reluctantly agreed to allow the scheme to continue.

I was next contacted by Philip Harris who advised me that he was our new account manager as Swift had again reorganized its salesforce. Philip was very positive about our agreement and we also had lengthy discussions about our proposed Visa card purchasing programme, but he did warn me that he didn't expect to be looking after our account for too long as he knew of yet another reorganization. I told him that this disappointed me and that I felt we were being treated badly by Swift and he promised to make sure things improved.

Towards the end of last year, I happened to meet your Sales Manager, Arnold Whitfield, who was talking at a conference I was attending. Arnold was doing a good job of telling us all how innovative and customer, focused Swift are. However, when I told him about our problems over lunch he was most disappointed and indeed shocked to hear of the service levels we were experiencing. He promised to make it a priority of his to look into the issues when he returned to the office and to report back. I am still waiting to hear from him nearly twelve months later.

Next, I received a phone call from a gentleman called Simon Brett who informed me that he had taken over as account manager. I explained my concerns to him and suggested methods that could be adopted by Swift to significantly increase the business they received from us. Simon accepted that all the changes were "unacceptable" and "disappointing" but he assured me that he was here to stay and things would improve. Needless to say, I was somewhat shocked when you called in June to explain that you were our new account manager – our sixth in four years!

I think that there is a real difficulty with the manner in which Swift categorize customers and thus how they are serviced, i.e. account manager, local representative, telesales, etc. This seems to be done purely on their level of expenditure, i.e. those that spend above a certain amount get an account manager but those that spend little only receive telesales calls. While I can understand your logic for setting these procedures, I would expect there to be a degree of flexibility, or if your prefer, "customer focus". We have 18 manufacturing locations nation-wide, ranging vastly in size and each one categorized by Swift depending upon their current spend levels, not their potential spend levels. Thus sites with a large potential are not being supplied by Swift because you are not prepared to have local representatives call them. I have suggested therefore, on several previous occasions, that selected Jennings sites receive an initial visit from a local representative. I am confident that this would generate considerable growth for Swift.

Hopefully, the contents of this letter will serve as a reminder that we at Jennings Construction have the potential and desire to develop our relationship with Swift, but only if you are prepared to put some effort in yourselves. If you are not prepared to offer this commitment then I'm afraid it really is time for us to go our separate ways.

I await your reply with interest.

Yours sincerely

K N Townsend
Purchasing Manager

Solution

An offering is a supplier's own view of the package it has developed. A customer will have a different view of it and will only be concerned with how effective the offering is as a solution to its problems.

There are many potential solutions to each business problem including the different offerings of potential suppliers. To be successful, a business marketer must be able to do the following:

- Consider his offerings as solutions to customers' problems and not in terms of his own abstract criteria of "quality" of product or service.
- Compare his offerings, through the eyes of the customers, with other potential solutions of whatever type and from whatever source.
- Advise customers on the choice of available solutions. Of course, business marketers also have to sell and convince the customer that their offering actually is a good solution to its problems. But in doing this, the marketer must be aware that its relationship with a particular customer will depend on its ability to fulfil the offer as a continuing solution.
- Actually deliver that offering to each customer, at the promised time and location, performance and consistency. In other words, a marketer's offering is of no value, unless it is *fulfilled*.

The effectiveness of the solution that a customer receives will of course depend on the characteristics of the offering and the supplier's skill in actually delivering it to the customer. But the effectiveness of that solution will also depend on the customer's skills. These customer skills have a number of aspects:

- The clarity with which it can define and describe its problems.
- Its skill in building relationships with suppliers and in communicating its problems to them and in motivating them to supply. In other words, in *selling* itself to potential suppliers.
- Its skills in working with the supplier to develop its offering and to ensure that it is fulfilled.
- Its skill in integrating that offering with the offerings of other suppliers and its own operations.

This means that the effectiveness of the solution that a customer receives will depend on the nature of the relationship between the supplier and customer, *irrespective of the technical quality of the supplier's offering*.

Figure 1.3 illustrates the process of analysing customer problems and developing offerings to solve them, rather than simply trying to sell products. The analysis was carried

```
" The machine has broken down."

" I have to carry out a programme of Planned Maintenance."

" I'm responsible for making sure that the machines are safe."

" I have a multitude of machines to maintain."

" I haven't got the skills to do all the jobs."

" We have very poor Maintenance Stock management."

" My budget is reducing all the time."

" I have fewer maintenance staff."
```

Figure 1.3   Some problems of a maintenance person.

out by a supplier of maintenance equipment and components. Figure 1.3 lists some of the problems that are faced by those responsible for maintaining equipment in a company. The company then analysed these problems in more detail and this is shown for four of them in Figure 1.4.

This further analysis led the company to consider extending its existing product offering by adding a "part-finder" service, a maintenance help-line, a separate

The machine has broken down

```
• I need to identify the right part

• I need to know whether to mend it, buy the
  part, or take it from stock

• I need to find sources for the product

• I have to choose the right source

• I need the right tools

• I need instructions to do the job
```

Figure 1.4   Detailed analysis of target problems.

I have fewer maintenance staff

- I need to find temporary staff

- We want to improve our productivity

- We need simpler processes

- We must reduce our non-productive time

- I must prioritize better

- I want to outsource some activities

- My staff and I need broader skills

- We need more external support

Very poor Maintenance Stock management

- I need to make it easy – dump the problem

- I need someone to analyse my stock and requirements

- I need to reduce my stock value

- I want better stock systems

- I need ease of access to products

- My suppliers need to provide consignment stocking

- I require replenishment information

I have a multitude of machines to maintain

- I need to schedule planned maintenance

- I would like to rationalize my suppliers

- I want to use a single source of supply

- I'd like to dump the problem

Figure 1.4   *Continued.*

planned maintenance company and a maintenance and inventory management consultancy.

Customer Uncertainties

It is quite straightforward for a company to solve a problem by making a purchase when:

- It is sure of the precise solution that will meet its needs.
- It has relationships with several suppliers, each with offerings that match those needs.
- It is quite sure that it will actually get exactly what it was offered by suppliers at the right time and when it is sure that it will not have to pay more than it originally thought.

But this ideal situation is unlikely to occur in practice and companies can face a number of *uncertainties* in their purchases, irrespective of the problems that their purchases are intended to solve. These uncertainties affect the requirements that customers have of their suppliers and it is vital for a business marketer to understand them. Figure 1.5 provides a categorization of buyer and supplier uncertainties.[7]

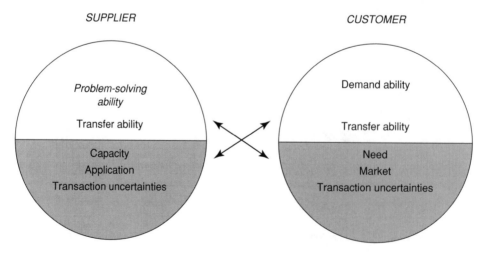

Figure 1.5   The uncertainties and abilities of buyers and sellers.

[7] This discussion of customer uncertainties is based on H Håkansson, J Johanson and B Wootz, Influence Tactics in Buyer-Seller Processes, *Industrial Marketing Management*, vol. 5, 1976, pp. 319–32. The ideas on supplier uncertainties are taken from David Ford *et al.*, *Managing Business Relationships*, Chichester, John Wiley, 1998.

Need uncertainty

Very often the company has difficulty in defining its problem, or it may not know precisely what solution will best solve its problem. In this case the company has *need uncertainty* and this will strongly affect the way the customer approaches the supplier and the purchase itself. Customers with need uncertainty are likely to seek advice from a supplier as to *how* they can solve their problem and what they should buy. This means that:

- They are likely to favour "close" suppliers – those that they trust, either because they have a strong brand or because they already have a relationship with them or because they are local to the customer.
- They are likely to concentrate a large proportion of their supplies to solve that particular problem with a single supplier – to "get into bed" with that supplier.

We can see a similar situation to this in our own individual behaviour when we are unfamiliar with a purchase, such as when buying a laptop computer for the first time; or when we lack self-confidence, such as when buying an "important" article of clothing. Brand and reputation are likely to be important in both cases and loyalty to previous, trusted suppliers is likely to be strong.

Market uncertainty

A company will often face a wide variety of potential solutions to a particular problem or find that the technology in the area is changing rapidly, so that new and different solutions are arising all the time. In this case the company will not have a relationship that will provide an obvious solution to its problem and we say that it has *market uncertainty*. A customer with market uncertainty is likely to behave very differently from one with need uncertainty:

- They are likely to devote considerable efforts to scanning the available suppliers and the different potential solutions.
- They are unlikely to concentrate their purchases from a single supplier, because that would lock them into that supplier's technology. Instead, they are likely to develop relationships with a number of competing, parallel suppliers.

Again there is a parallel between business buying and our own consumer purchasing, when faced with a wide range or rapidly changing set of complex products. Journals such as *What Hi-Fi?* or *What Computer?* are one way for us to cope with our market uncertainty.

A marketer faced with a potential customer with high need uncertainty will find it worthwhile trying to increase its share of the customer's purchases. But if that customer has high market uncertainty, then those efforts are unlikely to be worthwhile, because the customer will wish to avoid concentration and spread its purchases around.

Transaction uncertainty

On other occasions, a customer company may be quite sure about the right solution and about the available offerings from different suppliers. However, it may be uncertain about whether the supplier will actually *fulfil* the promise of its offering; whether on time, in the right place, with the right performance, at the promised price or do these things consistently. Another aspect of transaction uncertainty occurs in many routine or non-critical purchases when the customer seeks a solution involving the least cost and effort. In each of these cases the customer has *transaction uncertainty* and this will strongly affect its purchase behaviour:

- The customer is likely to investigate the supplier carefully, check aspects of its operations and performance and monitor its deliveries.
- The customer may seek to develop the supplier and try to improve its abilities to satisfy the customer's requirements.
- Alternatively, the customer may try to minimize its dependence on any one supplier and "play the market", by buying on the most advantageous terms from a range of suppliers on a short-term basis. The first of these approaches would involve investment by the customer in building a relationship with the supplier, while the second would avoid the costs of this relationship investment, but without the benefits.

Manipulating customer uncertainties

The uncertainties that a customer feels when contemplating a purchase are affected by the relationships that it has with different potential suppliers. This means that it is possible for a business marketer to manipulate the uncertainties that customers feel. For example:

- A supplier may try to increase a customer's *need uncertainty* by emphasizing the complexity of the problems on which the purchase is based and the range of considerations that the customer needs to take into account in making a choice. Alternatively, the supplier may reduce that need uncertainty by simplifying the considerations it draws to the customer's attention.
- Similarly, a supplier may try to increase a customer's *market uncertainty* by highlighting the variations between its own offerings and those of different suppliers. In contrast, it could reduce market uncertainty by talking about the similarity between the technical standards of the different offerings.
- This supplier could then stress that although the offerings of different suppliers were apparently very similar, it was important for the customer to be able to trust a supplier to live up to promises on delivery or price or to be consistent in its performance over time. The supplier could then contrast the record of different suppliers in these ways, thus increasing the customer's *transaction uncertainty*.

Supplier Abilities

A supplier may try to manipulate a customer's uncertainties so that they relate more closely to its own abilities. These abilities take two forms: problem-solving ability and transfer ability.

Problem-solving ability

This is a supplier's ability to design and develop an offering that will provide a solution to a customer's problem. The offering is a *promise* of a solution for a customer.

Problem-solving ability is likely to be costly for a supplier to build and sustain. The ability to design and develop the product, service or logistics elements of an offering may involve considerable investment in staff and research facilities. Similarly, adapting an existing offering to a customer's individual requirements may also be costly. Providing advice may require an expensive, technically qualified sales force. The costs of the supplier's problem-solving abilities will have to be reflected in the price that the supplier charges for its offering. A supplier's problem-solving ability will be important to some customers with complex or unique problems or with high need or market uncertainties. But other customers with more simple or standardized problems will not be prepared to pay the high prices charged by suppliers that are seeking to recover the high costs of developing or adapting complex offerings.

Transfer ability

This is a supplier's ability to actually deliver its offering to the customer. It is the supplier's ability to fulfil the promise of its offering, so that the customer actually receives the anticipated solution to its problems at the time and at the price it was anticipating. The emphasis here is on timing and consistency of supply, on conformity to the specification of the offering and on cost control. These also require investment by the supplier to develop its production and service processes, its systems, its logistical sophistication, its efficiency and to reduce its costs. A supplier's transfer ability is particularly important to a customer with high transaction uncertainty. Fulfilling an offering for some customers will be straightforward and will involve few operational problems. For others, the requirements of cost, consistency, timing or location will place great demands on the supplier.[8]

Some suppliers have strong problem-solving abilities. They can provide a sophisticated solution to complex or difficult problems. But these companies may be weak in their transfer abilities and the actual fulfilment of their offering may be inconsistent, late

---

[8] Many of the ideas of "Lean Production" with minimal inventories involve using suppliers with strong transfer abilities to be able to cope with the challenge of tightly timed, complex deliveries, perhaps to a number of locations and with "zero defects". For a discussion of these issues, see, JP Womac, DT Jones and D Roos, *The Machine that Changed the World*, New York, R A Rawston Assoc. 1990, and Richard Chase, Nicholas Aquilano and Robert Jacobs, *Operations Management for Competitive Advantage*, New York, McGraw-Hill, 2001.

or subject to cost over-runs. Other companies may be better at transfer ability. Their offerings may be similar to those of other suppliers, or standardized for all customers, but they are skilled in delivering the offering to the customer on time, on budget and to specification. This may involve extremely complex and challenging operations or logistics, such as simultaneously delivering with minimal inventory to several production lines in different countries.

Suppliers in business markets must choose how to divide the investment of their scarce resources between developing their problem-solving or their transfer abilities. These choices will affect both their offerings and fulfilment and also the type of customers they attract. Customers will seek those suppliers whose problem-solving or transfer abilities most closely relate to their own problems and uncertainties. Similarly, suppliers will seek those customers whose requirements most closely match their own abilities. This adds to the complexity and variation that exist in business markets and to the tasks facing the business marketer. We will examine the tasks involved in building and transferring offerings in Chapters 6 and 7, respectively.

Problems and Uncertainties for the Supplier

Earlier in this chapter we pointed to similarities between business marketing and business purchasing. These include similarities in the problems and uncertainties of customers and suppliers and how they deal with these. We outline them as follows:

- Suppliers also have to assess the available customers and consider how business with each of them will relate to their problems and requirements.
- Suppliers also face uncertainties and often look to customers for ways of coping with them. But customers, just like suppliers, may try to manipulate the uncertainties of their counterparts.
- Both suppliers and customers have to balance their own short-term interests in a relationship against those of their counterparts and against the long-term interests of both of them.

Supplier problems

An important aspect of business marketing is for the marketer to assess his company's problems and judge how a portfolio of customers can provide a solution to some of them. For example, a supplier may have a cash-flow problem and rely on one particular customer to provide the revenue to reduce this. This same supplier may consequently face the problem of low profitability and seek other customers with different problems to solve that may be the source of higher-margin business. Another supplier may have the problem of technological obsolescence in one area of its business. A particular customer may not be profitable for this supplier, but may be an important source of new technology to help the supplier in its relationships elsewhere in the network.

Supplier uncertainties

Irrespective of its problems, a supplier will face uncertainties in its dealings with customers. It is as important for a business marketer to understand his own uncertainties as it is to know about those of his customers. It is also important for the marketer to think about how his customers may try to manipulate these uncertainties. A supplier's uncertainties have much in common with those of a customer and we can outline them as follows:

- **Capacity uncertainty:** Very often a supplier is uncertain about how much of a particular offering it is likely to be able to sell in any time period. Capacity uncertainty is likely to be high in those suppliers with high fixed costs of production or development, or those that are dominated by a small number of major customers. A supplier faced with this uncertainty is likely to try to form close relationships with a number of customers in order to provide some assurance of sales volume.
- **Application uncertainty:** Suppliers often face uncertainty about *how* their offering can be most effectively used by customers, or for which particular applications or problems it is most suitable. This is likely to be the case when the offering is based on recent technological development or when it needs to be integrated into customers' operations in a complex way, or when customers' problems are changing rapidly. The way that customers' problems will evolve is often difficult to predict, but it will have a strong effect on the requirements they have of their supplier. A supplier faced with high application uncertainty will need to develop effective mechanisms to scan how a wide range of different customers are applying its offering.
- **Transaction uncertainty:** This is a similar uncertainty to that faced by a customer. The supplier may doubt that the customer *actually* knows what it should be buying and it may not trust the customer to *actually* take delivery of the volume it ordered, on time and or to pay the price that was agreed. Transaction uncertainty is likely to be high when the supplier undertakes considerable development work on behalf of its customers or where demand for its offerings is concentrated in few customers. A supplier faced with high transaction-uncertainty has a similar choice to that of a seller. It can either try to establish a close relationship with its customers to learn more about their requirements and likely behaviour, or it can seek to reduce its dependence on a small number of customers by broadening its portfolio.

What its own uncertainties mean for a supplier

A customer can seek to manipulate the uncertainties of a supplier in the same way that a supplier can manipulate the uncertainties of a customer. For example, a customer can increase the capacity uncertainty of a supplier by emphasizing the unpredictability of demand from customers for the supplier's offering. In contrast, it can reduce a supplier's application uncertainty by simplifying the specification of its requirements. It can also increase a supplier's transaction uncertainty by pointing to the extent of company failures among users of this type of offering.

A customer also brings two types of abilities to its interactions with a supplier. These are as follows:

- **Demand ability:** A customer's demand ability enables it to advise the supplier of the type of offering it should produce and to offer the supplier the volume and type of demand that it requires. In this way the customer assists the supplier to develop its offering. In this way it may appear to be a valuable customer. A customer's demand ability would be important to a supplier with high capacity uncertainty and high application uncertainty. A customer's demand ability may arise because of its high-volume requirements, but it may also be based on its knowledge of how the supplier's offering should be developed and integrated into its own operations. This ability is likely to be particularly important to a supplier trying to solve a new customer problem, or one that has recently developed an offering based on innovative technology for which the application may be uncertain, or where the supplier needs to recover high development costs. A supplier might have to "pay a price" for the customer's demand ability by extensive interaction with the customer, or by adapting to its requirements, or by granting the customer a low price.
- **Transfer ability:** In the same way that a supplier's transfer ability is about reliably making sure that the customer receives the promised offering, so a customer's transfer ability is about its reliability in providing the promised type and volume of orders and information to the supplier, or more generally in managing a relationship. A customer with strong transfer ability will be valuable to a supplier as it will be little "trouble". In other words, by using its own transfer ability, it will require less of the supplier's transfer abilities.

Interchangeable abilities

Customers and suppliers share an interest in ensuring that mutually satisfactory transactions take place between them. Their discussions and disagreements are likely to concern which of them should do what and who should incur the costs that are involved. The abilities of suppliers and customers are to some extent interchangeable in a relationship and both companies can benefit from this. For example, many retailers provide the design and specification for the offerings of suppliers, based on their knowledge of their own consumers. They also decide *how* the offering should be produced. Both of these are based on the customer's demand ability. Retailers also often take responsibility for inspecting produce on farms or clothing in factories to see that it meets their requirements and they control logistics to ensure timely delivery, based on their transfer ability.

On the other hand, many suppliers design complete modules of a customer's final product, in which their components and those of others are parts. This is based on their problem-solving skills. These suppliers may also carry out inspections of their own and others' components and supervise delivery of components directly to the place on the production line where they are to be assembled, to ensure that no delays occur. This is based on their transfer skills.

This substitution of activities is only likely to occur in well-developed relationships. We will examine the process of relationship development in Chapter 5, where we will see that the involvement of companies in business relationships can lead to a situation where it is difficult to separate the activities of buyer and seller from each other.

Conclusion

This chapter has tried to set the scene for the book by examining some aspects of the world that faces business marketers. The chapter has emphasized that business marketing in one company is only part of the total set of activities in many companies that lead ultimately to the availability of offerings for consumers. Business marketing occurs between two *active* companies that are important to each other, in a relationship that is often close, complex and long-term. We can only understand each business purchase within the context of the relationship of which it is a part. Each single relationship does not exist in isolation and can only be understood within the wider network of relationships.

Business marketing is a very similar activity to business purchasing. Both buyer and seller have similar uncertainties and abilities. Both must search for and evaluate the right counterparts based on the abilities, problems and uncertainties of both companies. Both need to adapt themselves and invest time and resources to develop relationships with their counterparts. Relationships with counterparts are major assets for both suppliers and customers and both need to maximize their long-term return on those assets.

This chapter has emphasized some of the differences between the world facing the business marketer and that of the consumer marketer. Unlike business marketers, consumer marketers often deal with thousands or millions of individually insignificant customers who can be grouped into relatively homogeneous segments for the purposes of analysis, communication and targeting. Traditionally, consumer marketers assemble a market offering that only varies for individual customers within very narrow parameters and "talk" to their customers via complex and usually impersonal channels such as television and press advertising. Similarly, consumer marketers "listen" to their customers only via market research surveys.

Nevertheless, there are a number of similarities between business and consumer marketing and these seem to be increasing as markets evolve. The traditional divisions between manufacturers, wholesalers and retailers are breaking down and both consumers and business customers now buy computers, airline tickets or hi-fi components directly from a manufacturer, from a web supplier or from a traditional retailer. The availability of call centres and the Internet has meant that consumer marketers and their customers have a greater opportunity to interact with each other – just like business buyers and sellers. Advances in process technology have enabled suppliers to tailor offerings to the requirements of individual consumers. The availability of more detailed data on each customer's life-style and purchase behaviour has also meant that consumer marketers can take a longer-term view of their customers. They increasingly see their task as building and exploiting a relationship with them over the longer term. Just as in business marketing, the unit of analysis for the consumer marketer has shifted from the product, the sale, the segment or the market to the relationship and the portfolio of which it forms part.

Our immediate task in these first chapters of the book is to develop skills of analysis for business marketing. In Chapter 2 we introduce ideas on how business marketers can analyse the wider network in which they operate. Then in Chapter 3 we develop ideas on how a marketer can analyse his own company and its abilities and technologies. In Chapter 4 we look in more detail at the problems of customers and how they develop supply strategies to overcome them.

Further Reading

David Ford, Lars Erik Gadde, Håkan Håkansson, Anders Lundgren, Ivan Snehota, Peter Turnbull and David Wilson (1998) *Managing Business Relationships*, Chichester, John Wiley.

Michael Hammer and James Champy (1993) *Reengineering the Corporation*, New York, Harper Business Books.

Michael Hutt and Thomas Speh (2001) *Business Marketing Management*, Fort Worth, Dryden.

Wesley Johnston (1981) *Patterns in Industrial Buying Behaviour*, New York, Praeger.

Arch G Woodside and Niren Vyas (1987) *Industrial Purchasing Strategies*, Lexington, MA, Lexington Books.

BUSINESS MARKETING AND NETWORKS

2

Aims of this Chapter

- To show how in business marketing it is essential to develop relationships.
- To show how these relationships between suppliers and customers can develop in a network.
- To describe the characteristics of business networks.
- To identify the main problems that marketers face, how they can be structured and analysed and how the marketer can take advantage of the network in which he operates.

Chapter 1 explained that a business marketer is likely to have far fewer customers than a consumer marketer. Some customers may be relatively unimportant to the marketer, but others may be responsible for a large share of his total business and be vital to the success of his company. We also explained that the transactions between a business supplier and its customers are not isolated events that are unrelated to each other. Instead, each of these transactions takes place in a *relationship* and each is related to the previous experience of the companies and to what they plan for the future. Rather than meeting as strangers, the companies tend to know each other quite well and may adapt different aspects of their offerings and operations to suit each other's requirements.

A business marketing company will also have relationships with its own suppliers and these relationships are critical if the marketer is to build a valuable offering for its customers. Each of the company's suppliers will also have relationships with their suppliers and with their other customers. Each of its customers will have relationships with other suppliers and with their own customers. All these relationships are affected by the others and are intertwined in a *network*. This network is the arena in which the business marketer must operate. The relationships in the network enable the company to grow and develop, but they are also a constraint on that development and may restrict its activities.

We start the chapter by using two different types of network to illustrate some of their general characteristics. Following from this we build a set of tools for network analysis. We start by examining the content of companies and relationships in networks and then look at the overall patterns that exist within them. Finally, we look at how the marketer can examine each single relationship in a network.

This chapter is based on the idea that if we want to understand the behaviour of a business company then we have to look at its relationships with other companies.[1] Rather than being a free agent able to develop and implement their strategy alone, each is dependent on others in order to act and each has to react to or accommodate the aims and strategies of others. In other words, the basic assumption of network thinking is that, "no business is an island".[2]

The growing technological intensity of companies' offerings and the rising costs of technological development have led companies to specialize in fewer of the skills needed to satisfy the requirements of their end-customers. This has increased the interdependencies between component producers, assemblers, distributors, service, logistics suppliers and others. At the same time, problems in managing relationships and the interconnections between them have led to a greater interest in networks by business people.

Different Types of Networks

A good way to identify some important properties of business networks and the issues they raise for business marketers is to look at typical cases. Two of the most distinctive examples are supplier and distribution networks.

Supplier networks

The Toyota supplier network, illustrated in Figure 2.1 was developed by one large customer over a very long period of time. Toyota would not be able to work with all of the 50 000 companies that contribute to its own offerings. So instead, it chose to work closely with a small number of "system suppliers". Each of these is responsible for both the design and production of a certain part of the final car. Each system supplier has in turn a restricted number of suppliers that deliver parts of the system to it. On the third tier are suppliers that deliver standardized, non-adapted components. The example shows several significant features of networks:

- **Indirect relationships:** These allow a customer in a network to be systematically related to a large number of suppliers, in this case over 50 000, even though it only has

---

[1] A comprehensive review of ideas on business networks is provided in Geoff Easton, Industrial Networks: A Review, in Bjorn Axelsson and Geoff Easton, *Industrial Networks: A New View of Reality*, London, Routledge, 1992, pp. 3–27.

[2] Håkan Håkansson and Ivan Snehota, No Business is an Island: The Network Concept of Business Strategy, *Scandinavian Journal of Management*, vol. 14, no. 3, 1990, pp. 177–200.

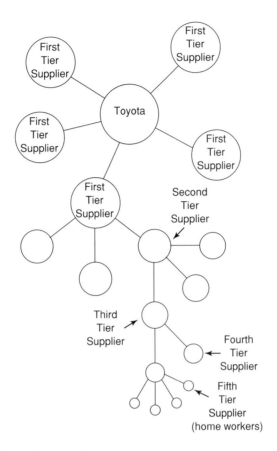

Figure 2.1   Toyota's supply network.

Source: D Blenkhorn and AH Noori, What it Takes to Supply Japanese OEMs, *Industrial Marketing Management*, vol. 19, no. 1, 1999.

direct contacts with a small number of them. Because its suppliers are all working in the same way, the network branches out to allow a customer access to a wide range of suppliers both geographically and technologically. It can achieve this with just a few well-developed relationships. However, the existence of a structure of relationships is not enough. Toyota has to be sure that even the relationships in which it is not directly involved are working effectively. This has taken Toyota several decades to achieve.

- **Co-ordination between relationships:** The development of a customer's relationships with its immediate suppliers must be co-ordinated with the suppliers' own relationships with others. It is only when the relationships all work well together that they will create substantial value for the customer. Some customers try to manage these interdependencies by building a linear "supply chain" through a network.
- **Influence of large companies:** The example demonstrates that a large company can have a very significant role in the overall development of a network. A large company

can combine different relationships with each other in a productive way, provided that it is prepared to understand the perspective of others in the network, to invest in relationship development and take a long-term strategic viewpoint.

- **Problems with a single perspective:** Despite the influence that a large company can have on a network, it is important to stress that a network drawn from the perspective of a single company can never capture the total situation. The network in Figure 2.1 is described from Toyota's point of view. If we described the network from the perspective of a system supplier, it would have been quite different, with different customers and suppliers. The picture of a network changes depending on our starting point and there are as many networks as there are starting points.

Distribution networks

Figure 2.2 illustrates a distribution network. It describes the distribution of computers from the perspective of a large supplying company, IBM. The figure shows the different ways that computers can reach its customers in Italy. This example shows a number of different features of networks, when compared with the supplier network:

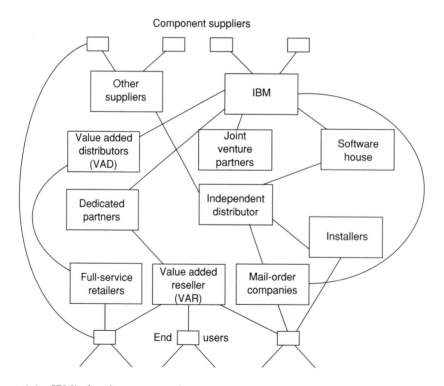

Figure 2.2   IBM's distribution network.

Source: Ford (ed.) *Understanding Business Markets and Purchasing*, London, Thomson Learning 2001.

- **Variety of companies:** Figure 2.2 shows a variety of different types of companies that appear to be performing more or less the same activity – selling computers to customers. The companies vary in terms of size, technical capabilities and competencies. They also vary in the way that they relate to and service customers. These companies have evolved to provide different solutions to a variety of customer problems. All these problems centre on computing, but they require offerings consisting of different combinations of product, service, logistics, adaptation and advice. This variety of companies enables the supplier to have its own offerings combined with the distributors' different skills to produce a wide range of offerings for end-users. But the variety of companies is also a problem for the supplier, as it will have to select the ones it wishes to work with and provide them with a variety of offerings to suit their particular problems and requirements.
- **Variety of relationships:** Not only will the supplier in this network have to provide a range of offerings, but it will also have to manage a range of relationships with its distributors. This range of relationships is needed because the distributors are different themselves, and also because they have different relationships with their customers.
- **Difficulties of control:** This network shows how difficult it is for even a very large company to determine who takes part in a network and how they should relate to each other. This may appear to contradict one of the conclusions about the first network. But although a single company has some discretion in a network, it certainly is not the only one trying to influence its development. The evolution of a network is the outcome of all of these efforts, rather than the dictates of any one company.

The features we have identified in the two examples can be summarized as follows:

- In order to examine a network we need to choose a focal point, for example, a company. We can then examine the network from this perspective. As soon as we change this focal point, then we will see a new set of relationships and companies and the network will be different. It is useful to examine a network from the perspective of different companies. For example, it is often instructive for a marketer to examine a network from the perspective of a major customer or one of that customer's customers. By examining a network carefully, a creative marketer can achieve a realistic understanding of his own position in the minds of customers and suppliers. He can also start to understand the dynamics of the network and even help the company to "design" a new one by seeing the potential interdependencies that others have overlooked.
- A network provides both opportunities and restrictions for any company, but no one company controls the network. A company may try to design its own network, as Toyota has done, but it may find out that others are also trying to influence the network in such a way that even the strongest companies have to adapt, as both IBM and Toyota have found out.
- The existence of a network does not alter the fact that the key task of business marketing (and purchasing) is to manage each single relationship. It is through its relationships that a company learns and adapts to the surrounding network. It is through them that a company exploits and develops its own abilities and gains access to those of others. It is also through relationships that a company can influence different companies elsewhere in the network.

- A network structure means that it is possible for a single company to influence a large number of other companies, even if it has a limited number of direct relationships. It also means that the company can be influenced by a large number of companies. It is not unusual to find examples of companies trying to systematically relate to companies up to three tiers away, such as Toyota in the example above.

- Each company in a network needs to establish connections between its different relationships. A company's relationships with its suppliers, when combined with its own resources, contribute to the offerings that form the basis of its relationships with its customers. The company's relationships with all its customers also contribute to the development and fulfilment of those offerings and form the basis of its relationships with its suppliers.

- There is a danger that when drawing a network from the perspective of a single company, that the company may believe that it is more important to others than it actually is and that it can control the network more than it actually can.

The value of a network analysis can be seen in the example in Box 2.1.

Box 2.1   A Financial Services Network

"Lender"[3] became a major player in the HLTV business – High-Loans-to-Value. HLTV loans are secured on the equity that the consumers have in the value of their homes, just like normal loans. But the difference is that HLVT companies will lend up to 125 per cent of that equity. This means that the loans provide less security to the lender than more conventional ones and hence they are often referred to as "sub-prime". The HLTV market in the United States grew from less than US$1 billion in 1995 to US$10 billion in 1998. Lender accounted for a large share of this market.

Lender can be viewed as a conventional consumer marketing company. It makes loans through retail channels, including its own "loan shops" and via commercial banks that act as distributors for its loan products. Its marketing employs mail-shots and television advertising, fronted by a well-known and trusted personality. However, another view of Lender's business is shown in the network diagram in Figure 2.3. This network diagram also helps to explain the severe difficulties that the company hit in 1998, despite its marketing success.

Lender describes its business as follows: "Lender originates, services, securitizes and *sells* consumer receivables". In other words, Lender originates loans *from* its consumers and sells them *to* other companies in the network. In fact, consumers are at least as much its *producers* as its customers. Lender does not have access itself to a large volume of low-interest, long-term funds that it would need if it were to hold its loans on its balance sheet until they matured. So it uses *securitization* to bring together seemingly unrelated actors in the network – those investors that have money to lend and those consumers who are "credit-challenged". In return, Lender receives revenue from consumers for initial charges on the loans and it also receives

[3] The name of the actual company has been changed. This case was developed from the work of an undergraduate project group at the University of Bath.

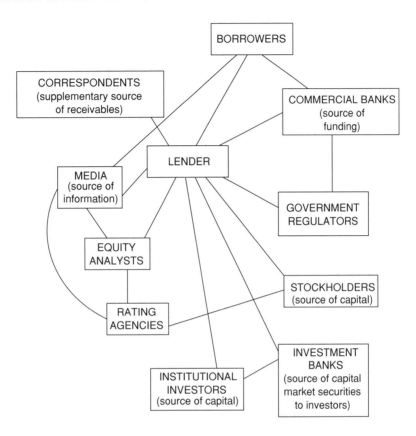

Figure 2.3   The High-Loans-to-Value network.

a margin from the financial institutions. As well as investment banks and institutional investors, the network also includes rating agencies, the media and government regulators. Each brings its specialized resources in the form of expertise and finance:

- Institutional investors, such as insurance companies and pension providers buy a set of risk and return characteristics when they buy a security and the price depends on their perception of risk.
- Investment banks act between borrowers and lenders in the network. They will not buy any securities that investors do not wish to purchase as this would leave them with costly assets they could not sell.
- Rating agencies play both a direct and an indirect role within the network. Before Lender can securitize any loans, regulators such as the SEC (Securities and Exchange Commission) require them to obtain a rating from one of four private rating agencies. Indirectly the agencies try to bring shape and order to the evolving network.

How it went wrong for Lender

Lender was a marketing success. Demand was strong and Lender was able to create and develop relationships with "quality" consumers, i.e. those likely to pay their debts. However, the increasing volume of lower quality loans generated by their competitors increased concerns within the network among the media, regulators, rating agencies and investors.

Then the Asian financial crises broke in 1998 and Russia defaulted on its debt. The attitudes to risk of US investors changed immediately and they flocked to the safety of US Treasury Bonds. Investors in Lender's securities required ever-higher rates of return and new securitizations became more difficult or impossible. A number of Lender's competitors went bankrupt and this caused investors to retreat further. Lender's share price fell sharply and it was forced to put itself up for sale and seek massive financial restructuring.

Lender had a wide portfolio of relationships with a number of investors and investment banks and produced a torrent of general press releases to explain its activities. But, unlike some other companies, it had not developed strong relationships with individual investors, who would take a long-term view of their relationship when investment conditions deteriorated. Nor was it adept at communicating its current situation and plans *within* its relationships. One journalist expressed this as follows:

> [Lender] has not been hobbled by rising delinquencies, loan losses ... or fraudulent accounting ... rather, [Lender] seems to have been dragged down by surrounding ... forces, botched communication with analysts and investors and a whirlwind of rumours.

This case shows how a company's activities can only be understood by looking at the wider network. Lender was a successful consumer marketing company, but this is only one part of the network and it is closely related to all the other things that happen in it. Lender had an unclear view of its position in the network and it failed to appreciate the dynamics of the network. Nor had Lender developed the relationships that it needed to build its position. It built its business on the basis of a static view of an unstable network.

The Content of Companies and Relationships

We now turn to the analysis of companies and relationships in business networks. The two networks that we have described above consist of companies and the business relationships that link them. Each company does not have relationships with all of the others but there is a clear pattern of linkages in the network. In order to analyse a network we first need to examine the content of the companies and their relationships and then look at the wider pattern of the network.

Companies and relationships in a network are inter-dependent. This is because relationships evolve to meet the requirements of companies and to link their resources and skills and to solve their problems, but also because companies evolve to meet the requirements of their relationships with suppliers, customers and others.[4] Without its relationships a company could not operate and without the resources and skills of both companies a relationship would have no purpose or value.

This inter-dependence has important implications for understanding the content of companies and relationships. It means that we cannot make sense of companies by looking at them in isolation, but only in relation to each other. It also means that we can gain more insight into a network by looking at the pictures that the companies have of each other, their resources and their relationships. It is these views that form the basis of their actions in the network.

There are two important aspects of the way that the companies in a network view each other. The first aspect has to do with a company's general interest in particular relationships. Companies will vary widely in the importance that they attach to individual customers, suppliers or others. Each company must set priorities for its relationships as well as try to understand the priorities of others and this can be both difficult and time-consuming. When both of the companies have the same view of each other's importance or lack of importance, then it is easy for them to find the right way of working with each other. However, it is much more difficult when one company sees the relationship as much more important than the other does. Relationship priorities cannot be set once and for all, but need to evolve with companies' experience of each other, their problems and network position. Nor are these priorities set on a single dimension of "high" or "low", but in terms of a range of issues that are important to the company. In Chapter 5 we will examine the management of customer relationships in detail. We will see that an important task of business marketing (and purchasing) is to manage a portfolio of relationships, each of which may be important for different purposes, such as for technological development, or the sale or purchase of large volumes of low-price standardized offerings, etc. A realistic assessment of the relative importance of customers on a number of carefully assigned dimensions is an essential preliminary for business marketing management.

The second aspect has to do with what actually happens in a relationship, given a certain priority. In order to be of value to each other the companies in a relationship must be able to perform particular *activities* and in order to do so they need *resources*. Thus, an analysis needs to describe the activities that each company performs in relation to the other and the resources that they have internally, or have access to. The activities include development and operations, logistics and administration. A relationship is the way that these activities are co-ordinated in the two companies. The resources can be of many kinds, both physical and human. They include the offerings and facilities of both companies. They also include the human resources used to design the offering and to fulfil it. The relationship itself is also a resource in two ways: first, a relationship bridges the resources of the two companies and influences their development by directing them towards each other. Second, the relationship provides each company with access to the resources of other companies elsewhere in the network, via the relationship.

[4] Håkan Håkansson and David Ford, How Should Companies Interact?, *Journal of Business Research*, vol. 55, 2002, 133–139.

Patterns in a Network

Analysis of companies and their relationships provides a number of insights into a network for the business marketer. For a more complete picture it is important to examine the overall patterns that exist in the network and how these influence what the companies can do and how they should do it. We can examine these network patterns by looking at two dimensions: types of content and types of inter-dependency.

Types of content

Our analysis of the content of companies and relationships is built on three dimensions: *activities*: how activities within the companies are linked through the relationship; *resources*: how the resources in the companies are tied to each other through the resources that are built through the relationship; and *priorities*: how important each relationship is to those involved.

The relative importance of these dimensions can be used to describe the patterns in different networks. Some networks are dominated by activities; some by particular resources and some by powerful companies that are high on all the companies' priorities:

- **Activity-centred patterns:** Some business networks are dominated by the existence of an extensive set of activities of either production or transportation. One example is the automotive industry, with a large number of firms producing different parts of a finished car in a co-ordinated production system. Another example is the airline industry, where many companies provide fuel, baggage handling, catering, air-traffic control, check-in, etc. The timing and synchronization of activities are a central issue for most of those involved. These networks are dominated by the search for efficiency gains. The numbers of items being produced means that a small improvement in one activity will produce a large total effect. Activity-centred patterns are increasing as companies are concentrating on performing fewer activities in-house and contracting out more to subcontractors.
- **Resource-centred patterns:** Other networks are dominated by a large, fixed resource. Examples include those in petroleum production, mining or many process industries. The capital costs of the resource will have to be met almost irrespective of output and this means that it is important to maximize its utilization. The characteristics of the resource and the way that can be linked to other resources to improve utilization will be central aspects that form the network pattern. There are often large activity structures in this situation, as a consequence of the need to utilize the resource.
- **Company-centred patterns:** Finally, there are networks where the configuration is dominated by the existence of some powerful companies. Examples include the fashion industry where companies such as Nike, Benetton and Marks and Spencer dominate a network of material suppliers, garment makers and designers. Other examples are in insurance and other services. The reasons for this dominance can be functional, such as the importance of large volumes in order to operate as in banks and insurance

companies. But it can also be due to government influence or the power of a brand or for historical reasons.

None of these three types of content are exclusive and it is possible to find some elements of each in most networks but one type usually dominates in each case and affects the pattern of the network and the way in which all companies and all marketers must operate.

Types of inter-dependencies

The inter-dependencies in a network can be classified into three types: series, pooled and mutual inter-dependency, based on Thompson[5] and Stabel and Fjelstad:[6]

- **Series inter-dependency:** This type of inter-dependency exists in most series or chain types of production process, such as the automotive and white goods industries, and other value chain-dominated industries. Each activity in this situation is dependent on some previous activity having been performed and value is created step by step as the product is produced. Both value and supply chain models build on this type of inter-dependence. Companies aim to increase efficiency and reduce the overall costs of production by adapting the activities of all of the companies involved to each other. If one activity is improved, then this will benefit all companies in the series.
- **Pooled inter-dependency:** This type of inter-dependency exists between activities when they are dependent on the same resource. Examples include the telecommunications and power industries. In this situation the physical structure of the industry itself often takes the form of a network and the value of that structure increases as more units are connected to it. Pooled inter-dependence can lead to both co-operative and competitive action by the companies. Competition can arise if there is lack of capacity in the common resource while there might be co-operation if the costs of different companies can be reduced through sharing.
- **Mutual inter-dependency:** This type of inter-dependency between activities in a network exists when the performance of each of them is dependent on the other. A typical example is major construction projects where resources from many companies are used at the same time and where the success of the project depends on the interaction between the different companies. Other examples include hospitals or major airports, where a range of different departments or companies have to interact effectively to create value.

These three types of interdependencies exist in all networks, but one of them is likely to be dominant, either because of the type of technology involved or the way that the companies have chosen to relate to each other. Each type will affect the activities of a marketing company and the problems that it is called on to solve for its customers and the

[5] JD Thompson, *Organisations in Action: Social Bases of Administrative Theory*, New York, McGraw-Hill, 1967.

[6] C.B. Stabell and O.D. Fjeldstad. 1998, Configuring Value for Competitive Advantage: On Chains, Shops, and Networks, *Strategic Management Journal* vol. 19, no. 5, pp. 413–37.

nature of the relationships in which it is engaged. We will now turn to the examination of individual relationships in more detail.

Single Relationships

We now need to develop a way of analysing the content of a single relationship within a network. In Chapter 1 we described how relationships evolve and how they solve the problems of both sellers and buyers. We will now use the ideas on the patterns in networks that we have just developed.[7] These will help to identify in more detail the effects of a relationship on both supplier and customer companies.

Activity links

A relationship can systematically link the inter-dependent activities performed in a supplier and a customer. This can include basic service or production activities, as when a company overhauls a customer's equipment on site, rather than have it returned to its depot, or when a cable producer delivers cables to a ship-builder ready-cut to a required length, rather than in a roll. It can also include the activities that facilitate or control a production process, such as Just-in-Time co-ordination to reduce stocks at both companies. It can also include logistics or design as when a software supplier links its software development to the service design of an insurance company. The activity structures, links and patterns between five companies are illustrated in Figure 2.4.

A business marketer faces the important question of which activities to link with its customers. This will depend on the nature of the customer's problem and its view of the relationship, as well as the supplier's strategy for that relationship. For example, a customer may see its problem as the need to reduce its overall operational costs, rather than simply to buy suitable products or services. In this case a supplier that is prepared to invest in developing complex activity links may be suitable. But such an approach is unlikely to be successful where a customer is unwilling to commit itself to the costs and dependence on a single supplier that would be involved. In this case a more limited linking of activities is likely to be appropriate. Another question facing the business marketer concerns how the linking should be done. This will involve the marketer working closely with his own operating staff, who will also be dealing with the customer to relate investment levels and likely pay-offs to overall strategy for a relationship.

Resource ties

A relationship can also tie together resources in both of the companies, as in Figure 2.5. These resources may be the products, service capabilities or facilities that are built together through the relationship. The tie can be physical, such as when a pipeline

[7] This discussion is based on Håkan Håkansson and Ivan Snehota (eds), *Developing Relationships in Business Networks*, London, Routledge, 1995.

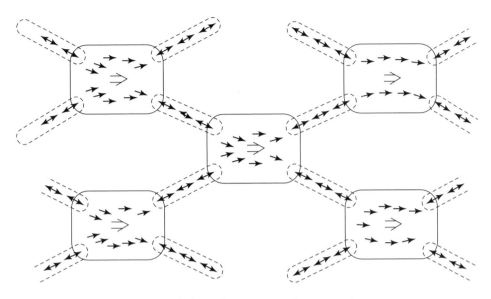

Figure 2.4   Activity structures, links and pattern over five companies.

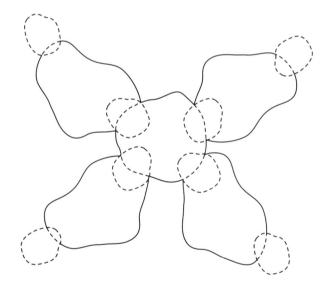

Figure 2.5   Resource ties between five companies.

connects the two companies but more commonly it is the knowledge resources of the two companies that are adapted to each other. This occurs when a retailer has its call-centre operated by a telecoms company or an automotive company has its system suppliers take responsibility for the development of certain parts of a car. This process of systematically relating the resources of each side to the other has an important effect on the resources themselves. As they become better developed in relation to one company, they become less developed in relation to others.

For the business marketer, this means that resource investment decisions or even ways of thinking about technical or operating issues can tie a company to a particular customer and adversely affect its ability to relate effectively to others. Resource ties can develop gradually and unconsciously as problems are solved within a relationship. These ties can be substantial and important in old relationships, without the companies being aware of them. In contrast, innovation often occurs when resources are tied together in new ways between companies and this can lead to the development of offerings with wide application. Both of these issues emphasize the importance for the marketer of auditing each important relationship. We will deal fully with the process of relationship audit in Chapter 5.

Actor bonds

Business relationships always have a social content. People in the two companies get to know each other through interaction and this is important in the growth of trust, which is necessary for the relationship to develop. Sentiments, attitudes, norms and values are affected by the evolution of the relationship and the two companies become part of the same social system. These social dimensions add up to the bonds existing between the two companies. These bonds are a central part of the identity of a company and of its ability to work with others. Figure 2.6 shows a schematic illustration of actor bonds between individuals in five companies.

A relationship is a way of connecting situations separated from each other by time. The current situation in a relationship is built on what has occurred in the past and it forms the basis of what will happen in the future. By managing relationships in a conscious way, the business marketer is taking advantage of history. But the marketer must also manage the expectations of the individuals involved and developing inter-personal relationships has long been an important part of business marketing.

Characterizing relationships

It is possible to investigate the content of relationships in a network by interviews and by inspection of offerings, facilities and routines and in this way build a picture of the links, ties and bonds that they contain. An example of this is provided in Figure 2.7 for a single customer and three of its largest suppliers. The volume of transactions within each relationship is indicated by the diameter of the circles. Figure 2.7 illustrates a number of differences between the relationships, as follows:

- Relationship 3 is the largest in terms of volume and consists mainly of actor bonds. It is described by the customer's purchasing manager as very positive: "There are never any problems with this supplier." But despite good inter-personal relationships the companies have done little to integrate their activities or to make resource investments in their relationship.

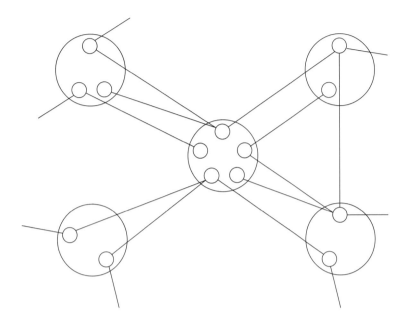

Figure 2.6 Actor bonds between five companies.

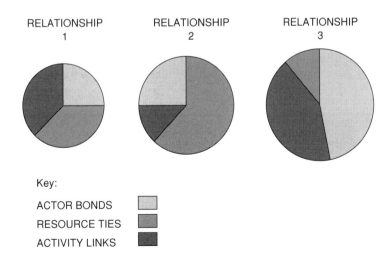

Figure 2.7 The substance of three relationships.

Figures 2.4, 2.5, 2.6 and 2.7. *Source*: Håkansson and Snehota, *Developing Business Relationships in Industrial Networks*, Routledge, 1992.

- The customer considered that Relationship 1, with the smallest supplier, was much more difficult to handle. Actor bonds are relatively undeveloped and there had recently been a major conflict with the supplier about how to commercialize some technical developments that had been made within the relationship.
- Relationship 2 is different from the other two as it includes more resource ties without corresponding activity links. An example of this would be in the case of a supplier of equipment or of design or development services. Here the design of the offering itself is critical, but this can be carried out without strong links between the supplier and customer. Such relationships are often quite easy to handle because they can be isolated from other aspects of the two companies' operations and it is easy to form a project group to handle them. However, these relationships can lead to problems in other relationships. The resource ties between the companies mean that some of their resources have been affected by the relationship. These resources have to be used in other relationships. Even if the design of the resource is good in itself, it might not be appropriate for these other relationships.

A comparison of these three relationships illustrates the following important points for the marketing manager:

- There are significant differences between relationships even if each is well developed and mature. Relationships are not single-dimensional and the business marketer needs to analyse them multi-dimensionally. The content of a relationship is the outcome of a number of factors: the strategies of the two companies; the characteristics of the network; the two companies' problems and resources; and the evolution of the relationship itself. Differences in the content of a relationship will affect the relationship management task for the marketer.
- The absence of conflicts or difficulties in a relationship is not necessarily a good sign. It can also be an indication that there is insufficient interaction taking place. All relationships where there is a lot happening will have difficulties and conflicts. These difficulties also give supplier and customer the opportunity to learn more about each other. Conflicts that are handled well by the marketer can contribute to the development of a relationship.
- Marketing companies often have relationships in which they have worked hard to build the social bonds with a customer. However, they may not have worked so hard to build activity links and resource ties. These relationships are probably not fulfilling their potential, because the value of a relationship is directly related to the links and ties between the companies. Also, "nice and friendly" relationships that are built solely on actor bonds are much easier to break than those with strong activity links and resource ties.

Connected Relationships

A relationship is developed through interaction between two companies. Yet in this interaction the two companies cannot just think about developing this relationship by itself, but must also relate it to the other relationships they have. Managing and developing a relationship is not an isolated activity, but just one piece in a larger puzzle that we call a network. A marketing manager responsible for developing a single relationship must consequently look at in this larger context and how it affects a larger *activity pattern*, *resource constellation* and *web of actors*.

Activity pattern

Figure 2.8 shows an activity pattern involving a supplier and a customer and some of their other relationships. The activities that the supplier and customer perform in relation to each other must synchronize the two companies' operations, but all their other relationships provide restrictions and opportunities for this process. Production, logistics, administration, design can all be moved, redesigned or connected to each other in different ways and different relationships, on both the supplier's and the customer's side. The overall outcome of this activity pattern is determined by interaction between all of the companies involved. This determines the efficiency of the network as a whole and the well-being of each company.

Figure 2.8 might give the impression that it is possible to get a single, complete picture of the total activity pattern. However, this is not the case in most situations for two main reasons:

- The sheer number of different activities restricts the analysis. Each activity can be broken down into greater detail and each can be re-integrated into new larger

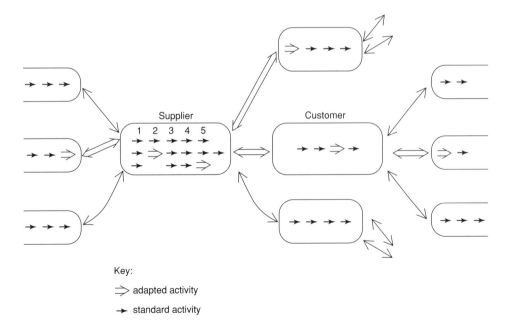

Figure 2.8   **Activity pattern for a supplier and customer.**

activities. Increases in the cost of acquiring the skills and technologies to develop and fulfil offerings add to this complexity. These mean that companies must now concentrate on fewer activities, in which they excel. Many of the activities they previously carried out are being spread among many other companies in the network with which they have relationships. Developments in information technology contribute to the co-ordination of this wider spread of activities.

- There is no clear boundary that can be drawn around an activity pattern. Every border or limitation must be arbitrary and will depend on the starting point. For the activities in Figure 2.8 the border will probably only appear reasonable for those in the centre of the pattern. If the pattern were examined from the perspective of one of the peripheral activities, then another boundary, including other activities, would be necessary.

This might appear to be bad news for a business marketer. It reinforces the need for the marketer to constantly re-examine relationships and patterns. But it does mean that the marketer must be realistic in his expectations of analysis and that this analysis must be carried out with the clear objective of looking at specific activities or problems. It also demonstrates the enormous potential that exists in a network to develop all existing activity patterns. There will never be a final and optimal pattern.

Resource constellation

The resources involved in a relationship are also parts of a larger whole. The offering of a single company will depend on its own resources and those of other companies. The ties between these different resources are important as they affect the characteristics of each of them. Through interaction, the different resources are systematically related to each other, embedded in each other's operations and developed in order to cope with each other's characteristics and requirements. In this way the two companies "co-evolve". For example, a logistics company's distribution depots and vehicle fleet may evolve to accommodate the different requirements of large or small users, those that have their own central warehouses or those that have no facilities. These resource investments will in turn affect decisions by the company's customers about their investment in their own facilities and distribution expertise and their relationships with other providers.

The resources in the evolving constellation will be complementary, but there will always be some contradictions, such as those customers that continue to invest in their own facilities while also using those of a contractor. Previous examples of resource combination illustrate the difficulties and complexities of resource combination. Thus it took more than twenty years from the introduction of computers before they were combined with the keyboard, something that today seems absolutely natural. The keyboard itself has had the QWERTY design since the end of the nineteenth century. This design was related to the mechanical functioning of the machine. It was intended to make it impossible to type quickly, so that the typing levers did not become entangled with each other. Thus, an early resource combination still exists despite the fact that one part has been completely changed.

An understanding of resource constellations has important implications for business marketers. It means that they must examine their existing offerings and resources. What has influenced their development? Are they the product of history or determined by convenience in existing relationships? Can they be developed to solve customers' problems more effectively or to reduce costs through new resource combinations with those customers, or our own or the customer's other suppliers?

Web of actors

The companies in a network do not just consist of a set of resources that perform activities. They are purposefully directed by many individual actors. These individuals form a social structure and have views of each other in relation to the total network and they act on those views. The individuals bring the network to life. As in all social structures, there are elements of friendship, closeness, distance, antagonism, prejudice, and so on. The individuals may belong to professional associations, they may change their employment between companies in the same network. Their companies may be connected through ownership or there may be strong cultural or operational links between them. These individuals try systematically to influence each other as their companies co-evolve. This process of individual influence is both an effect of the co-evolving relationships between companies in the network, but also an important influence on it.

The actor bonds in a network are closely related to the development of trust and commitment between individuals and their companies. Individuals gain from the efforts of others and learn from their experience of success and failure. Like all aspects of a network, actor bonds are multi-dimensional. Companies relate to each other in many ways and for many reasons. So it is meaningless for the marketer to try to make an overall ranking of his interactions. Instead, every customer and supplier must be seen to have value on some dimension. Large-volume customers are certainly important but so might be lower-volume customers. These may have special requirements and because of the bonds between them, both companies can develop new skills to meet these requirements. Others may be valuable, even though there are few bonds between them, because they contribute much more revenue than they cost. Business marketers must examine the nature and value of the bonds between their company and its customers and between others that surround it. These bonds to a large extent determine the pattern of resource allocation and the activities between companies. This is often in ways that may not make immediate economic sense, but have a strong logic in terms of trust, confidence or reliability. In the same way the absence of these bonds can confound the development of relationships in the face of an overwhelming technological or economic logic.

Positions in a Network

So far in this chapter we have developed a number of concepts that will help us to understand and describe the network of relationships in which a business marketer operates. In this final section we will bring these together to make sense of a single company's *position* in the network. A network is a special organizational form that relates companies to each other in a particular structure based on their relationships with others. Each company in a network has a unique position in relation to all the others:

> A company's network position is defined by the characteristics of the company's relationships and the benefits and obligations that arise from them.

A business marketers' activities will depend on his company's position in the network and we can illustrate this by looking at the system suppliers in our earlier example of Toyota. System suppliers have a complex direct relationship with Toyota through which they are obliged to supply a major part of a vehicle. They also have relationships with companies in the second and third tiers of the network. Toyota expects them to use these relationships to provide it with access to the skills and resources of other suppliers without it having to manage the relationship itself. In turn, the second and third tier suppliers expect the system supplier to provide them with access to a major customer. This access is of course conditional on the system supplier maintaining its relationship with Toyota. The system supplier's position provides them with the benefit of being able to strongly influence the operations, revenues and prices of their suppliers. Also, because of their access to the wider network and their integration and development skills, they are much more important to Toyota than a second tier supplier of a single commodity, with which they have no direct contact.

An assessment of network position is an important basis for the business marketer to achieve change in that position. For example, a system supplier to Toyota may choose to invest in a wider range of relationships with its suppliers to strengthen and increase the scale of its relationship with Toyota. Alternatively, it may try to develop a similar relationship with another major customer, perhaps in another country. A second or third tier supplier may decide to invest in the technological resources to design its own dedicated offerings so that it can build direct relationships with other major customers. Similarly, Toyota could seek to change its position by establishing direct relationships with a number of currently second tier suppliers to increase its flexibility and reduce dependence on a few system suppliers. All these changes would involve building relationships, all involve the acquisition of resources or technologies and all will affect the company's current relationships and position.

Conclusion

This chapter has introduced some of the complexities of business marketing. Business marketing is not just about developing good offerings and selling them well. It is not just about developing and managing many different relationships over time and taking difficult decisions about resource allocation between them. All of these are important but the activities of a business marketer take place within the wider context of a network. The network affects each relationship in the same way that each relationship affects the transactions that take place within it. It is vital for the business marketer to be aware of these network effects. This is so that he can consider the effects on a customer relationship of that customer's relationship with its other suppliers and its own customers, as well as those between the marketer and its other customers and its suppliers. Even more importantly, a company's network position determines the opportunities and restrictions that it faces. A realistic understanding of these is an essential preliminary to developing and changing that network position. Analysing network position, deciding and achieving change are the essence of business marketing strategy.

Relationships are more complex than single sales and networks are more complex than single relationships. There is always a temptation for the marketer to deal at the simplest level and try to make short-term sales at the expense of a longer-term relationship or to concentrate within a single relationship and ignore the wider influences on that relationship.

Similarly, there is often a tendency for the marketer to try to build the inter-personal bonds between his own company and the customer as a basis for a relationship and to neglect the development of time-consuming, costly, but potentially more durable, activity links and resource ties between the companies.

Further Reading

Wroe Alderson (1965) *Market Behavior and Executive Action*, Homewood, ILL, Irwin.
RM Axelrod (1984) *The Evolution of Cooperation*, New York, Basic Books.
Bjorn Axelsson and Geoff Easton (1992) *Industrial Networks: A New View of Reality*, London, Routledge.
Wim Biemans (1992) *Managing Innovation within Networks*, London, Routledge.
David Ford (ed.) (2001) *Understanding Business Marketing and Purchasing*, London, International Thomson, especially readings 3.1–3.9.
Håkan Håkansson and Ivan Snehota (eds) (1995) *Developing Relationships in Business Networks*, London, Routledge.

UNDERSTANDING TECHNOLOGY IN BUSINESS NETWORKS

3

Aims of this Chapter

- To show how business marketing is inextricably linked to the technologies on which a company's offerings are based, as well as those of the company's suppliers and customers.
- To analyse different types of technology and provide a structure to help marketers understand the technological strengths and weaknesses of their company.
- To describe how companies acquire, manage and exploit their technologies and the implications of these activities for business marketing.
- To examine the role and effect of technology in business networks and in individual relationships.

Introduction: The Impact of Technology on Business Marketing

It is not enough for business marketers to understand the offerings that they supply to customers. They must also know something about the technologies on which those offerings are based as well as the technologies on which their customers and suppliers depend. Business marketers also need to be involved in decisions on the management of their company's technologies, which are critical for its future success.

Business marketing companies face a number of issues that relate to technology:

- Companies are likely to need an increasingly wide range of know-how, skills, abilities or technologies in order to provide the offerings that their customers need. For example, car manufacturers once depended on the relatively simple technologies needed to design the body and to bend sheets of steel to make it. They also needed the technology to design simple engines, to cast cylinder blocks, to forge metal for the springs and to assemble simple components. Most cars are still built with sheet steel, but aesthetic and performance requirements mean that they are now designed with the aid of complex software. Car manufacturers now have to incorporate computerized engine management systems, computer-controlled suspensions, climate control and devices to tell us if the tyres are flat, to navigate us to our destination and soothe us on our way with the music of our choice.

- The cost to the company of developing its technologies is likely to increase with each new generation of offerings.
- The rate of technological change outside the company is accelerating and competitors are engaged in a desperate race to introduce new technologies into their operations and offerings. For example, aluminium is increasingly replacing steel in the construction of car bodies. This poses major design and production challenges for car companies who have no experience of using this material.
- New competitors often arrive in established industries using innovative technologies that have been developed in quite different applications. For example, the traditional banks face severe competition from grocery retailers, insurance companies and entirely new entrants, all of whom are skilled in managing call-centres and web-based sales. Many banks respond by using the services of specialist customer-service companies. In other words, technological innovation has led them to contract a central area of their business to an outside supplier.
- Companies cannot afford to develop and maintain in their own company all the skills and technologies that they need for their offerings. Nor do they have the time to develop their own version of each new technology that affects them. Instead they have to concentrate on fewer technologies and activities and they are increasingly dependent on the skills, technologies and resources of suppliers, development partners and their customers to enable them to provide offerings to those customers. The development and fulfilment of an offering that is finally supplied to an end-customer are likely to be carried out in more and more different companies in the network. For example, an aluminium-bodied car may be designed by an independent design house, its body will be welded and assembled using the skills of the aluminium suppliers. It will incorporate components designed and produced by thousands of different companies, all of which will be assembled into larger modules by system suppliers in the car company's factories. The "manufacturer" of the car will in fact only be responsible for final assembly and marketing to the customer.

All this means that companies face critical decisions on which technologies they will develop and retain in-house and those where they will rely on others. For example: a confectionary company may decide to stop designing and producing its own packaging. Instead, it may source packaging from a range of designers and producers, to achieve lower costs. Meanwhile, developments in the technology of packaging will continue elsewhere. The company may then find that its competitors are introducing innovative packaging. But if the company wishes to restart its own design and production, it will have to incur the costs, difficulties and risks of trying to catch up with current packaging technology.

On the other hand, before deciding to develop a particular technology a company must be sure that the technology is central to its competitive position in the network. It will also have to make a commitment to continued investment in staff and facilities and it is unlikely to see a return on that investment in the short term.

Technology in a Company

Technology decisions are very long term and can profoundly affect a company's ability to develop and fulfil its offerings for many years. Business marketers cannot just confine their attention to their current offerings or to new ones that are based on existing technologies. Instead, they must be able to understand the technological position of their own company and those of its customers and suppliers and be able to use that understanding to develop their approach to their customers.

Tasks in technology

As a first step it is useful to separate out the three principal tasks of companies concerning technology. These are first, to *acquire* the technologies that the company needs for its operations and its offerings. Second, to fully *exploit* these expensively acquired technologies in their offerings by other means, and third, to *manage* these two processes effectively in a complex organization. These three tasks are shown in Figure 3.1.

Acquiring technology

Companies have three alternative ways of acquiring technology:

- **Internal acquisition:** This is when the company "makes" its own technology by developing it in its own research and development facilities. This method may be slow, risky and expensive, but it is an important way of maintaining the company's research capability, "stock" of technologies and its competitive position.
- **External acquisition:** A company can externally acquire technology in a number of ways. First, it can take a licence on the technology of another company. This is what happens when a company buys the right to manufacture gas-turbines to the designs of General Electric or to supply fast food using the skills and technology of the McDonald's corporation in a McDonald's franchise. Licensing is often a much quicker way to acquire a technology than by developing it internally. However, using licensing means that the company may only acquire obsolete technology or technology that is also available to its competitors.

  A company can also buy another that has the technology it needs. This is likely to be an expensive method and it may not be possible to successfully transfer the technology from the acquired company. These problems are often expressed in the saying, "Don't buy the dairy, just because you want a glass of milk". On the other hand, buying a company may also provide access to its relationships and to a new part of the network.

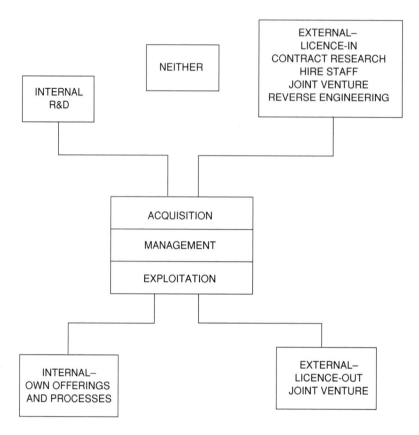

Figure 3.1 Tasks in technology.
Source: Developed from David Ford and Mike Saren *Managing and Marketing Technology*, London, International Thomson (2001), p. 43.

A company can also commission a contract-research company to develop a technology for it. Contract research is likely to be relatively quick, but expensive, and the acquiring company does not gain the ability to develop future generations of technology for itself.

Alternatively, it can hire staff from a company that has skills and technology that it wants. This is a very common method, but to be successful, it is essential that the company has or can develop a culture in which the new staff feel comfortable and can develop further.

It can enter into a joint venture with another company, where each contributes part of the funds and/or part of the expertise needed to develop a technology. Joint ventures are useful where the company has some, but not all of the skills or finance available for a development. But by entering into a joint venture the company will have to give up some control over the direction of that technological development.

Finally, it can try to copy or "reverse-engineer" the technology from another company. Copying may be low cost, but it can cause problems if the company falls foul of patent laws. It also means that the company becomes a technological "follower" and may also lose some of its abilities to solve customers' problems.

- **Don't acquire the technology:** A third alternative is simply not to acquire a needed technology! Instead, the company can buy an offering from a supplier, based on the supplier's technology. In this way it gains the benefits of the supplier's technologies, but it does not acquire the technologies themselves, nor does it incur the costs of developing them. We refer to these technologies on which a company depends, but does not own as "external technologies".[1] This method has the obvious advantage of saving the time and costs of its own development and its R&D budget can be used for other and perhaps more important technologies. Also, the supplier of the offering will be able to spread its costs of developing the technology over a number of customers and thus may be able to charge a low price for the offering. But buying an offering, rather than developing a technology, has the disadvantage that the company will be dependent on a particular supplier and its technology. Also, the company is likely to receive an offering which is technologically indistinguishable from those of other customers who may be its competitors, unless it has a very special relationship with the supplier.

Decisions on which technologies to acquire are critical for a company. Its ability to develop and fulfil its future offerings will depend on having the right technologies at the right time. Decisions on how to acquire them will affect the timing of their availability, their costs and their suitability. It is important that companies choose the appropriate method, depending on their own skills, the future requirements of its customers, the urgency of the situation, the availability of alternatives and the age of the technology.

But these decisions are often taken by companies without clear strategic analysis and earlier studies indicate that few companies take a coherent approach to technology acquisition decisions.[2] A number of functions need to be involved in these important decisions, in addition to the company's most senior management:

- R&D staff are obviously the most qualified people to assess their own competence in a particular technology and those of potential external suppliers. Unfortunately, R&D people also invented the not-invented-here syndrome! They are often keen to convince management that they should develop their own version of a particular technology in-house. A wrong decision to develop in-house can lead to delays, high costs or failure.
- A company's purchasing staff should have an important role in decisions on whether to acquire technology. They are responsible for the company's actual or potential

---

[1] A useful example of this process is the watch on your wrist. By buying it you acquired the benefits of the technologies of the producer. You have a beautiful and reliable timepiece but you did not acquire the technologies themselves. You cannot reproduce the watch for yourself. The technologies remain with the supplier. As far as you are concerned, they are external technologies.

[2] Earlier studies in both the USA and the UK indicate a sharp difference between a small number of companies that use a variety of technology acquisition and exploitation methods and the larger majority that use licensing as an ad hoc way to cope with a technological inadequacy, see D Ford and M Saren, *Managing and Marketing Technology*, London, International Thomson (2001), p. 29.

relationships with suppliers. They should be able to advise on whether suitable technologies exist in suppliers and whether these could be translated into valuable offerings as a substitute for in-house development or external acquisition.

- Business marketers should also be involved in technology acquisition decisions. Their input should be based on their knowledge of what customers are likely to require in future offerings, what technologies they currently use and plan to acquire and how these relate to the technologies of the company and its suppliers.

Exploiting technology

Companies face similar choices in exploiting their technologies:

- **Internal exploitation:** This is the most obvious way for a company to exploit its technologies, by using them in its own processes and offerings. Internal use of technologies is likely to lead to lower costs and improved offerings. But it is only a limited way of recovering the company's investments in its technologies.
- **External exploitation:** This is where the company exploits its technologies by selling them to others, most commonly by licence, but also by offering a "turnkey" package where it provides the production equipment and product design and the customer simply has to "turn-the-key" to start operations. External exploitation has the advantage of generating additional revenue for the company. The disadvantage is that it may involve selling to competitors those technologies that are critical to the company's future. This is often referred to as "selling the seed-corn". A different sort of external exploitation is a joint venture with another company where both companies contribute their own technologies and gain the benefit of those of each other. A joint venture can develop new technologies through the efforts of both companies, as well as solving customer problems that would be beyond the resources of one company acting alone.

The wider, external exploitation of their technologies is often disregarded by companies and many opportunities thus can be missed. Companies often take individual exploitation decisions without sound strategic analysis. It is relatively easy for a company to spot an inadequacy in its technologies when its sales start to slump. It may then look around for a company from which to license an up-to-date technology. Few companies actually analyse their inventory of technologies and develop ways to exploit them fully. Few companies actually have a clear idea of what skills and technologies their company has and what value they might have to other companies. This is illustrated by studies in the USA and the UK that show that in the majority of licence deals, the initiative was taken by the buyer, rather than the seller.[3]

Full exploitation of technology is likely to be achieved only by using it in-house and externally at different stages in the life of the technology, with different counterparts and in different applications. Business marketers need to be involved in planning for this

[3] Ford and Saren, op. cit. p. 37.

phased exploitation. For example, a company may use a new type of design in its own offerings for a period of time and then license it to others in different countries or for different applications. The car industry has many examples of this. General Motors licensed the designs of earlier models of its Opel Kadett and Ascona to Daewoo, Mitsubishi licensed designs to Proton that it was no longer using and Fiat have licensed obsolescent technologies to both Poland and Russia.

Unfortunately, marketers are often too preoccupied with generating sales from the company's offerings, rather than being concerned with maximizing the return on its technological assets. Also, the potential customers for a technology licence are very often the company's competitors and marketers are often unwilling to take any risk of helping a competitor even if the revenue prospects are attractive or the technology is old.

Managing technology

This third task includes the important issue of how the company can speedily and economically commercialize new technologies and bring them to its customers. It also includes how the company can transfer knowledge around the company so that each operating unit can gain from developments elsewhere in the company so that the same problems are not solved several times. Finally, it also includes the critical task of developing and implementing policies for technology exploitation.

In many companies, these activities are fragmented and this causes considerable problems for the business marketer. Often, a marketer when responsible for solving the problems of customer in a particular relationship will have difficulty in finding out whether similar problems have been solved elsewhere and how it was done. Also, the business marketer will have to take an active part in the commercialization of technology both across different relationships and in specific offerings.

We will revisit these problems in Chapters 6 and 7 when we look at the development and fulfilment of offerings.

Box 3.1 The Problem of Using Technology Effectively

This problem has been highlighted by many managers in the saying, "If we knew what we know, we would be unbeatable". However, Siemens is attempting to deal with the problem among its 470 000 employees in 190 countries by setting up "Sharenet", an internal system on which knowledge is posted for use throughout the company. For example, Siemens Malaysia used this system when it wanted to bid to supply a high-speed data link between Kuala Lumpur and its new airport, but lacked the necessary know-how. Through the sharenet it found that Siemens was already working on a similar project in Denmark. The Malaysian company was able to adapt what had been done there and won an order for a pilot project. The chairman of Siemens hopes that the system will enable him to say in future, "Siemens knows what Siemens knows." (*The Economist*, 2 June 2001, p. 103)

Examining technologies

An offering that will solve a customer's problem will be based on a number of different technologies. This means that it is important for the business marketer to differentiate between different types of technology and to understand their respective role in the company's competitive success. This can be achieved as follows.

Types of technology

A company's technologies can be separated into two broad types:

- Product technologies provide the ability to design a particular type of offering. These technologies are the basis of the company's *problem-solving abilities*. For example, McDonald's have product technologies that they apply to the design of offerings that solve the customer problem of needing to eat quickly and speedily. A "Big Mac" is one of the many current outputs from these technologies. McDonald's could apply the same technology to the design of a pizza. Similarly, Bic have the product technologies to design small, disposable, plastic products. They have applied these technologies to a range of products such as pens, razors, lighters, etc.
- Process technologies provide the ability to produce or fulfil an offering, on time, in the right place to the right specification, at the right price and to do all these things consistently. Process technologies are the basis of the company's *transfer ability*. Black and Decker claim to have strong process technologies in the production of small electric motors. The process technologies behind this sophistication have had a strong effect on their marketing strategy. They have exploited these technologies by finding many different things to "wrap round" these electric motors and introduce innovative, affordable and reliable electric drills, lawnmowers, hedge cutters, paint strippers, electric saws, etc. McDonald's have process technologies that enable them to produce their fast-food *fast*. For example, they designed a scoop that allows their operators to stack French fries neatly in a carton with only two hand movements. The scoop is not the technology, but it is an *output* from it. McDonald's have recently started to exploit their product and process technologies more widely in two areas; closer to their original business in setting up coffee shops and further away in opening the first "Golden Arches" hotels.

A combination of product and process technologies is always needed to satisfy the requirements of a customer. Thus, the design of a car is of little use to a motorist unless someone has the process technologies to produce it. In the examples that we have given above, both types of technologies are located in the same company that supplies the offering. But this is not always the case. In many situations it is the *customer* who possesses either or both of the necessary product and process technologies. For example, many retailers specify the design (product technology) of the offerings that they wish to buy and manufacturing methods (process technologies) that will be used to produce the offerings. In this case the customer has incurred the costs of developing the offering and so will expect to pay a much lower price than for an offering that has been developed by a supplier.

In other situations a company may design an offering (product technology), but either by choice or necessity it may rely on another company with the appropriate process technology to manufacture it. For example, when Amgen developed Epoetin alfa, its first treatment for anaemia (product technology), it did not have the ability to either manufacture or distribute it, so it launched a 50:50 joint venture with Kirin Brewery which had the manufacturing and distribution presence in major Asian markets (process technology).[4] The use of the technologies of different companies may be coordinated by a third company that has a relationship with end-customers. This is common in the fashion industry. Here retailers liaise closely with independent designers on what garments are required and then use suppliers that "cut-make-and-trim" garments to those designs for their stores.

In some networks a number of combinations can exist. For example, Boeing has traditionally designed the undercarriages of its airliners itself (product technologies). It has then contracted with US manufacturers, who have the necessary process technologies, to produce undercarriages to that design. In contrast, Airbus has used suppliers who both design and produce undercarriages to its requirements specified in terms of dimensions, weight of aircraft and landing speed.

The product and process technologies of a company affect its position in a business network, its relationships with its customers and suppliers and its ability to compete. But these networks are not stable and marketers must be aware of the constantly shifting relationship and technological situation. For example:

- The US producers of undercarriages we referred to above will have a particular relationship with Boeing, based on their own process technologies and Boeing's product technologies.
- European companies will have a different relationship with Airbus based on their own product *and* process technologies.
- The European suppliers may find it difficult to work with Boeing because both supplier and customer would have similar product technologies. They would also find it difficult to compete on price with US suppliers who did not have to cover the same overheads of research and development.
- The US manufacturers would find it difficult to build a relationship with Airbus, unless they invested heavily in their own product technology. But recently a US supplier, BF Goodrich, has committed itself to these investments and won a major order from Airbus for the main landing gear for the A380, "Super-Jumbo". However, Airbus has sought to maintain its relationship with a major European supplier by awarding it the contract for the nose-wheel mechanism for the aircraft.
- Boeing faces many of the technology issues we have described above. It cannot continue to develop in-house many of the technologies on which it depends, so it is seeking relationships with suppliers where *they* are responsible for developing the necessary product and process technologies and for carrying the financial risks associated with that development.

[4] Alberto Torres. Unlocking the Value of Intellectual Assets, *The McKinsey Quarterly*, 1999, no. 4, pp. 28–37.

Business relationships integrate the product and process technologies of the two companies involved, so it is vital for business marketers to know what technologies their companies have and how they are assessed by those around them. This assessment will affect a company's relationships with its customers, its suppliers and its development partners.

Basic and distinctive technologies

Not all technologies are of equal importance to a company and business marketers need to know how their company's technologies are viewed by customers and which are more or less important to their competitive success. We can examine this important issue by differentiating between *basic* and *distinctive* technologies:

- **Basic technologies:** These are the technologies on which a company depends and without which it could not operate in a particular network. For example, car companies must have the necessary process technologies to run an assembly line. They must have the product technologies to design a passenger compartment and the seats in it. But for most companies, these are basic technologies that are a necessary, but not sufficient condition for competitive success.
- **Distinctive technologies:** These are the technologies of a particular supplier that are seen by customers as somehow "special" and are the source of that supplier's competitive advantage. These distinctive technologies are likely to be different for different competing suppliers. So, for example, when other companies had similar, basic process technologies, Toyota developed distinctive technologies in vehicle manufacture. Not only did these reduce its inventories, but they also improved the "build-quality" of its cars. For many years customers saw these distinctive technologies as the basis of the reliability of Toyota cars. In contrast, Volvo has a distinctive product technology in safety engineering. In both cases, customers do not necessarily have to understand the technologies, as long as they can recognize their effects. Also, it does not matter whether or not the company's technology in these areas is actually better than that of other companies, at least in the short term. If customers believe it to be better, then it is distinctive!

The separation between basic and distinctive technologies has important implications for business marketers. A company's offerings will depend on all its own technologies as well as those of its suppliers. Nevertheless, its distinctive technologies are likely to be the basis of its competitive success. It is important for marketers to have a realistic view of which of their company's technologies are seen by its customers as basic or distinctive – and how they relate to customers' problems. For example, a company may produce electronic components whose performance is identical to those of its competitors (based on basic product technologies), but it may have distinctive process technologies that enable it to supply components with very low failure rates. The company may be able to build productive relationships with those customers for which absence of failure is far more important than absolute level of performance.

Customers do not buy products, they buy offerings to solve their problems. These offerings are based on the technologies of the supplier and its suppliers. Very often a customer will establish a relationship with a supplier rather than develop and produce a similar offering for itself. These "make-or-buy" choices are often long-term decisions for customers as the technologies involved become "external" for it.[5] It is important for marketers to understand that these choices are not just made on the basis of the supplier's price, "quality" or features but on the basis of the supplier's current technologies and its perceived ability and willingness to continue development.

More strategically, once a company has assessed which of its technologies are distinctive, then it can decide whether to continue operating in some of its basic technologies. Often a company can reduce its levels of investment and operating costs by sub-contracting activities to other companies, so that the technologies involved become external to them. This practice is increasing as companies try to limit the costs of technological development and managerial activity. Marketers need to be involved in these decisions in their own companies, based on their understanding of customer requirements and how these relate to the company's technologies. They also need to be aware that increasing pressure on companies to contract out activities can lead to major marketing opportunities. An example of these opportunities can be seen in the growth of "contract manufacturers", such as Flextronics, Solectron, etc. These type of companies undertake production for other companies and currently account for about 11 per cent of world production of electronic hardware. Contract manufacturing is growing at around 20 per cent per annum. Contract manufacturers have developed relationships with component suppliers and buy their own material. They have distinctive process technologies and they are able to advise their customers on product design to ease manufacturing. The largest have factories in several countries. This enables them to ramp up production quickly to get new products to market for their customers. Also, if demand in one country increases rapidly, they can literally fly in an entire production line from somewhere else.

Box 3.2   An Analysis of Basic and Distinctive Technologies in a Food Ingredients Company[6]

The matrix in Figure 3.2 was produced for a supplier of food flavourings, seasonings and ingredients. It shows the percentage of the company's total gross-profit contribution generated by offerings that were based on distinctive or basic product and process technologies. The majority of its contribution came from offerings based on basic product and process technologies, (Cell 1, 66 per cent). An example of this is the seasoning for sausages, for which the technologies of formulation (product) and production are well known. In contrast, the design of flavourings for snack foods is an area where customers recognized that the company had some distinctiveness, although there was nothing special about its production skills. These offerings accounted for 19 per cent of total contribution. Emulsifiers are used to bind water and

---

[5] For a discussion of the concept of External Technologies, see Ford and Saren, op. cit., pp. 64–6.

[6] Developed from the work of Richard Brewer, Research student, University of Bath.

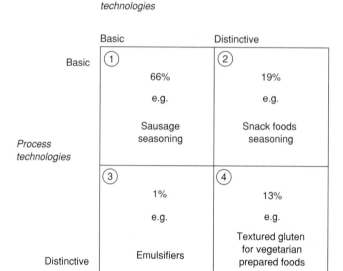

*Product
technologies*

Figure 3.2   The contribution of different product and process technologies.

Source: Ford and Saren, *Managing and Marketing Technology*, International Thomson, 2001.

fat together in food. The technology for designing these is widely known, but the company was seen to have distinctiveness in their production (Cell 3). But these offerings only represented 1 per cent of gross contribution. Finally, only 13 per cent of the company's gross contribution came from offerings based on technologies where it had both distinctive product and process technologies. This was in the area of textured gluten for the relatively new area of prepared vegetable meals.

Despite being heavily dependent on low-margin offerings, based on basic technologies, the company was financially successful. Further analysis indicated that this success was based on the speed with which it was able to spot emerging trends amongst ultimate consumers and on its good relationships with food producers. These enabled it to develop new flavour offerings to meet these requirements, often within 48 hours. However, the company was concerned that too much of its efforts were devoted to short-term customer response and it was locked into the low-margin Cell 1. It addressed this by putting more effort into longer-term relationship building and particularly technology acquisition programmes.

Technology, offerings and life-cycles

Most business marketers are familiar with the idea that a company's offering is likely to move through some sort of "life-cycle", during which sales increase, reach some sort of stable level and then decline as the offering has been adopted by most potential customers or is replaced by better offerings from competing suppliers. These simple life-cycles are not predictive devices and the pattern of a company's sales can depart from an expected pattern for many reasons, such as changes in customers' problems, competitive innovation or wider macro-economic factors. But life-cycles do explain important elements of the business marketer's task and this is illustrated in Figure 3.3.

Suppose that a company develops an offering (1), either alone or in co-operation with a customer. The company will then seek to introduce the offering to a number of customers, perhaps in a different form to each one. In this way it will try to achieve a return on its development expenditure. The costs of this development are likely to be considerable. For example, one major electronics company estimated that on average it needed to achieve 15 per cent of the world market for an offering just to recover its development costs, before taking into account production or marketing expenses. The offering will progress through a life-cycle of sales. At some point, the company will withdraw or radically change the offering.

It is important that the business marketer is able to do this *before* the offering is outdated by the competition, to the detriment of her relationships with customers. But the marketer faces two problems:

• The time that the offering is likely to provide the best solution to customer problems is likely to be short, either because the problems themselves change or because competitors develop better offerings. Another major electronics producer refers to "six-month markets". Clearly, if the company in this situation is two months late with its offering, then it has missed a third of the available market.

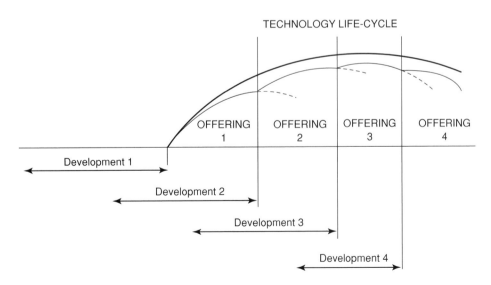

Figure 3.3 Technology and offering life-cycles.

- The length of time that a new offering takes to develop means that the development of offering 2 must start *before* the first offering has been launched.

Figure 3.3 also shows the sales curve for offering 2. If the company has managed the development and transition process well and the new offering relates well to customer problems, then this curve will show an upward trend. Similarly, the marketer will need to develop and time the transition to offering 3. Each succeeding offering will largely be based on modifications to earlier offerings and thus is likely to require less development expenditure than its predecessors. This may lead to higher profits, even though sales growth may be lower. However, each of the offerings will be based on one or more technologies that will themselves have a life-cycle and those technologies will become increasingly outdated. This is illustrated in Figure 3.3 by the Technology Life-Cycle that overlays the offering curves.[7]

Marketers must face the decision of whether to develop a further generation of offering based on existing technology or whether to switch to new or different technologies. Obviously, the time taken to make a major change in technology is likely to be longer and more costly than that required simply to introduce a new version of an offering based on "old" technology.

This means that business marketers must not just be involved in the development and introduction of successive generations of offerings. They must also be involved in much more critical decisions about the technologies on which their offerings depend. Business marketers need to be involved in decisions on the development and internal exploitation of the company's technologies in its own offerings. But they must also be concerned with their wider *external* exploitation. They need to co-ordinate both internal and external means of achieving a return on the company's technological assets. For example, it is often possible to exploit technologies that are no longer usable internally by licensing them to other companies, in other countries, or for different applications.

Technology in supplier and customer

In Chapter 1 we saw that companies seek suppliers to solve their specific problems. Also, we showed that the way that they approach these suppliers will depend on the *uncertainties* that they face. Often they are unsure about what is the right solution for them, or they face a very wide range of alternative offerings or they are unsure about the fulfilment of the offering. These uncertainties relate to the technological understanding of the supplier and customer and this is illustrated in Figure 3.4.

The supplier in a relationship is likely to have a greater knowledge than the customer of the technologies on which its offering is based at the start of that relationship. Its limited understanding is likely to be an important factor in the customer's need uncertainty. Over time, the supplier's knowledge will increase, but so too will that of the

---

[7] David Ford and Chris Ryan, *Taking Technology to Market*, Harvard Business School, March–April 1981, pp. 117–26.

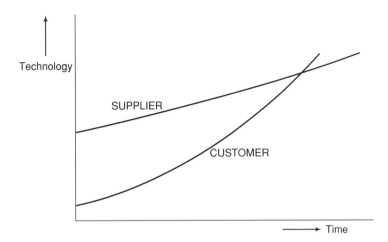

Figure 3.4 Technology in supplier and customer.

customer. The gap between the two curves is likely to narrow and they may eventually cross. In this case, the customer knows more about the technologies on which the supplier's offering is based than does the supplier itself. This situation is common in business markets. For example, many retailers will be involved in development and will specify both the product and the process technologies on which their purchases of textiles and other products are based.

The gap between the two lines indicates the relative technological contribution of the two companies to their relationship and is likely to be reflected in the supplier's profit margin. It is important for business marketers to continuously monitor their position on these curves. Suppliers who move close to or past the intersection of the lines are unlikely to earn high margins and will need to invest in their technological contribution to the relationship to do so – effectively moving their position to the left.

Technology and Networks

A network consists of companies, each having different product and process technologies. A company in the network is dependent on the technologies of its suppliers that are incorporated in their offerings and which it transforms using its own technologies to provide offerings for its customers, and so on. A combination of the technologies from many companies is needed to provide an offering that will meet the requirements of an end-consumer. The relationships between the companies in a network enable this process to take place. Companies operating in complex business networks can only make sense of their marketing by understanding how different skills and technologies are distributed throughout the network and the impact of this on the priorities of customers and suppliers and on the company itself.

Stability and change

The impact of the network on a company and its technologies is neither simple nor predictable. At least two dimensions can be identified:

- First and perhaps surprisingly, technology tends to stabilize the networks in which business marketers operate and restricts their freedom to innovate. The technologies that a company develops will lead it to invest in operational facilities and a range of offerings to exploit those technologies. Its customers and suppliers will make similar investments using their technologies. There is an incentive to use these investments, once they have been made and paid for. Each of these investments will be influenced by investments in surrounding companies. This leads to pressure on marketers from their own companies to produce offerings that use existing process facilities or product designs, so as to maximize the company's return on its technological investments. It also leads to pressure from customers and suppliers for the company to work within their technological boundaries. This pressure for continuity may also affect the direction of the company's future development.
- In contrast, successive refinements of existing technologies and the birth of new ones are probably the most important factors for change affecting companies. Developments can occur at any point in a network and affect even distant companies through the inter-connections of relationships. This makes it important for the business marketer to scan the wider network for technological developments that may be significant for her company and also to look for opportunities to exploit the company's technologies in new applications. Developments in technologies change the internal operations of a company but they also affect the relationship between the company and its counterparts. For example, a supplier may be able to reduce a customer's costs of inspection of delivered items by developing its own process technology to produce more consistently to specification. Similarly, by introducing new process technology, a supplier may be able to undertake activities previously carried out by the customer.

Adapting to the network

Companies operating in business networks develop technology themselves but they must also adapt to the technological development of other companies around them. Indeed, they rely on this technological development by others to complement their own. Consequently, business marketers need to be concerned with the technological developments that their company can and should be doing and what surrounding companies are also doing. In other words, they must know how the company can influence what is going on in the network and how it should take part in what others are initiating. A company's developments must take place in interaction with important counterparts. Every company has to take part in a sequence of actions, reactions, counteractions, co-operation in which companies' technologies and offerings are developed in relation to each other. We referred to this process in Chapter 2 as "co-evolution".

The company's own developments

In order for a company to take advantage of technological opportunities, it is important that it has a number of development projects as well as an intensive internal discussion about what are suitable development directions. Both the projects and the discussions must systematically include external parties such as customers and suppliers. Marketers have a primary role on the interface with external parties by discussing the company's intentions with its customers and also with its suppliers, who often need to be involved in major developments.

Relating to developments elsewhere

Business marketers also have an important role alongside that of purchasing and development staff to monitor the current and potential developments in counterpart companies. This includes both existing and potential customers, as well as developments in competing or complementary suppliers as well as within research institutions of different kinds. These developments elsewhere in the network can be of vital importance for the company.

Technology development between customer and supplier

The active involvement of customers has frequently been shown to be one of the key factors in successful new product development and launch. Indeed, Håkansson[8] has shown that the majority of technological development in business networks does not take place in either supplier or customer, but interactively between them. Often the potential users of an offering initiate its development, by searching out and working with potential suppliers. At other times suppliers seek a "lead-user" to be closely involved in the development of a product or process technology or an offering based on them.[9] Customers are important to suppliers in development for several reasons:

- Customers have to face the problems of using current offerings and have the greatest knowledge of how a new offering can provide an improved solution.
- Customers know how a single offering can be used in combination with others from different suppliers.
- Customers know about alternative and substitute offerings and how a new offering compares to alternatives.
- Customers know how the offering will be used by their customers and at other points in the network.
- Perhaps most importantly, customers are likely to be committed to the development process because they will benefit from improved performance.

[8] Håkan Håkansson, *Industrial Technological Development: A Network Approach*, London, Croom Helm, 1987.

[9] EA von Hippel, *The Sources of Innovation*, New York, Oxford University Press, 1988.

It is the business marketer's task to locate potential development partners among customers, to establish a relationship with them and to manage interactions with them during the development process. In doing this, it is important that the marketer understands and is able to communicate the benefits *to the customer* of a developmental relationship with a supplier. Some of these customer benefits are as follows:

- Suppliers have a range of different technologies that the customer can never match.
- By using the efforts of several suppliers, the customer can gain the benefits of their combined technologies.
- A company can increase its total development capacity substantially by mobilizing its suppliers, without having to make all the required investments itself.
- A customer's suppliers may in turn be able to mobilize their suppliers to create a large development network to support the customer's own development activities.

In this way, suppliers can relate the developments in their fields to the evolving requirements of a customer. However, for this to be successful, both companies must effectively manage the relationship between them.[10]

Box 3.3   Effective Development Between Customer and Supplier

A good example of the benefits of suppliers and customers working systematically together is provided by Toshiba and Cummins.[11] Ceramics have excellent insulating and high-temperature strength properties. Cummins is a producer of diesel engines and it started the development process with the idea of using ceramics to make a diesel engine without a cooling system. After some initial contacts with other firms Cummins directed their attention to Toshiba. Cummins was impressed by Toshiba's competence and concluded that it was the most progressive company and that it seemed to have the best material in its hot-pressed silicon nitride. Toshiba became a supplier of several engine components that were tested by Cummins.

It then became clear to Cummins that substantial gains in energy efficiency could be made by improving the design of conventional engines. They also realized that fine ceramics were very resistant to wear and could be used in applications other than insulation. Cummins made a thorough survey of all the potential materials and suppliers. The result of these efforts was that silicon nitride was selected as the most promising material and a patent search showed that Toshiba had by far the best patent position in regard to this material. The studies also indicated a good fit between Cummins and Toshiba. Both companies seemed to have staff with similar personalities, ways of working and common business objectives. After a number of meetings Cummins decided to choose Toshiba as partner for this programme.

---

[10] Lars Erik Gadde and Håkan Håkansson, The Changing Role of Purchasing: Reconsidering Three Strategic Issues, *European Journal of Purchasing and Supply*, vol. 1, no. 1, pp. 27–36, 1994. A Lundgren, *Technological Innovation and Network Evolution*, London, Routledge, 1995.

[11] J Laage-Hellman, *Business Networks in Japan: Supplier-Customer Interaction in Product Development*, London, Routledge, 1997.

The negotiations between the companies were extensive and difficult. Despite this, a joint project team was put together. The core group consisted of 3–4 full-time people from Cummins and 8–9 part-time people from Toshiba. This group had already started to work together before the formal agreement was signed. The group jointly decided which components to develop. The wear resistance of the components was tested on both sides and the joint project team evaluated the results. One important factor in the selection of components was their development costs in relation to expected revenue benefits. This led the project team to decide to go for the simplest components in order to minimize the design and manufacturing problems. Cummins concentrated on design technology and Toshiba on that of manufacturing.

The two companies felt that together they were breaking new ground. Despite this, there were a lot of uncertainties about what would happen in the engine, such as how the interaction between ceramic and metal would work. If these questions were not answered, there would be no business. Despite a number of problems, the joint development effort was considered a success and a joint company was established, Engineering Ceramic Technologies Inc. (Enceratec). The main task of this company is to market ceramic components in the US market. The reasons for this move were as follows:

- Both Toshiba and Cummins felt that together they had developed a unique distinctiveness in the product and process technologies for ceramics.
- Toshiba had idle production capacity and wanted to bring in new customers.
- Cummins was also interested in this, even though the potential customers were some of their main competitors. They believed that by exploiting the technologies widely they could reduce the costs of the components that they had purchased for their own use.

This case study shows how productive co-operation between supplier and customer can advance technology and can also develop new businesses to exploit that technology more widely. However, it also shows that these benefits are not achieved easily or without a great deal of effort.

Technology in relationships

The interaction between supplier and customer companies can result in relationships with features similar to an organization. Relationships have often been described as "quasi-organisations".[12] There are even companies that view their most important business relationships as entrepreneurial units. Technology is an important aspect of these quasi-organizations:

- Relationships act as pipelines bringing the technologies of the two companies together.

[12] Keith Blois, Quasi Vertical Integration, *Journal of Industrial Economics*, vol. 20, no. 3, pp. 253–72.

- They create the frame within which technological development takes place and they influence the direction of technological development in and between both companies.
- They become a technological resource for the two companies.

However, to be successful, the process of technological development within a relationship needs to be carefully managed and business marketers have an important role in this. In some cases a customer will accept the offering from a seller and adapt itself to it. In this case the customer accepts the product and process technologies on which the offering is based as a given. In other situations the supplier will provide an offering that is completely designed by the customer, including the way it is delivered. Most situations are somewhere between these extremes, with both parties involved in development and in making adaptations. These adaptations can range from those when two technicians meet to exchange ideas and decide on some changes to those where the whole workforce on one side visits the counterpart to learn about its operations or requirements and then adapts or develops their technology or operations completely.

Business marketers face important questions about the developments and adaptations that they and their customers should make and about how to manage the process of adaptation. If the technological strand of a relationship does not work, then the whole relationship will be in trouble. We can identify some of these questions for each relationship as follows:

- **Who should be responsible for adaptations and changes?:** These are not the responsibility of marketing or technical staff alone. Instead there must be a continuous discussion between marketing and technical departments about the costs and benefits of specific adaptations for different customers.
- **When and how can the technical staff of the customer be activated?:** A common problem for business marketers is to find ways to get more people from the customer's company involved in a relationship. Greater involvement can lead to wider opportunities to develop the relationship and to gain from the technological strengths of the customer. But at the same time, greater involvement will mean increased investments by the supplier and customer and it is important that this leads to new solutions. Interaction without new or improved solutions will always be seen as a waste of time and can easily damage a relationship.
- **When and how should the technological issues in a relationship be evaluated?:** It is important to evaluate the level of technological investment in all important relationships and its contribution towards new solutions and the relationship as a whole. In order to increase objectivity, this analysis should be carried out by someone who is not closely involved in the relationship.
- **How should the company organize itself to cope with the technological issues in a relationship?:** Marketing companies often organize themselves using key account managers or key account departments. This approach assigns responsibility to a single individual or group for co-ordinating all the interactions with a customer. However, it does not automatically solve the problem of the interface between marketing and R&D. Innovations in offerings and in processes will always affect customer

relationships and vice versa and there is a need for a close link between the two. It is also vital to realize that both a company's relationships and its technologies are equally important and neither should be de-emphasized. Key issues in both must be addressed together. Similarly, there is an important interface between marketing and operations. Most obviously this concerns questions of fulfilment, such as the daily problems with deliveries and minor customer complaints. But the longer-term issues of the link between developments in relationships and the company's process technologies also demand close liaison between marketing and operations staff.

There are also a number of issues that concern adaptation and development across several similar relationships:

- **How can the company handle relationships that are very different from each other?:** This is a key issue in the interface between the internal organization of a marketing company and its portfolio of relationships. On the one hand it is important to maximize the technological similarities between relationships so as to reduce development costs and take advantage of previous investments in the design of offerings or in production processes. Yet, on the other hand, standardization reduces the opportunities to gain knowledge from the unique features of the customer or the relationship. This means that business marketers need to think carefully about the potential and costs of a relationship and liaise with technical staff to assess the technological benefits of adaptation.
- **How should the technological content of different relationships be related to each other?:** Each relationship will be based on one or more offerings from the supplier that will in turn be based on some of the supplier's technologies, development efforts and physical resources. Business marketers need to be involved in continuous discussion with technical staff about the best use of scarce resources in different relationships and the possibilities of starting new relationships to make better use of spare resources or of investments that have already been made.
- **How can developments in different relationships be related to each other?:** Each of a company's relationships is a potential source of technological development. A major challenge for business marketing is to capitalize on this potential, so that developments in one relationship can be applied elsewhere. All too frequently, problems solved in one relationship have to be solved again in others because the company has not transferred the learning across its operations. This problem is particularly acute in companies that operate internationally. It can only be reduced by good flows of information between those responsible for different relationships and for technical issues in each operating area.

Conclusion

Most or at least many business marketers are not technologists and there is no necessary reason why they should be. Nevertheless, they do need to have an appreciation of the issues that their companies face in technology. This chapter has shown that a company's technologies and its relationships are its prime assets. Neither are a free resource. Each must be expensively acquired and each has no value without the other. Relationships are essential to exploit and develop technology.

Technology is essential if a relationship is to have any value to customer or supplier. A relationship can add to the technologies of both customer and supplier as well as solving an immediate problem for them and generating short-term revenue. It is true to say that much of the technology of business companies actually exists *in* their relationships.

One view of a company's technology is that it is the sum total of all that exists "between the ears" of its staff. Technology includes patented designs of physical products and services and complex operating processes. But it also includes the company's experience of how to put offerings together that will solve customers' problems, how to make things work and how to consistently and accurately fulfil the promise of an offering. Business marketing has the responsibility, with others, of maximizing the rate of return on these assets.

Technology is a widely but loosely used term. All too frequently managers talk of "high-tech", "core technologies" or "distinctive competences" without thinking what they really mean. Business marketers need to be pro-active in making sure that their companies have a clear idea of the technologies they *really* have, both product and process. They must realistically assess which are truly distinctive and which are basic and common across all their competitors. This understanding is essential as a basis for exploiting technologies in a portfolio of relationships, whether for the sale of an offering or for external exploitation via licence or joint venture.

Finally, when a customer takes a decision to buy an offering from a supplier it is doing so because it believes that the supplier has the ability to design, develop and fulfil an offering that will solve a particular problem for it. This ability is based on the problem-solving and transfer abilities of the supplier. These abilities in turn depend on the supplier's technologies, when combined with those of the customer. All of a supplier's technologies must be related to the problems, operations, buying processes and organization of its customers. It is to these issues that we turn in Chapter 4.

Further Reading

David Ford and Mike Saren (2001) *Managing and Marketing Technology*, London, International Thomson.

Håkan Håkansson (1987) *Industrial Technological Development: A Network Approach*, London, Croom Helm.

Håkan Håkansson (1989) *Corporate Technological Behaviour: Cooperation and Networks*, London, Routledge.

Eric von Hippel (1988) *The Sources of Innovation*, New York, Oxford University Press.

I Nonaka (1990) Redundant, overlapping organisation: a Japanese approach to managing the innovation process, *California Management Review*, Spring, pp. 27–38.

CK Prahalad (1993) The role of core competences in the corporation, *Research Technology Management*, November–December, pp. 40–7.

P Smith-Ring and A van de Ven Development Processes of Cooperative Interorganisational Relationships, *Academy of Management Review*, vol. 19, no. 1, (1999) pp. 90–118.

U N D E R S T A N D I N G
C U S T O M E R S

4

Aims of this Chapter

- We examine the importance of the purchasing function in a company and how this affects suppliers.
- We analyse the nature of customers' problems and the role of purchasing and suppliers in solving these.
- We look at the actual behaviour of customers in solving their problems. The core of our argument is that customers mainly find the solutions to their problems within their portfolio of *existing* relationships. We explain why this happens and highlight when customers are likely to look for new solutions and new suppliers.
- We examine three important dimensions of the purchasing strategy of a customer and their implications for suppliers. These are the nature of its relationship with its suppliers; the size and organization of its supplier base; and the extent to which the customer relies on its suppliers.
- The customer is the starting point for all business marketing. In fact, the main task for a business marketer is to support the procurement activities of customers. The main aim of this chapter is to help business marketers to understand what happens in these procurement activities.

The Importance of Purchasing and Suppliers

Purchasing is of major strategic importance to most companies. This is because a substantial amount of the resources available to a company are handled by the purchasing function. For example, in 1999 Ford spent $76.54 billion, General Motors spent $62 billion and General Electric spent $34 billion on purchases. Purchases from suppliers account for more than half of the total costs of most companies and in some industries such as electronics, telecommunications, construction and automotive, this portion can be considerably higher.

The importance of suppliers has grown as companies have concentrated more of their efforts on a limited part of the total activity structure of the business network in which they are involved. Specialization reduces a company's costs of technological development and leads to economies of scale in operations but it means that a company becomes more reliant on inputs from suppliers. Effective purchasing is vital to reduce a company's costs. It is also important as a way of ensuring that a company's offerings are competitive, by making the best use of the skills or technologies of suppliers. The importance of suppliers in developing customers' offerings is illustrated by Box 4.1.

Box 4.1 Suppliers are Increasingly Involved in Design Activities

A US survey revealed that suppliers have become important sources of product design. In this study 44 per cent of the companies declared that they had handed over design responsibilities to independent suppliers. Component design was the main task for suppliers.

78 per cent of customers had outsourced the design of components.
48 per cent of customers had outsourced the design of sub-systems.
19 per cent of customers had outsourced the design of total systems.

Purchasing, 1 May 1997, p. 32.

The supply side of companies has also come more into focus because what happens at the interface between firms has gained in importance. Ideas such as "just in time deliveries" (JIT), total quality management (TQM) and the zero-defect principle increase the importance of the relationships between a company and its suppliers. Applying these techniques make the boundaries between firms unclear. It means that a customer's internal costs are greatly affected by what goes on at the interface with its suppliers. Efficiency improvements related to JIT and TQM require the active involvement of both buyer and seller and affect benefits and costs for both parties.[1]

Dimensions of supply

A customer's set of supplier relationships reflects the nature of its operations and there are no "average" or "typical" relationships. Some suppliers are important because of their immediate financial effects, while the contributions from others only become

---

[1] The importance of supplier relationships in ensuring the success of JIT is shown in Karen L Brown and R Anthony Inman, Relationships with Vendors: A Critical Factor in JIT Implementation, *Journal of Business and Industrial Marketing*, vol. 8, no. 1, 1993, pp. 5–13.

apparent over time. The impact of each individual supplier relationship depends on how it fits into the operations of the customer and the way it affects the customer's other supplier and customer relationships. There are large variations in supply relationships across industries and companies, but also for an individual firm over time. The variety of customers' approaches to their suppliers can be described in three dimensions:

- **The scope of its supply:** This describes the extent to which a company uses external suppliers. Purchasing accounts for the dominant portion of total costs for many firms but other companies have a higher internal value-added and purchases have much less impact on their total costs.
- **The configuration of its supplier base:** This refers to the make-up of a customer's supplier portfolio. Many companies require a large number of different offerings provided by many specialized vendors. But even if a company uses hundreds or even thousands of suppliers, the offerings of only a few of them may account for the major portion of purchasing costs. It is not unusual for ten major suppliers to account for about two-thirds of total expenditure. Some suppliers may be important for other reasons, such as being responsible for offerings such as components, raw materials or services that are critical to the operations of the customer.
- **The nature of its relationships with suppliers:** A customer's supplier relationships will vary substantially in the level of activity links, resource ties and interaction between the individuals. Some relationships are characterized by extensive inter-personal contacts, some by joint development of offerings. Some suppliers are kept at arm's length with minimal interaction. Some work solely to the customer's specification. Some suppliers deliver "just-in-time", while others deliver to the customer's inventories. This variety can be illustrated by three examples: a high-volume commodity such as cement will involve intense interaction between many individuals at different production plants and construction sites, particularly regarding deliveries. The production scheduling of the two companies will be tightly co-ordinated, but there will be few, if any, adaptations of the product supplied.

  Second, a relationship involving specialized components may have extensive mutual adaptations of the offering and equipment, but only moderate levels of activity co-ordination.

  Finally, a relationship that involves JIT deliveries will entail very tight co-ordination of the activities of the two companies, but the products may be standardized and there may be only limited interaction with other functional areas in the companies.

This leads to a distinction that we will use throughout this chapter between *high* and *low involvement relationships*. High involvement relationships are those with either extensive activity links, resource ties or actor bonds, while low involvement relationships score low on all of these.

The Customer's Problems

We emphasized in Chapter 1 that business marketing is about providing solutions to customers' problems. These problems can arise for many reasons, but they all relate to two basic activities of customers, which they will look to their suppliers for support in achieving. The two activities are rationalization and development.

Rationalization

Rationalization concerns the customer's need to carry out its day-to-day operations as efficiently and economically as possible. Faced with a particular operating problem, a customer may consider changing the specification of the offering it buys from a supplier or the way that it is produced or delivered. It may change suppliers, or it may choose between making what it needs or buying from a supplier. Purchasing can contribute to these decisions through its knowledge of the capabilities of different suppliers and by relating these to the internal needs of the company's development, design and operations.

Rationalization requires customers to be concerned with both the *variable* and *fixed* costs of what they buy. Variable costs comprise the amount of the invoice from a supplier and the other costs that can be directly traced to the specific transaction, such as transportation costs. Concern with variable costs is likely to be greatest when the customer's need and transaction uncertainty are low and the specific problem is not closely related to other problems. When faced with this situation, it would be important for a supplier to benefit from economies of scale and offer a low purchase price by adopting a standardized offering.

Fixed costs are all the other costs of purchasing. They include the costs of running the specific relationship in which the purchase is made and the more general costs of its purchasing operations. Fixed costs are more difficult to trace than variable costs because they do not normally show up in company records, but they are often substantial, for example, Kodak estimates that these "hidden costs" are 250 per cent of its variable costs of purchased items. Hence, in many cases a customer is likely to gain more by reducing its fixed costs than by chasing for lowest price. We will examine the supplier's costs in detail in Chapter 8 when we consider pricing in business markets.

Companies often try to reduce the fixed costs of their purchases by changes in the logistics element of a supplier's offering. For example, Frito Lay, a major producer of snacks, had problems with deliveries from suppliers to its plants. The company took the logistics element out of the offerings of all its suppliers and appointed a specialized logistics provider to supply all inputs to Frito Lay's 38 plants. The provider reduced transportation costs by 12 per cent and improved delivery reliability.[2]

The administration of purchases, from enquiry to order to payment, also provides opportunities for reducing fixed costs. These fixed costs may be greater than the total value of the purchase, especially for frequent purchases of low-valued items. One US study estimated the costs for handling a single purchase order for uncomplicated items

---

[2] We will return to the issue of third-party fulfilment of an offering in Chapter 10.

such as for maintenance, repair, or operations (MRO supplies) to be at least $20. For more complex purchases the costs ranged from $75–150. This emphasizes the importance for companies to develop effective routines to deal with a huge number of transactions rather than to concentrate on optimizing each one. However, because each purchase is relatively unimportant, many companies have neglected to undertake these rationalization efforts. Hence they struggle with a huge number of fragmented purchases from a large supply base and an unnecessary administrative burden. Other companies have analysed and reduced their supply base, and concentrated their small purchases with a single supplier that then buys offerings from other suppliers on their behalf.

Development

The second source of a company's problems is its need to develop its operations and its offerings. Purchasing has become more important in development as companies have concentrated their own operations and relied more on suppliers as an important resource. This means that the internal development activities of a customer need to be co-ordinated with those of its suppliers and so purchasing must be involved in developments at an early stage and then bring the right suppliers into the process. Early supplier involvement means that the vendor's product and process technologies can be fully exploited to enhance design and to reduce later costs. The importance of this is emphasized by studies that show that up to 80 per cent of the total costs of a new offering are determined in the design phase. Early supplier involvement can also reduce development lead times. This thinking has led companies such as Ingersoll-Rand to involve its important suppliers when new projects are "only a gleam in the eye of the marketing manager"! Suppliers can also influence design, as shown in Box 4.2.

Box 4.2   How Suppliers Improve Design

By getting involved early in the design process, the Rittal Corp. of Springfield, Ohio, saved a computer manufacturer money by adapting its standard enclosure to enable it to ventilate the computer. Previously, the company would choose a separate climate-control system after getting its enclosure.

   Square D Corp helps equipment designers to decide whether to use a proximity sensor or a conventional switch, by presenting users with software with multiple decision paths that quickly narrow the number of available selections.

Purchasing, 1 May 1997

Who is Involved in Purchasing?

Purchasing is complex; it is not a simple process of search, evaluation and ordering. It often does not have a clear beginning and end. It is not just concerned with a set of discrete and separate transactions. Each purchase is affected by those that have been made before and ones that are planned for the future. Purchasing is not something that only buyers do. Instead, its importance to the rationalization and development of a company's operations means that many of the company's staff and functions are involved in it. The idea of the "buying centre" provides a way to make sense of this complexity.[3] A buying centre is not a formal group that exists in the company, but a way to classify different roles that individuals can perform in purchasing.

Buyers are likely to have a major role in *managing* an existing supplier relationship and dealing with the contractual arrangements in most purchases. They are also likely to have a role with others in selecting and establishing relationships, but they rarely act alone when important problems arise in either case. Sometimes a customer will have relationships with a group of suppliers that have been approved by others in the firm. Then the buyer will often be responsible for negotiation about the offering and fulfilment for a particular episode. In other cases a supplier has been chosen from within a portfolio by someone else in the company and the buyer's task is then to administer the order.

Influencers are those who can affect choice between existing suppliers in a portfolio. They can also introduce new suppliers into consideration or question the presence of existing suppliers in the portfolio. They can be found in almost any part of a customer. For example, the marketing department may have preferences for certain suppliers, because their offering can improve the customer's own offerings for its customers. Development staff can be important influencers based on their evaluation of the technical content of different offerings. Buyers can also influence supplier choice because of their experience of the reliability of suppliers, so can accounting staff who know about the financial position of suppliers. Individuals who are potential *users* of suppliers' offerings can be important influencers. The importance of users has increased as companies have appreciated that listening to them is a good way to enhance future productivity. *Gatekeepers* control the flow of information into the customer. Buyers often act as gatekeepers because they often are the customer's primary interface with existing suppliers and they are likely to receive sales efforts from new ones.

Finally, in some cases it is possible to identify one or more *deciders*. These may be individuals who specify a supplier, or an offering in such a way that choice is limited to only one company. Sometimes development staff or senior managers take on this role and there is no "choice" for the buyer. In other cases it may be difficult to identify either a single decider or the point at which a decision is taken. Alternatively, a particular purchase may be made within an existing relationship without additional evaluation.

It is important for business marketers to be aware of the roles of different individuals in a customer company and who is carrying them out. The more difficult or important the problem, the larger the supplier portfolio, the more complex the process and the more

[3] FE Webster and Y Wind, A General Model of Organisational Buying Behaviour, *Journal of Marketing*, vol. 36, no. 2, 1972, pp. 12–19.

people are likely to be involved, especially as influencers. Any one individual may occupy several roles, especially in small companies. Sometimes more formal multi-functional groupings exist in companies as illustrated in Box 4.3.

Box 4.3   Multifunctional Teams in Purchasing

General Motors has 150 "Creativity Teams" that form part of its globalization efforts. They combine people from purchasing, engineering, design, quality, marketing and finance. Their main task is to co-ordinate sourcing decisions for everything from door handles to anti-lock braking systems on a global basis. The members of the teams live in different countries and have telephone meetings twice a week. According to the purchasing director, these people together, "bring the skill levels up for our buyers" and often uncover new strategies and sourcing opportunities. When developing parts and systems for future models GM relies on "advanced purchasing teams" of buyers and engineers during the design stage for a new vehicle. Together they decide on the functional requirements and ask suppliers for proposals. Based on these proposals, the advanced purchasing team makes a final recommendation to the sourcing committee.[4]

Purchasing teams at Genentech are usually led by purchasing and are made up of members from quality assurance, quality control, manufacturing, process development, process sciences, inventory, materials planning, production planning and top management. Formal teams are in place to discuss performance of existing suppliers and to work toward continuous process involvement. These teams meet weekly to review the performance of suppliers with whom high-volume or single-source agreements have been made and discuss specific incidents of non-conformance of raw materials and delivery. Less formal teams are often formed to handle new projects or sourcing of a new raw material.[5]

The people in the buying centre will have different information needs because of their different responsibilities, so a buyer is likely to be more interested in price and contractual details than a user is. Yet behind these roles there are individuals who will have their own perceptions, expectations and objectives based on their personalities and backgrounds. Thus an analysis of the different roles in a buying centre needs to take personal as well as functional characteristics into account.

How Companies Buy

When academics try to explain how companies buy they usually describe a number of stages in a rational decision-making process for a *single* purchase. This process moves from need-recognition to the selection of a supplier and subsequent delivery of an offering.

---

[4] *Purchasing*, 15 August 1996.

[5] *Purchasing*, 8 February 2001.

However, the example of the software customer in Chapter 1 showed that customers do not treat each purchase as an isolated event. Instead, they will relate the purchase to a number of factors particular to themselves, as follows:

- the particular problems they are addressing and the uncertainties they face;
- their experience of dealing with this problem or similar problems in the past, within each of their relationships;
- their expectations of the future of those relationships;
- their own organization and resources;
- their view of the wider network and of the other relationships in which they are enmeshed.

These factors help to explain why business customers most commonly start by looking for solutions to their problems in their existing supplier relationships. We refer to this process as Buy-cycle 1: "business as usual".

Solutions from existing relationships – Buy-cycle 1

A customer will have a supply base made up of a variety of existing relationships and it will vary widely in its involvement in them. Both high and low involvement relationships provide different opportunities for customers to solve their problems and this variety also reinforces continuity.

The customer (and the supplier) in a high involvement relationship use some of their limited resources to adapt their offerings and operations to suit each other's requirements. Because of this, the customer will have an incentive to stick with its current supplier to gain the benefits of these investments.

A low involvement relationship requires only limited co-ordination of activities between the companies, few adaptations and little interaction. However, a customer will still be inclined to continue with it for routine problems, provided that it is effective and requires little attention. In this way, the customer avoids the costs of searching for and evaluating potential new suppliers. For example, one study found that some customers had low involvement relationships that had lasted for more than 30 years.[6]

Table 4.1 shows the age of relationships with varying characteristics in the portfolio of a vehicle manufacturing company. The 17 important suppliers account for about one-third of the customers' total purchasing costs and supply components and materials of varying complexity. Some of these relationships involve extensive adaptations. However, in some the supplier has delivered standardized offerings with no specific adaptations, every year for more than 25 years. In another case, two competing suppliers have been used for one of the same components and each of them has delivered each year.

An existing relationship may be important because it involves large payments or contributes to technical development or is valuable to another company in the customer's network. Both high and low involvement can be important and all important relationships tend to be long term. This is so even when there are no apparent barriers

[6] M Bensaou, Portfolios of Buyer-Supplier Relationships, *Sloan Management Review*, Summer 1999, pp. 35–44.

Table 4.1 Duration of supplier relationships.

Relationship duration in years	Number of suppliers
1–4	2
5–14	5
15–24	4
25+	6

to the entry of other suppliers. It does not mean that a customer will continue with its less important relationships just for convenience. Often it will have two or more relationships simultaneously and alternate purchases between them. But it does mean that a customer will consider the value of its existing relationships, its previous efforts to develop them, its evolving problems and the costs of searching for, evaluating and developing new ones, before it makes a change.

Business-as-usual is a rational approach in most cases. A customer will often have made major efforts to find the best solution to its problems and find a suitable supplier. Often this will involve adaptations towards specific suppliers and so it would be rather surprising if a customer turned readily to a new solution and new supplier.

However, Business-as-usual does not mean a lack of change. Customer's problems constantly evolve in even the most "stable" of relationships. Suppliers' offerings also shift as both companies look for opportunities to improve the fit between them. The amount of change depends on how important both of them think their relationship is. Sometimes the revisions are initiated by the customer as new problems emerge. But often it is the supplier that proposes a change, perhaps based on its experience in other relationships. Often it is difficult to trace a clear origin to these changes and they simply arise from the continuous interaction between the firms. Altogether this means that the process of seeking solutions from existing relationships in Buy-cycle 1 is highly dynamic.

Searching for solutions outside existing relationships – Buy-cycle 2

Sometimes a customer may look for solutions *outside* its existing supply base, even though this may require investments of time and money. We refer to this as Buy-cycle 2 and the cycle can start for a number of reasons:

- The customer may face new problems, or it may find it necessary to change its requirements for internal reasons. For example, it may decide to change the organization of its operations and search for a supplier of a new business system.
- On other occasions problems and solutions are redefined because of changes outside the customer, for example, it may be presented with offerings from new suppliers. These may provide new types of solutions or lead the customer to see some of its problems in a new light. Sometimes the customer's own customers may change their

requirements or its competitors may introduce new offerings. Hence the customer will have to change its offering and thus seek new suppliers. Sometimes a customer may use an innovative offering from one supplier to solve a particular problem and then other problems and solutions may need to be redefined.

- The customer may simply not be satisfied with the way that established suppliers are fulfilling their promised offerings. Perhaps deliveries or service provision have declined or prices have become uncompetitive.
- The existing supplier itself may cause a relationship to end. This could be because the supplier considers that the required investment in the relationship outweighs the potential benefits, or because it wishes to devote more resources to other customers. Suppliers have a portfolio of customer relationships and they have to evaluate how individual relationships contribute to the portfolio as a whole. Suppliers must *choose* the customers with which to be highly involved and investments in one relationship may hinder investments in others. Once a supplier has made its evaluation, it may not stop supplying the customer, but simply stop investing in the relationship until the customer itself chooses to switch.

Buy-cycle 2 involves a customer in searching outside its existing supplier-base. Depending on the reason for this, the customer may start with any one of those activities:

- re-evaluating potential solutions;
- re-defining the problem;
- seeking an alternative supplier.

Business marketers must be prepared to be involved in any of these activities if they wish to develop a new relationship or break into an existing one. The marketer will have to compare the solution that her offering provides to a range of other potential solutions, some of which may be unfamiliar to her. She must also be prepared to help the customer to define its problem, especially if this has changed. She must relate her offering to this problem, rather than simply describe its features.

Finally, she must be able to compare her offering with those of alternative suppliers *as a potential solution to the customer's specific problem*, rather than simply contrast their specifications.

No relationship will exist between the customer and the potential supplier in Buy-cycle 2 and both companies are likely to have considerable uncertainties. Both will need to invest time and possibly make adaptations to suit each other's offerings and operations.

Individual episodes and information

The relationship between a customer and a supplier may encompass only one transaction, such as when a utility company buys a new generating station from a particular supplier or an insurance company employs a consulting firm for a major culture-change project. More commonly each relationship involves a number of transactions or episodes, such as the regular delivery of batches of components or monthly payment for a public relations contract. Each of these episodes can only be understood in the context of the relationship of which it is part and each relationship can only be understood in the context of the network in which it is enmeshed. Despite this, business marketers still need to be aware of each single episode.

A single episode can vary in the time that it takes and in the number of functions and individuals from the customer and supplier who are involved. It can also vary in the type and amount of information that the customer and its supplier need. Business marketers have a prime role in managing information in a relationship. This is to provide what the customer needs and what they need in order to monitor the relationship and to develop, communicate and fulfil their offering. It is useful to distinguish between three different types of information: administrative, commercial and technical.[7]

- **Administrative information** is needed for a transaction to be fulfilled. It covers a chain of activities from inquiries, offers and orders, to delivery notifications and invoices. This is the major portion of the information that is exchanged between supplier and customer in simple episodes in Buy-cycle 1. When transactions between companies are frequent and the offerings are low-value, then the costs of handling the flow of information will be a large proportion of the customer's total costs. In these cases, customers will be interested in suppliers that can help to reduce these costs.
- **Commercial information** is necessary to identify existing and potential suppliers and to continuously evaluate their offerings and their ability to fulfil them. A substantial amount of information will be needed to evaluate new, potential suppliers in Buy-cycle 2. Customers often use comprehensive rating schemes for new suppliers, but they may still find that they can only assess how well they fulfil their offerings after they have been used for some time. Convincing new customers of their fulfilment abilities is often a major challenge for marketers. In contrast, many customers omit to continuously evaluate their existing relationships. This can mean that an existing supplier can "get away" with things if the customer does not check on how up-to-date is its offering or how well it is being fulfilled. It can also mean that supplier's best efforts are "taken-for-granted" by its existing customers. Both cases can mean problems for the marketer.
- **Technical information** is often critical for a customer when making an initial evaluation of both offering and fulfilment. Once established, a relationship can be stable for a long time, so the need for technical information is not necessarily determined by the complexity of an offering. For instance, technical exchanges between a car manufacturer and its component suppliers are much less complicated once a model of car is in serial production, then administrative information becomes more crucial for a time. An intense exchange of technical information may follow when the customer seeks a new solution or the supplier plans to modify its offering and each tries to take advantage of the technologies of the other.

[7] Lars Erik Gadde and Håkan Håkansson, *Professional Purchasing*, London, Routledge, 1993.

Resources for purchasing

The importance and complexity of business purchases mean that customer companies have to face the difficult issue of how they should allocate resources of people, time and money to particular episodes in each relationship. Figure 4.1 illustrates some of the factors in this resource allocation.

Uncertainties

A customer is likely to devote more resources to a purchase episode when it faces greater uncertainties:[8]

- **Need uncertainty** is likely to lead a customer to involve more staff to try to establish its requirements and relate these to available offerings and to liaise with potential suppliers.
- **Market uncertainty** means that a customer will need to gather commercial information about technological changes in the network and about a number of potential suppliers, unless it already has relationships with those suppliers.
- **Transaction uncertainty** may lead the customer to either devote resources to improving the fulfilment performance of its current suppliers or to search for new suppliers.

The importance of an episode will also affect the resources that a customer puts into it. For example, a purchase may involve little risk such as when it is just one of many similar purchases, or it may be of low monetary value. In this case it is likely to involve few resources within an existing relationship, following Buy-cycle 1. In contrast, a purchase

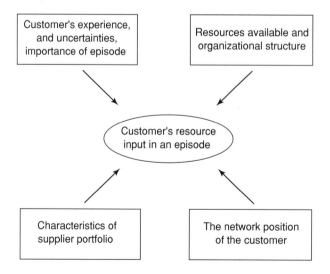

Figure 4.1 Purchasing organization and resources.

[8] For a full discussion of customer and supplier uncertainties, see Chapter 1.

may be risky because the problem involved is difficult to solve or is critical to the company's operations, or it may be of high value. In this case the company is likely to devote considerable resources to it. It may even use consultants or it may restrict its detailed discussions to only a few trusted suppliers to try to reduce its need uncertainty.

Centralized or decentralized organization

A company can organize its purchasing activities in two different ways, either centralized or decentralized. By bringing all its purchasing activities into one centralized function, a company will hope to co-ordinate all its contacts with each supplier and achieve cost savings through large order quantities. Centralized purchasing also improves resource allocation and professionalism because purchasing staff can specialize in buying particular items, such as professional services or components. In decentralized purchasing the various business units within a company can make the supplier choices they prefer. This has the advantage that buyers can relate more closely to the particular requirements of the users of their purchases but it does mean that they have to work across a broader range of offerings.

The choice between centralization and decentralization will always be a compromise and many companies try to combine the advantages of both approaches. For example, a decentralized purchasing organization may be supplemented by a central unit that is responsible for group agreements so as to benefit from economies of scale. Similarly, centralized purchasing can be supported by local buyers who are in close contact with the company's operations. An example of this approach is illustrated in Box 4.4.

Box 4.4   Purchasing Organization at Dupont

To overcome the many challenges of purchasing in the specialty and fine chemical areas, Dupont has combined the specific market knowledge of buyers in each of its separate business units with the leverage and perspective possible only with a centralized sourcing structure.

Dupont's purchasing structure has buyers and contract administrators at each of its locations and within each of its 18 strategic business units. These buyers handle the purchasing task of the business on a day-to-day basis.

Sourcing personnel focus on the more strategic procurement task and are grouped in the company's global services business unit. Headed by the chief procurement officer and three directors (two for sourcing and one for logistics), the global services business unit includes many purchasing professionals. These specialize in various areas of strategic sourcing, including energy and raw materials, specialty chemicals, contract manufacturing, equipment, transportation, and logistics.

In addition to the sourcing and purchasing divisions within Dupont's central and localized purchasing models, sourcing personnel are also stationed within the business units, having dual responsibility – to the business units and to the company's central sourcing structure.

Purchasing, 6 May 2001

Supplier portfolio

We have emphasized that a customer's existing supplier relationships affect the evolution of its problems and the solutions it seeks. The characteristics of these relationships also have a major impact on the resources that a customer puts into its buying operations. Most of these resources will not be devoted to single episodes, but are used to maintain the relationships and also to develop long-term exchanges with suppliers. High involvement relationships are resource demanding, not only at the beginning, but need continuous maintenance. It is important for a customer to manage its portfolio so that it has a range of suppliers that relate closely to its existing and emerging problems. At the same time it is important that the customer does not incur the costs of maintaining a wider portfolio of supplier relationships than is needed to meet its requirements. The effects of poor portfolio management and the costs of trying to manage too many suppliers were highlighted in a study of purchasing in German electronics companies. These indicated a considerable difference between successful and less successful companies in the number of suppliers per purchasing volume. Details of this are shown in Figure 4.2.[9] Figure 4.2 shows the numbers of suppliers per DM 100 million purchasing volume, machinery and component producers.

Network position

Other companies can affect the way that a customer allocates its resources to its supplier relationships. These companies can include the customer's own customers or its other suppliers, or companies operating elsewhere in the network, that may be dealing with similar problems. For example, an important customer may pressurize a supplier to invest more heavily in its relationship with a particular component supplier. On the other hand, the network position of some major companies, such as Microsoft or Intel can more or less dictate many aspects of the way that surrounding companies do business.

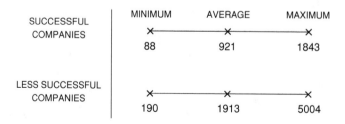

Figure 4.2   Number of suppliers per purchasing volume.

[9] Jürgen Kluge, Lothar Stein, Edward Krubasik, Ingo Beyer, Dieter Dusedau, Wolfgang Huhn, Eberhard Schmidt and Rupert Deger, *Shrink to Grow: Lessons from Innovation and Productivity in the Electronics Industry*, Basingstoke, Macmillan, 1996.

Strategic Choices in Purchasing

We saw in Chapter 2 that the choices facing a single company are strongly affected by the surrounding network. This means that the ability of a company to develop an independent purchasing strategy is severely limited by its existing relationships and the wider network that impacts on these.[10] Despite these limitations, companies do face clear choices in their purchasing strategy and these have important implications for business marketers. We can examine these using some of the terms we have developed in this chapter.

Determining the level of involvement with suppliers

It is possible to see two simultaneous but contrasting approaches to a customer's involvement with its suppliers: low involvement relationships and high involvement relationships.

Low involvement relationships

When a customer and supplier establish close activity links, resource ties, or actor bonds, then both will become dependent on each other. Sometimes customers strive to avoid this dependence on individual suppliers to give themselves freedom to change. So-called "arm's-length relationships" have four major advantages:

- They are cheap to operate.
- A number of suppliers can help overcome short-term problems of fulfilment, such as delivery failures, problems with product or service "quality" or fluctuations in demand.
- Too much investment in a single relationship might mean that the customer is "locked in" to that supplier in the long-term.
- High involvement with a single supplier makes it difficult to encourage different suppliers to compete by improving their offerings or reducing their prices.

The low involvement approach to supply relationships considers suppliers as more or less efficient producers of *identical* inputs. This view is implicit in purchases by competitive tender, which is common in government buying and in the construction industry. Each project tends to be evaluated in isolation and on the basis of each supplier's price for a *defined* offering. This price orientation ignores the effects of the fixed costs of a purchase. It is also rather adversarial, so that a price reduction is a gain for the customer and a loss for the supplier and vice versa. In practice, a low involvement approach can work when the customer's problem and the required solution are clear and need not be questioned and there are a number of suitable suppliers available. Examples include contracts for waste removal or office cleaning. Although, even in these cases, differences between the way that each company fulfils its offering can cause problems and cost increases for the customer.

---

[10] We deal fully with overall issues of strategic choice and limits to independence in Chapter 10.

High involvement relationships

These are based on another idea of purchasing efficiency and a different view of the role of suppliers and the nature of relationships. Companies increasingly have to rely on the resources of outside suppliers and this means that many of the customer's activities must be co-ordinated with those of its suppliers. This need for co-ordination means that the two companies will have to adapt some of their activities and invest dedicated resources in the relationship. These adaptations create inter-dependencies and when this happens, it is not possible for a customer to switch suppliers frequently.

Box 4.5   High Involvement Relationships at Sun Corporation

John Shoemaker, Vice-President for Purchasing has witnessed how supply management at Sun has evolved: "When I first got here, Sun had a highly tactical strategy with suppliers. We did not work with them. We had adversarial relationships with them." However, Sun began forging long-term relationships with suppliers and took a more strategic approach to supply management. It signed long-term agreements with suppliers who were travelling down the same technology path as Sun. It developed an "open kimono" approach to suppliers who became involved earlier in Sun's new product developments. "It's totally changed from the old days when you didn't want suppliers to know too much. Now it's the opposite. They know as much of our business as we do. That's how you maximize their value-added."

Purchasing, 19 September 1996, p. 38

A customer taking a high involvement approach will not try to optimize the price it achieves in each single transaction. Instead, it will aim to improve its operations in the long term by using the resources of its suppliers more effectively. This involves attempts to reduce the total variable and fixed costs of the relationship by effective adaptations by both companies. Examples of this include building activity links to enable a data company to process a customer's data overnight in a low-cost location such as India, or introducing Electronic Data Interchange (EDI) to enable a textile supplier to reduce the in-store inventories of a fashion retailer.

This approach also involves a customer in using suppliers in the development role of purchasing, to enhance its offerings for its own customers. An example of this would be a supplier and a customer working together on joint developments to improve the service level in the customer's call-centre, or joint development of the product design in a supplier's offering to enable the customer to change its product to provide a higher performance offering to its customers.

Joint development with suppliers has become increasingly common over time. Integrating resources with suppliers can reduce the lead-time in developing new offerings and decrease total development spending. It can also increase the profits of both companies by contributing to better relationships between the customer and its own customers. However, a high involvement approach is always costly. Achieving the benefits of integration requires adaptations of offerings and resources, co-ordination of activities and intense personal contact between individuals.

A marketer must find out the approach that a customer is likely to take to involvement in their relationship and adjust her own approach accordingly. But her task is also to develop and manage a portfolio of customer relationships and she faces a limit to the resources she has available. She must determine the opportunities and problems of each relationship, based on the customer's approach to it, the approach she would prefer, the resources the relationship will require and its contribution to the portfolio as a whole.

Configuration of the supply base

Low involvement relationships often lead to a large supplier base as customers use multiple competing suppliers to try to drive down prices. However, customers have become increasingly aware of the fixed costs of handling suppliers and this has made them eager to reduce the number that they use. One way that they have done this is to encourage some suppliers to become systems suppliers and take responsibility for bringing together the activities of a number of sub-suppliers, as we saw in Chapter 2 in the case of Toyota.

The trend to high involvement relationships has also affected suppliers' portfolios. This is because customers often have to use a single source for each problem or offering in order to achieve the benefits of integration. Business marketers will often only consider investing heavily in a relationship in return for exclusivity. High involvement relationships are resource-demanding for customers and suppliers and companies cannot handle too many of them. This was very clear when Sun entered high involvement relationships some years ago. Five years before the strategic change, Sun spent 80 per cent of its purchasing budget with about 100 suppliers. After the change, 89 per cent went on 20 suppliers and the top five account for 65 per cent of its total spending.[11]

Even greater benefits of high involvement can be achieved if it can be extended to cover the supplier's suppliers and the customer's customers. This can promote activity co-ordination and resource combinations throughout what is often referred to as the customer's "supply chain". However, the major benefits for customers are likely to be attained if a wider "supply network" perspective is used. Customers need variety in the level of their involvement in their supplier relationships and it is the combined efforts of *all* suppliers that comprise the external contribution to them. *This means that it is vital for suppliers to understand their position in the total network that surrounds a customer and how that customer sees the relationship between that supplier and the rest.* Encouraging co-operation between the total network of complementary suppliers can produce major benefits and a number of major companies are following this route. The best-known example is Nike's supply network. Nike's production system is entirely based on outsourcing. It no longer manufactures any shoes in-house, but relies on a variety of suppliers and subcontractors with different characteristics, illustrated in Figure 4.3.

[11] *Purchasing*, 18 September 1996, p. 35.

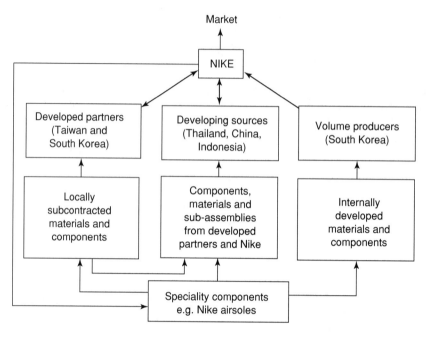

Figure 4.3   The supplier network of Nike.
Source: M. Donagh and R. Barff (1990) Nike Just Did It, *Regional Studies*, vol. 24, no. 6, pp. 537–52.

Nike's suppliers are classified into three different groups:

- Volume producers provide economies of scale in production by supplying a number of different footwear producers.
- Developed partners are exclusive Nike suppliers and produce the most advanced and latest models.
- Developing sources can manufacture shoes at a very low cost.

In order to improve the performance of this supply network Nike shares its knowledge and resources with suppliers and actively intervenes in their operations. One way of doing this is through an "expatriate programme" whereby former Nike technicians become permanent staff in supplier factories. Some suppliers are also encouraged to participate in joint product development activities. However, some suppliers in low-cost countries have very limited skills and these must be improved to meet Nike's global standards. Nike asks its more advanced suppliers to take an active part in this process and to transfer technology through joint ventures with Nike and less experienced partners.

The scope of supply

The final set of strategic choices in purchasing concerns the extent to which the customer should make-or-buy the inputs to its operations. This has been an issue in companies for a long time, but was traditionally handled at a relatively low level in purchasing organisations. Decisions were mainly based on the expected level of capacity utilization and historical cost data. Depending on conditions, the make-or-buy decision could be changed from year to year. Such changes caused no major problems because the sub-contracted items were either highly standardized or designed by the customer.

Only recently has make-or-buy been regarded as a strategic issue, based on the sort of technology analysis we described in Chapter 3. This has led companies to rely more and more on "buy" rather than "make". Outsourcing has extended far from the sub-contracting of manufacturing operations to other activities such as administration, logistics, market intelligence, process design and product development. In the previous chapter we explained how the reasons for this centred on companies' need to concentrate on a small number of distinctive technologies, rather than attempt to maintain a presence in all of the technologies needed to produce their offerings. Specialization means that a customer can use suppliers that can achieve economies of scale in their operations, so that focused suppliers can contribute to the rationalization role of purchasing. A supplier working with several customers is also likely to be better at choosing and following the right direction for technical development, when compared to a customer with its narrower experience and focus on its own operations.

Corporate attitudes towards resource control have also been modified. Owning resources provides a high level of autonomy in their utilization and companies have traditionally shown preference for ownership control, but investments in highly specialized resources can lock a firm into a structure which might become obsolete as technologies develop. On the other hand, outsourcing can provide flexibility. Companies increasingly realize that they can still achieve some control over the direction of development and the operations of their supplier's resources within high involvement relationships.

The increased level of outsourcing places greater emphasis on the relationship management skills of both buyers and business marketers. It provides opportunities for supplies as their customers ask them to take on more responsibilities. Changes in attitudes to resource control have also fostered new ways for suppliers to connect with customers through links, ties and bonds. A supplier can actively promote customers' outsourcing activities by making its wider capabilities available, but this requires marketers to move away from a narrow orientation towards their offering and take a greater interest in their company's operations, their resources and their technology. All of these are increasingly brought into play in their relationships with customers.

Conclusion

This chapter has examined some of the complexities of business purchasing and their implications for business marketers. Customer problems are at the core of business marketing. These problems go beyond concerns about which offering to choose for each transaction. They include the wider questions of how to carry out the development and rationalization roles of purchasing, what type of relationships to seek and how to manage them effectively. Different types of relationships provide quite different kinds of benefits to a customer. High involvement relationships are costly, but may contribute more to rationalization and development. In other situations, a customer is likely to gain more through a low involvement approach. Sometimes a customer might benefit from having suppliers that compete with each other to offer the lowest price for a standardized offering. In other cases a customer might gain from staying with one supplier for a long time and perhaps developing a dedicated offering for its requirements. Every customer needs a mix of supplier relationships characterized by variety in the level of involvement. The main issue in supply strategy is how to handle this mix and to modify it as conditions change. Box 4.6 illustrates how Kodak categorizes its suppliers to achieve this mix.

Box 4.6   Kodak's Three Levels of Supplier Category

Level One – "World-Source Suppliers" have global capabilities; are a designated standard source for specific products; have established global pricing/discount contracts in place; and a formal variance process is applied to any request to purchase these specific products from other sources.

   Level Two – "Preferred Supplier" designates a few specific, selected suppliers per product who may have either global or regional pricing or discount agreements. Although their use is encouraged, it is not mandatory as it is for world-source suppliers. The opportunity exists for these suppliers to eventually become a world-source supplier.

   Level Three – "Niche Suppliers" are for specific applications in a specific manufacturing segment where it does not make good business sense to change the installed base. They may not be retained in the long run.

Purchasing, 7 March 1996, p. 46

The ways in which customers handle strategic issues in purchasing have profound implications for business marketers. Marketers must be closely in touch with varying customer problems and also make choices about how to handle customers, based on their own resources and aspirations. For some customers a standardized offering will be appropriate because any adaptations would involve it in more costs than benefits, or it may simply not be possible to convince the customer of the benefits of adaptations, or it may negatively affect the supplier's relationship with another customer. In some cases a customer may be interested in developing a high involvement relationship. In this case the marketer must evaluate the potential long-term costs and benefits of such an arrangement and, if it goes ahead, must continue to monitor the relationship throughout its life.

Further Reading

R Axelrod (1997) *The Complexity of Cooperation*, Chichester, Princeton University Press.
T Davis (1993) "Effective Supply Management". *Sloan Management Review*, Summer, pp. 35–46.

Donald W Dobler and David Burt (1996) *Purchasing and Supply Management*, 6th edition, New York, McGraw-Hill.

David Ford (ed.) (2001) *Understanding Business Marketing and Purchasing*, London, International Thomson, especially readings 5.1–5.6.

Lars Erik Gadde and Håkan Håkansson (2001) *Supply Network Strategies*, Chichester, John Wiley.

Richard Lamming (1993) *Beyond Partnership: Strategies for Innovation and Lean Supply*, London, Prentice-Hall.

T Nishiguchi (1994) *Strategic Industrial Sourcing: The Japanese Advantage*, Oxford, Oxford University Press.

Mari Sako (1992) *Prices, Quality and Trust: Buyer-Supplier Relationships in Britain and Japan*, Cambridge, Cambridge University Press.

J Womack and D Jones (1994) From Lean Production to the Lean Enterprise, *Harvard Business Review*, March–April, 93–104.

MANAGING RELATIONSHIPS WITH CUSTOMERS

5

Aims of this Chapter

So far in this book we have stressed the importance of a number of concepts that help us to understand what happens in business markets. These are as follows:

- the *relationship* between a supplier and customer company;
- the *interaction* that takes place in that relationship;
- the *network* of other relationships and companies that surrounds that relationship;
- the *resources* and *technologies* of both the supplier and customer companies;
- the *abilities*, *problems* and *uncertainties* of both suppliers and customers;
- the *offerings* of the supplier and the *solutions* for the customer.

We have also defined business marketing as the task of selecting, developing and managing customer relationships for the advantage of both customer and supplier, with regard to their respective skills, resources, technologies, strategies and objectives.

The aim of this chapter is to bring together these concepts to explain how a supplier company, whether it is nominally a manufacturer or a distributor, can be successful in managing its relationships with its customers.

The chapter starts by describing the six tasks that comprise business marketing management. The chapter emphasizes that the key to successful business marketing management is the management of individual customer relationships. It goes on to structure the tasks involved in relationship management. Finally, because of the importance of relationships to the business marketer, the chapter concludes with a system for auditing these relationships.

The Tasks of Business Marketing Management

The customer and its requirements are at the core of business marketing and as always, this provides our starting point. We will use the framework in Box 5.1 to analyse and describe the approaches that a business marketer must take and the tasks that he needs to perform.

Box 5.1   The Tasks of Business Marketing Management

1. KNOW YOUR CUSTOMERS.
2. KNOW YOURSELF.
3. MANAGE EACH RELATIONSHIP.
4. BUILD AND DELIVER AN OFFERING WITHIN EACH RELATIONSHIP.
5. MANAGE YOUR PORTFOLIO OF RELATIONSHIPS.
6. MANAGE YOUR NETWORK POSITION.

The customer

A customer will use its existing relationships or seek new ones to solve one or a combination of its own problems, such as the need to improve a production process, or to develop a new customer offering, or to increase the reliability of a key service. Each individual and sub-group in the company will also have their own problems and these will all affect the way that the company interacts within its relationships. For example, the operations department may feel overloaded by frequent changes in the company's offering, so it may be keen to develop a relationship with a supplier of flexible equipment. The development department may have difficulty in attracting technologists because the range of its work is too restricted to provide them with interest or career development. It may try to build relationships with new suppliers that use its development skills. The company's Head of Finance may be under pressure to contract out the accounting function to another company and thus may fear that he will lose status or salary. He may try to get the company to invest in new operating software that will "lock" it into doing its own accounting, or even try to damage the company's relationships with potential suppliers of accounting services.

Irrespective of its problems, a customer is likely to approach its relationships with *uncertainties* (see Chapter 1). It may be uncertain about what would be the best solution to its problems – its *need uncertainty*; whether potential suppliers can be trusted – its *transaction uncertainty*; or about how to cope with changes in technology or in the surrounding network of suppliers – its *market uncertainty*.

The customer will also bring its *demand* and *transfer abilities* to a relationship. Demand ability enables a customer to advise a supplier of the type of offering it should produce and to offer the supplier the volume and type of demand that it requires, either by itself or by providing access to other customers in the network. In this way the customer helps the supplier to build its offering and thus may appear a more valuable customer. A customer's transfer ability relates to its reliability in providing the promised type and volume of orders and information to the supplier, or more generally in managing the relationship. Finding out about the customer is the first task of business marketing:

> TASK 1 – *The business marketer must find out exactly what problems the customer brings to the relationship, whether or not these are recognized by the customer. The marketer must also find out what the customer's uncertainties are in the relationship so that he can determine which supplier abilities it requires. He also needs to analyse what abilities the customer brings to the relationship and whether these come from the customer's own resources or from others with which it has relationships.*

The supplier

A supplier will seek a relationship with a customer as a way of solving some of its own problems, such as the need to generate cash, or to earn profit, or to develop new skills that may then be applied elsewhere, or to cope with a loss of business from another customer. Individuals and sub-groups in the supplier will also have their own problems that can affect the interaction. Examples may include a salesperson down on his targets and desperate to make a sale at almost any price; or an operations department anxious about the reliability of its production and keen to learn from the skills of a customer; or a finance department keen to achieve quick sales to count in this year's financial results.

A supplier will approach all its relationships with uncertainties. These may be about the amount of its offering that it is likely to sell – its *capacity uncertainty*; about how customers might want to use the offering – its *application uncertainty*; and about whether a particular customer will actually do what it has said it will do in the relationship – its *transaction uncertainty*.

The supplier will bring to the relationship its *problem-solving* and its *transfer abilities*. Problem-solving ability will enable it to develop an offering with the customer consisting of a combination of product, service, logistics, adaptation and advice. Transfer ability will enable it to actually provide that offering and fulfil its promise. These abilities are not just based on the supplier's own physical and financial resources, but also on those of other companies in the network, with which it has relationships, such as component suppliers, finance houses, trucking companies or distributors. The supplier's relationships may be of great value to the customer. The supplier's own situation leads to the second task of business marketing:

> TASK 2 – *The marketer needs to be clear exactly which of his own problems a particular customer relationship can help to solve. He must also make clear his own uncertainties about the relationship, so that he knows which customer abilities he relies on. He also needs to analyse what abilities he brings to the relationship and whether they come from his own company's resources or those of others with which it has relationships.*

The relationship

Managing customer relationships is important for the business marketer for at least two reasons. First, making a single sale can involve considerable time and costs for both customer and supplier, even before the sale takes place. In order to recover these costs, both companies may have to deal with each other for a number of transactions over a period of time.

Second, a business marketer may only have a few potential customers for its offering and the marketer may have no choice but to invest time and effort in these over the long term. Even if a company has thousands of customers, a small minority may contribute the majority of its sales or profits. In this case, the company will still have to manage a small number of important relationships as well as a large number that are only important in total.

A relationship provides the following benefits for both customer and supplier:

- It eliminates the costs of searching for new customers or suppliers.
- It enables the marketer to learn about a customer's problems and uncertainties, as well as learn what abilities the customer can offer the supplier in return.
- It reduces the costs of adaptations, once the initial investments have been made in the relationship.
- It reduces the costs of interaction, such as time spent in selling and buying and in checking deliveries, etc.

The importance of relationships leads to the third task of business marketing:

TASK 3 – *The business marketer must select, build and productively manage his company's relationships throughout their life, rather than simply make sales, or run a territory.*

We will examine the task of managing a relationship in more detail shortly.

Offerings in relationships

Successful business marketing requires much more than high "quality" products and services. Products and services are only part of a complete *offering* of product, service, logistics, advice and adaptation. A customer will only value a supplier's offering if it is a potential *solution* to its particular problems and will relate the value of that solution to the total costs that it has to incur to obtain it.

Customers may find it difficult to identify or describe their problems or to identify a solution. The business marketer is often required to diagnose these problems, before an offering can be developed, adapted, transferred and integrated into the customer's operations. This can involve high costs and take a long time. It may involve the abilities, resources, technologies and network of relationships of *both* of the companies. As the relationship develops, the offering may evolve to meet the changing requirements of the customer and the supplier. Similarly, the fulfilment of the offering may be refined as the companies learn more about each other and their relationship develops. This leads to the fourth task of business marketing:

TASK 4 – The business marketer must build a coherent offering of product, service, logistics, advice and adaptation that relates to the customer's problems and resources as well as to his own. The offering is built, delivered and integrated into the customer's operations in the relationship between the two companies.

Portfolios of relationships

No single relationship exists in isolation. Both supplier and customer will have other customers and suppliers. Each relationship will differ in the problems it solves and the contribution it makes to the customer and supplier that are involved. Some relationships might be useful to both companies for the regular sale and purchase of standard offerings. They will contribute to the supplier's cash flow and to the basic operations of the customer. They may account for a major portion of each company's activities. These relationships may be safe and reassuring, rather like a marriage.

Other relationships may solve some particular technological or operational problems for the companies and lead to different ways of working or interacting. They may be exciting, but perhaps unstable and could damage both companies if things go wrong, just like an ill-considered affair.

Other relationships may be unimportant themselves, but together with other similar ones may constitute a vital part of the supplier's portfolio.

As with the relationships between people, it is likely that each of the parties to a business relationship will see it in a different way from each other. The customer might see the supplier as just an "extra", making a small contribution when compared with a main relationship, or the relationship may only be a way of solving a short-term problem. In contrast, the supplier may see the customer as an important source of future business and might be prepared to postpone short-term gain to achieve this. The supplier or customer may divert their resources into other relationships, in order to gain greater benefits when they consider that the first one is well established. Both might simply become bored with each other but both need to judge the value to them of each of their relationships, in comparison with the others in their portfolio. The fifth task of business marketing is about managing portfolios:

TASK 5 – The business marketer must manage his portfolio of relationships as a totality, according to the respective contributions of each one to its corporate success, the risks that each involves, the demands that each makes on his resources and the effects that each has on his other relationships.

Figure 5.1 outlines a simple categorization of relationship types that has proved useful for purposes of portfolio analysis.

Category 1: today's profits

These relationships generate current profits for the supplier. A full analysis of the costs of managing the company's relationships may show that only a minority of the company's relationships make a profit. These profits will be based on previous investments made in the

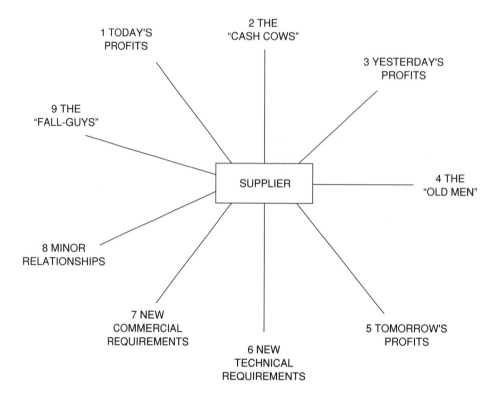

Figure 5.1   A relationship portfolio.

relationships, probably by both supplier and customer. If the customer's requirements change, then these investments may no longer be appropriate. In this case further investment may be required or the relationship will move into one of the other categories listed below.

Category 2: the "cash cows"

These relationships contribute the highest current sales volume for the company, but not necessarily the highest profit. This can be because these high-volume customers are likely to expect significant adaptations by the supplier and this results in very high relationship management costs. Also, because the relationship is important to the supplier, the customer might be able to force lower prices on it. Because of the costs and problems of these relationships, they have also been referred to by a manager as "bottomless pits"!

Category 3: yesterday's profits

Relationships in this category no longer contribute the same level of profits as previously. This can be because of changed customer requirements, or the efforts of competing suppliers, or the failure of the supplier (or the customer) to make the necessary adaptations. The sales volume may still be high and unless the marketer has good cost information he may not be aware of the reduced profits. This category emphasizes how important it is to constantly *manage* relationships throughout their life. It also emphasizes how important it is for marketers to know the real "cost-to-serve" of a relationship.

Category 4: the ''old men''

This category is a more extreme form of the previous one and includes many long-established relationships that have become "inert".[1] These relationships may be based on an offering and a way of interacting that suited the problems and conditions of long ago. These "old men" relationships are likely to be popular with long-serving sales staff, who value the personal interaction with old friends, but a full relationship audit could show that they tie up expensive resources that could more profitably be invested in other relationships.

Category 5: tomorrow's profits

These relationships have the potential for future growth. However, they are unlikely to be profitable at the moment because of the costs of investing in the relationship and developing the offering. This time-before-profit can be considerable and so it is important that the marketer makes a clear assessment of the development funds required, the potential of the relationship, the likely pay-back period and the risks involved. This category emphasizes how important it is for a marketer to *choose* which relationships to develop and which to discontinue, as opposed to simply taking whatever business is on offer.

Categories 6 and 7: new technical or commercial requirements

Customers in these relationships have demanding technical or commercial requirements. Satisfying them requires the supplier to invest in its product or process technologies; its order processing; or in its skills in managing relationships. Some of these types of relationships may currently or even *always* be unprofitable and no supplier could afford a large number of them. However, they are important because what is learned in these relationships could subsequently be valuable in others. In this case, a supplier may be prepared to offset the losses in these relationships against the profits to be earned in others.

Category 8: minor relationships

This is likely to be the largest category in many portfolios. The customers in this category may be small companies or new to the supplier. They may have limited requirements or neither company might see the other as an important part of their portfolio. It is often easier

---

[1] One study has shown that relationships can become inert after only a short time, if they are not properly managed. (David Ford and Philip Rosson, The Relationships between Export Managers and their Overseas Distributors, in Michael Czinkota (ed.) *Export Management*, New York, Praeger, 1982, pp. 257–75.

for a supplier to manage a single important relationship than many small, but potentially valuable ones. However, developments in operations and in electronic media have made it easier to develop and fulfil tailored offerings to even small users.[2] Relationships should not be judged solely on their size and this category should be separated into sub-groups according to their different requirements and their potential contribution.

A customer is likely to have a different relationship with minor and major suppliers, even for what is apparently the same type of offering. For example, the customer may use the major supplier for its large volume, day-to-day requirements. It may use minor suppliers for more flexible, more unusual, or more technically demanding problems, or simply to keep its main supplier "on its toes". There is an obvious analogy in this between the major supplier as husband or wife with the minor supplier providing excitement as a lover or mistress! More seriously, these differences mean that a company that is used to being a major supplier may not be able to cope with a minor supplier relationship. Conversely, a company that is used to being a minor supplier should perhaps choose to avoid major supply situations that may not match its skills or profit expectations.

Category 9: the ''fall-guys''

This final category emphasizes that managing business relationships is not solely based on mutual trust or "niceness". The category includes customers from which the supplier expects valuable volume, profit or knowledge *in the short term*. In the long term the supplier may either drop the customer or at least disinvest in the relationship, after it has learned as much as it can, or after alternative relationships have grown. However, when doing this the marketer should be aware that other customers in his portfolio are likely to hear about his actions and draw the appropriate conclusions!

Relationships and networks

All companies are enmeshed in a network of relationships. These relationships are major assets for the company and are the means by which it can benefit from the resources of its suppliers, customers and others and through which it gains access to the resources of the wider network. The idea of a network illustrates that companies are not linked in a neat straight line, comprising the "supply chain" of a single company.

The multiple links of all companies in a network also emphasize that a network does not just exist for the benefit of a single company. Although a relationship with a particular supplier may be important to a customer, that relationship may be quite unimportant to the supplier that has other far more important relationships.

A company's *network position* is comprised of its relationships and the benefits, obligations, rights and privileges that derive from them. Network position is an important resource for a company in its interactions with others and it complements the company's other physical and financial resources. For example, a company's relationships with its

---

[2] We will return to these issues in Chapters 7 and 9.

suppliers form part of its network position. These supplier relationships give it access to their skills and these complement its own skills enabling it to have productive relationships with its customers.

Strategy for the business marketing company is concerned with assessing and changing its network position. This leads to the sixth task of business marketing:

TASK 6 – The business marketer must assess the network position of his company and examine how his individual relationships contribute to that position. Business strategy involves changing individual relationships and the company's portfolio of relationships to achieve a new network position. Business marketers have an important role both in assessing network position and in achieving change.

Managing a Single Relationship

The six tasks outlined above amount to the core of business marketing management. At the heart of them is the management of each single relationship with its customers. We now turn to the tasks of relationship management in more detail. These tasks are summarized in Figure 5.2.

It is important to start by emphasizing that marketing people cannot carry out relationship management on their own:

Business marketers must liaise closely with other functional areas, such as operations, finance, purchasing and corporate strategy. Each of these is involved in a business relationship and many will interact directly with customers.

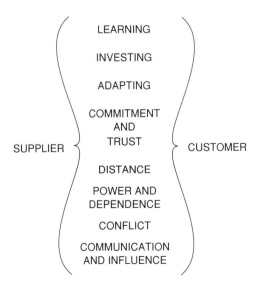

Figure 5.2 **Tasks of relationship management.**

Business marketers must also accept that a marketing company cannot *completely* manage or control a relationship:

> Business relationships involve interaction between two *active* parties. How a relationship develops will depend on the resources and actions of both customer and supplier. Each will have its own idea of what they want to get out of the relationship and what they are prepared to give to it. Both will have their own idea of its importance and both will look at the relationship in the context of all their other relationships.

Throughout this book we use the term "Relationship Management" rather than "Relationship Marketing". This is because both supplier and customer *interact* with each other and *both* will try to manage their relationship. Relationship marketing infers that it is only the supplier that is involved in the process. Any conversation with a business buyer will show how unrealistic this idea is! (See Box 5.2.)

Box 5.2   The Problem with Relationship Marketing

Many consumer marketing companies have adopted the ideas of "relationship marketing". Relationship marketing is based on the idea that a minority of consumers account for most sales and that the selling and promotional costs of attracting one new customer (establishing a relationship) are likely to be much greater than the costs of retaining an existing customer. Relationship marketing has been made possible by the availability of proprietary data-bases on customer life-styles, attitudes and overall purchase behaviour and on analysis of the company's own customer purchase data.

Some business marketers have also embraced the idea of relationship marketing, particularly those with a large number of small customers, such as those providing delivery services or office products. But throughout this book we will avoid the term "relationship marketing" and refer instead to "relationship management". The reasons for this can be seen in Figure 5.3 which lists some of the differences between relationship marketing and relationship management. Much of what is called relationship marketing has not really got much to do with relationships at all. It is based on a series of individual one-way communications with customers and an analysis of how effective each communication is in generating purchases. Each mail-shot or a phone call stands on its own and is not viewed as an episode in the development of a relationship.

But a relationship is interactive and both sides have a role in it and a view of what it means to them. A relationship marketing approach often fails to appreciate the customer's view of the relationship as part of its portfolio. An example from consumer marketing illustrates this. One supermarket wished to be the main supplier of groceries to its customers and used a variety of techniques to communicate its offerings. However, its customers had relationships with several stores, each of which they used to solve different problems. Many did not see this store as the source for their main grocery shopping, but instead as a source of emergency purchases, or fresh produce. Eventual realization of this led the store to change its strategy to work *with* their customers' views of their relationship.

RELATIONSHIP MARKETING	RELATIONSHIP MANAGEMENT
DISTANT	CLOSE
DISCRETE/ONE-OFF ACTIONS	EACH ACTION IS AN EPISODE THAT IS PART OF OVERALL RELATIONSHIP MANAGEMENT
AIMS TO INFLUENCE INDIVIDUALS IN COMPANY	SEES EACH INDIVIDUAL AS ONE ELEMENT IN RELATIONSHIP WITH THE COMPANY AS A WHOLE
CONCERNED WITH SINGLE TRANSACTIONS	CONCERNED WITH EPISODES IN A RELATIONSHIP
DOES THINGS *TO* PEOPLE	DOES THINGS *WITH* AND *FOR* PEOPLE
CONCERNED WITH ACHIEVING RESPONSE TO STIMULUS	CONCERNED WITH THE WHY AND HOW OF RESPONSE
CONCERNED WITH SUPPLIER'S VIEW OF RELATIONSHIP	CONCERNED WITH CUSTOMER'S VIEW OF HOW THE SUPPLIER FITS INTO THE NETWORK
MEASURES EFFECTS (DO YOU LIKE WHAT WE'RE SENDING?)	MEASURES REASONS (TELL ME WHY IT WAS USEFUL)
DEALS WITH A REDUCING SET OF ADDRESSES (RESPONDERS ONLY)	MAINTAINS AND BUILDS RELATIONSHIP

Figure 5.3 Differences between Relationship Management and Relationship Marketing.

Relationships acquire their own dynamics, norms and ways of working. In a very real sense, a business relationship is out of the control of either of the companies. Nevertheless, the business marketer and purchaser still have to work effectively in this situation – to control the uncontrollable and manage the unmanageable! In order to do this the marketer must be aware of the processes that occur in a relationship and the dimensions of each relationship that he must monitor and manipulate. These processes can be outlined as follows.

Learning from the customer

The way that a relationship develops and the interaction between the individuals will depend on what the two companies can learn about each other's uncertainties and abilities, and about what they need from the relationship and what they can offer it. The companies also have to learn about more subtle and complex issues, such as what their counterparts mean by the things they say and the attitudes they show. Learning helps the companies to reduce (but never eliminate) their uncertainties. They must also learn how to live with some uncertainties that cannot be reduced.

Relationships will vary depending on the extent to which the two companies feel that they need to learn, on their willingness to learn and on their ability to learn. This leads to the first task of relationship management:

TASK 1 – This business marketer must constantly learn about the customer and its operations, resources and technologies (including those that might be transferable to his own operations). He must learn about the customer's behaviour and how predictable it is. The marketer must also try to teach the customer. This includes providing information and advice to the customer about the marketer's company.

Investing in relationships

Business relationships require investments of tangible and intangible resources by marketers and by customers. These are likely to include human resource investment to develop contacts between the companies, to give and receive information and advice. They may also include investments to develop the different elements of either company's offerings or to make them more compatible, or improvements in the company's procedures to make interaction more effective and efficient.

This leads to the second task of relationship management:

TASK 2 – Investments build relationship assets. Marketers must constantly assess current and planned relationship investments against the benefits they can realistically expect to receive from them.

Making and controlling adaptations to each relationship

Most suppliers (and customers) will invest in each of their relationships to at least some extent. At one extreme, this investment may simply be the normal time spent by the supplier's sales force in advising each customer. At the other extreme, it could mean that the supplier always changes or develop a new offering for each customer. In contrast to these normal investments, *adaptations* are when a particular customer is treated in a unique way. Some formal adaptations will be laid out in the contract between the buyer and seller. Informal adaptations are those that are agreed to cope with a problem that arises or at the request of the counterpart. For example, the supplier may agree to reduce deliveries from the contractually agreed level for a short time to cope with a sales downturn at the customer, or the customer could change the design of its own product to cope with a production difficulty at its supplier.

Informal adaptations are often important in the development of a relationship but they are often made without a proper assessment of their costs or effects and this can cause problems for the marketer. Examples would be when a salesperson agrees to a price reduction for a single customer, without thinking through the effects on profits, or on other customers if they should find out, or when informal adaptations for different customers lead to uncontrolled proliferation of types of offering.

This leads to the third task of relationship management:

TASK 3 – The marketer must fully assess the costs and effects of each adaptation against the potential of the relationship. He must seek to monitor and control informal adaptations made by individuals. Where possible, the marketer should try to reduce the costs of adaptations for each relationship by making a single investment that can benefit a number of relationships.

The investments and adaptations of supplier and customer company build actor bonds, activity links and resource ties between them. They are also part of the process by which they come to rely on each other and to *co-evolve* (see Box 5.3). In other words, the companies actually change their characteristics and ways of working because they have a relationship with a customer or supplier.

BOX 5.3   An Example of Co-Evolution

The company in this example is an industrial wholesaler that has 30 000 customer relationships. Many of these are with small electronics companies involved in designing, developing or maintaining equipment. Many of the relationships are very long established. The company issues a comprehensive new catalogue every three months that contains 140 000 lines of maintenance, repair, development and operating items and customers telephone their orders for next-day delivery. The average value of orders is low and the company is not a competitive supplier of material in production volumes.

The company and its customers have co-evolved, but in different ways from each other:

- The supplier's operations and indeed its whole culture have been dictated by this large number of distant, impersonal relationships. Its operations are dominated by the need to constantly refine the efficiency of its interactions, each of which involves virtually no differentiation between individual customers.

> - The evolving efficiency of the supplier means that its customers no longer have to tie up capital in stocks of an ever-widening range of products on which they depend. Many development engineers in customer companies place great faith in the supplier's ability to "speak their language" and to select products for their catalogue that are "right" for them. Their relationship with this supplier means that they do not have to think ahead about their requirements. Unlike the supplier, their evolving culture does not emphasize planning, order and efficiency. Instead, the relationship means that they can react quickly to the random nature of their research, development or maintenance requirements.
>
> This co-evolution has also affected the supplier's other relationships with its few large customers that each place many low value orders. The company has found it difficult to develop an appropriate way of dealing with these large customers, each of which requires the supplier to adapt some aspects of its operations to suit their requirements. The supplier's management and staff are unused to the idea of dealing with separate customers in a differentiated way and its internal systems and procedures do not cope well with it.

Developing and demonstrating commitment and trust between customer and supplier

Many relationships fail to develop after an initial contact, perhaps because the problems of the customer or supplier disappear or can be solved more effectively in other relationships. Some relationships are long-lasting and may broaden in scope to solve a wide range of customer and supplier problems. Some potentially valuable relationships fail because either of the parties lacks the skills or resources to develop them, or because the companies do not understand their true value. A relationship can also fail because the companies do not demonstrate *commitment* to it, or do not trust each other.

A marketer demonstrates commitment to a relationship by agreeing to *adapt* his offering or promise. These show that he is willing to incur immediate costs for the prospect of later reward. A marketer builds up the trust of his customer by the way that he actually *fulfils* that promise.

It is easy for a marketer to demonstrate a lack of commitment to a relationship by declining to adapt a production schedule to suit a customer's requirements or by refusing to alter a fixed price for a volume order. Similarly, it is easy to destroy a customer's trust. For example, the marketer could reduce the calibre of staff assigned to a customer and divert them to other more profitable clients, or it could increase the price of an offering at a time of shortage.

But relationships are two-sided and even if the supplier shows commitment and fulfils its promises, that commitment may not be shared by the customer. For example, a customer may encourage the supplier to invest in their relationship, even though its requirements are likely to change in the near future.

Relationships vary widely: sometimes each company will willingly incur considerable costs so that both gain in the longer term. Sometimes the parties will be entirely trustworthy in their dealings, other times they will behave with guile. On some occasions they will show genuine altruism, but other times they will simply cheat.

The behaviour of the two companies will not always be predictable, or indeed make any sense when set against their stated individual aims or even their best interests. Every single relationship will have a history of how the parties have treated each other and the degree of trust and commitment that has been built up.

It is important for the business marketer to understand that trust cannot be built in a relationship by making promises, but only by fulfilling them. Unless the customer trusts a supplier to fulfil its promise, the customer will not value its offering as a worthwhile solution. A customer with high need uncertainty that is unsure about what is the right offering may initially trust a supplier's *brand*, or reputation from its other relationships but if the promise of that brand is not fulfilled then its trust will soon evaporate. Customers also have long memories of previous promises made by suppliers and whether or not they were fulfilled.

This leads to the fourth task of relationship management:

TASK 4 – The marketer must make a clear decision about whether he wishes to develop a particular relationship. If he does, then he must demonstrate commitment to it by a controlled process of formal and informal adaptations. He must also monitor how much the customer trusts the supplier and check the fulfilment of his offering to build that trust.

The marketer must also closely monitor the commitment of the customer and its investment in the relationship, as well as the customer's trustworthiness in carrying out that commitment.

Managing distance between the companies

The distance between companies in business relationships has a number of aspects that the marketer must be aware of and seek to monitor and control:[3]

- **Social Distance** measures how much the individuals in the two organizations are familiar with each other's ways of thinking and working and are at ease with them.
- **Cultural Distance** is the degree to which the norms and values of the two companies differ because of their place of origin, or because of their corporate cultures.
- **Technological Distance** refers to differences between the technologies of the two companies and indicates how easily they "fit" together. It also refers to their level of understanding of the technologies involved in the offerings in the relationship. For example, interaction between a retailer seeking to buy products to its own specification from an inexperienced, low labour-cost supplier is likely to be very different from that between a manufacturer of industrial robotics and an experienced buyer from the automotive industry.
- **Time Distance** is common in the early stages of a relationship, when there is a considerable time before either party is likely to have to deliver on its promises, or to

[3] Jan Johanson and Finn Wiedersheim-Paul, The Internationalisation of the Firm, Four Swedish Case Studies, *Journal of Management Studies*, vol. 2, no. 3, 1975, pp. 305–22.

receive benefits from the relationship. Hence, their interactions are likely to appear rather unreal and little trust will have developed between them.

The management of distance leads to the fifth task of relationship management:

TASK 5 – The business marketer must assess the distance between his own and the customer company and decide whether and how that distance should be changed.

Social, cultural and technological distance can only be reduced by social interaction between individuals and the development of actor bonds. Time distance can be reduced by arranging for the customer to receive some benefit from a relationship at an early stage.

It may not always be sensible for the marketer to try to reduce distance. The less distance between them, the more knowledge the customer has of him and hence the more predictable he may be. This may encourage a customer to take advantage of the supplier, based on knowing what it can get away with.[4]

Managing and exploiting power and dependence

A relationship allows both customer and supplier to gain more in benefits than the costs that they incur. A supplier incurs the costs of developing and fulfilling an offering but it receives revenue and perhaps it also learns from the relationship and gains access to other relationships. Similarly, a customer incurs the financial costs of buying the offering and also of any adaptations it makes to meet the supplier's requirements. But it can set these costs against the benefits of solving some problems through the relationship, as well as what it learns from the relationship and the access it gains to other parts of the network. Even though both sides gain, it does not mean that a relationship is always going to be close and friendly. Even the most productive relationships can exhibit power, dependence and conflict.

Both customer and supplier can simultaneously have power over each other in a relationship. Their power will vary due to the extent to which each is dependent on the other to solve their problems and the availability to them of alternative solutions. Dependence may be based on the difficulty of the problem and the technological distance between the two companies. It may also be due to the physical resources of the supplier or customer that enable it to solve a high volume requirement for the other. It may also be due to the investment that the companies have made to build the actor bonds, activity links and resource ties that are needed for an offering to be developed and fulfilled.

Power can also grow as a relationship develops and provides a solution to a wider range of problems for both parties. The more that a customer or supplier commits to a relationship, then the more dependent it is on the counterpart to solve some of its problems and the more powerful that counterpart becomes. Customer power over suppliers is common among large retailers buying from small producers of textiles or food

---

[4] David Ford, Håkan Håkansson and Jan Johanson, How do Companies Interact?, *Industrial Marketing and Purchasing*, 1986, vol. 1, no. 1, pp. 26–41.

items. Similarly, many customers in the automotive or aerospace industries have power over their subcontractors that manufacture to the customers' design and do not have their own design capability. Suppliers often have power over their customers when they have a strong technological position in an area that is important to a customer that has no similar ability itself.[5] Suppliers are also powerful when a customer needs an adapted offering from a supplier, but is unable to order in large volumes. Power and dependence form the basis of the sixth task of the business marketer:

> TASK 6 – *The business marketer must assess the extent of his dependence on a customer and on what that dependence is based; the revenue or profits generated by the relationship, or the learning it produces, or the network access it provides.*
>
> *The business marketer must decide whether to reduce his dependence on a customer, either by investing his resources in this, or in its other relationships.*
>
> *A marketer must also plan for exercising his power in a relationship. He may choose to take advantage of a customer's dependence for short-term gain, for example, by increasing price or requiring the customer to make adaptations in order to use the supplier's offering. Alternatively, the marketer may choose not to use his power in the short term, but to incur short-term costs as a way of increasing the customer's dependence on him and his long-term power. Before exercising power in a relationship the marketer must consider the extent of his own dependence on the customer, the purpose of the relationship and the long-term effects of any action.*

Managing conflict

There may be conflict about the overall direction of a relationship. For example, the supplier may wish both parties to invest in the long-term development of a relationship to solve a number of problems for both of them, but the customer may see this supplier only as a short-term stop-gap for an immediate problem. There can also be conflict over the division of activities between the two companies, such as when a department store wants a supplier of designer clothes to pay the salaries of sales staff in an area dedicated to that supplier's garments. Conflict can also occur because of the past or the future actions of either of the parties. An example would be because a problem with previous service delivery had meant that a customer lost one of its own valued clients, or because a customer insists on a guarantee of future compliance with specification. This leads to the seventh task of relationship management:

> TASK 7 – *When the marketer is faced with disagreement or conflict in a relationship, he must balance the exercise of his power to achieve his immediate aims against the chance that this will reduce the customer's trust and generate further future conflict. Any decision must be based on an assessment of the long-term value of the relationship to his company.*

---

[5] In other words, the technology is *external* for the customer.

Managing communication and influence

Communication and influence are frequently associated with the sales force. But these factors are not just used to persuade a customer to give the first or subsequent orders – or to sell the supplier's "product". Instead, communication and influence are important for *all* of the relationship management tasks:

- to learn about customers and their problems and abilities so that a suitable offering can be developed;
- to persuade the customer that the offering is the right solution to those problems;
- to discuss relationship investments and adaptations;
- to show commitment and build trust;
- to reduce distance – this is particularly important in the early stages of a relationship, or when the customer is overseas;
- to exercise power and manage dependence;
- to reduce or manage conflict.

The sales force is likely to be part of many of the critical "actor bonds" between the supplier and individuals in the customer company. This can lead to problems for the marketing company if it fails to control the sales force properly or allows a business relationship to become dependent on a single salesperson or an individual in the customer company.

In many relationships there are likely to be numerous contacts between individuals from different functional areas in both companies and within each customer about a single relationship. Figure 5.4 illustrates the scale of inter-company communication for a company supplying an international customer in the computer industry. Figure 5.5 shows the associated communication patterns within the supplier.[6] Each of these contacts involve communication and influence. Traditionally, the sales force had the job of co-ordinating these interactions. This co-ordination is important to ensure that each interaction fits into an overall approach to the relationship but it is the responsibility of the business marketer to determine what this overall approach should be, what resources should be invested and how the relationship should fit into the wider portfolio.

Companies face a number of problems in managing customer communications:

- The role of co-ordinating interaction has become difficult as more communications media are used such as call-centres, sales and service depots, web-sites and portals, etc.
- The problems of customers have become more complex and they rely more on suppliers to provide adapted solutions involving many different functions. For example, it is now common for major companies to contract out to suppliers their entire information technology or financial management. Many sales forces lack the technological competence or influence within their companies to co-ordinate this evolving interaction effectively.

---

[6] Figures 5.4 and 5.5 are from the work of Sally Hughes, postgraduate student, University of Bath.

SUPPLIER		CUSTOMER										
		Customer Corporate			Customer-Europe				Customer-USA			
		Commodity management team	Process project managers	Process development engineers	Fab general management	Site purchasing	Engineering project managers	Process engineers	Fab general management	Site purchasing	Engineering project managers	Process engineers
Corporate	General management	✓			✓				✓			
	Marketing Director	✓			✓							
Marketing	Key account managers					✓	✓		✓	✓		
	Customer care account handlers (UK)					✓						
	National sales centre (USA)	✓								✓		
	Onsite Managers at Customer	✓			✓	✓	✓	✓				
	Site service team						✓	✓				
	Customer Care account handlers (UK)	✓				✓			✓	✓		✓
	Site service team (USA)											
	Business development (Europe)	✓			✓							
	Product management (USA)	✓							✓			
Product Management	UK operations management team	✓	✓				✓					
	US operations management team	✓		✓		✓				✓	✓	

Figure 5.4 Customer–supplier communication matrix.

		Product Division, UK Operations Management Team				
		Operations director	Operations manager	Assembly cell leader	Project enginneers	Manufacturing support engineers
Corporate	General management	✓	✓	✓		
Customer Facing Divsion	Marketing director	✓	✓			
	Key account mangers		✓	✓	✓	
	Customer care account handlers (UK)			✓	✓	
	National sales centre (USA)			✓	✓	
	Customer site team manager (Europe)		✓	✓	✓	
	Site service team (Europe)			✓	✓	✓
	Customer site team manager (USA)			✓	✓	
	Site service team (Europe)					
	Business development (Europe)	✓		✓		
	Product mangement (USA)	✓		✓		

Figure 5.5   Internal communications matrix.

- Some companies have tried to overcome this problem by appointing technically qualified, senior relationship managers to co-ordinate continuing relationships, or project managers in the case of those relationships centring on a single major project. In this situation, the sales force becomes more of a service function working within the overall control of the relationship or project manager. This can lead to problems of low sales force morale and to poor communications between project managers and marketers.
- In many companies, marketing is only responsible for activities such as direct mailing and publicity. It lacks the stature in the organization to enable it to influence other

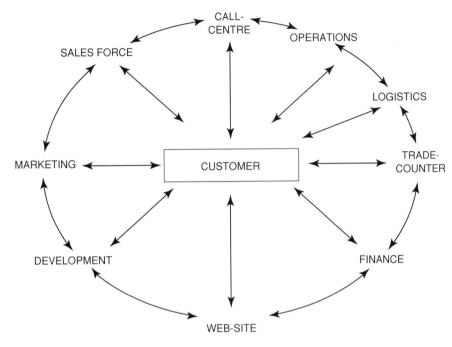

Figure 5.6 Co-ordinating customer communication.

functions, such as development, finance or operations. This problem is likely to be particularly acute when the company has a strong, experienced or senior sales manager or director.

Figure 5.6 illustrates the need to co-ordinate all of the interactions with a customer that involve different functional areas, each of which may have their own relationships with individuals and their own agenda to pursue. This is the eighth task of relationship management:

TASK 8 – The business marketer must co-ordinate communication between different individuals and functions in both companies so that each interaction in all media is in line with an overall approach to the relationship, as part of a portfolio.

Box 5.4 Five Things to Remember About Relationships

1 The customer will always have a different view from you about what the relationship is for, what they should contribute, what you should contribute, what you should receive, what they should receive, what you are doing and have done and what they are doing and have done.

> 2 If you think that the relationship is important, the other party may think it less important. If you think it unimportant, they may think it important.
> 3 The customer always has other relationships and will assess their relationship with you on the basis of their experience in those relationships.
> 4 Relationships are about time. In order to receive value from the relationship in the future, you must make investments today. The return on those investments is likely to take longer than you thought. The value that you may receive today is likely to be at the expense of the value that you could receive in the future.
> 5 Companies in relationships have long memories. If you take advantage of a customer today, they will remember the episode for a long time.

Auditing Business Relationships

A marketing company's relationships are its primary assets, without which neither its skills nor its physical resources can be exploited. The marketer needs to maximize the rate of return on these assets and a relationship audit of each important relationship is a useful starting point. Less significant relationships can be audited as a group. An outline of the questions in such an audit is provided in Figure 5.7.

History and Current Status

Questions in this section include which company started the relationship and why; what has happened in the relationship; what has gone right and wrong and why crises may have occurred. Customers have long memories of a supplier's good and bad performance which can strongly affect current and future business. An analysis of relationship history will explain much about current resource ties, activity links and actor bonds and contribute to a sound description of the current state of the relationship.

A customer and supplier are unlikely to have the same view of the purpose of a relationship. For example, the customer may see the relationship only as a source of basic items with a restricted potential, whilst the supplier considers it to be a potential source of technological learning. These differences in views will affect the marketer's assessment of the potential of the relationship and the tasks necessary to achieve his aims for it.

The financial performance of a relationship is an important indicator of the value of the relationship to the marketer. It is important that financial analysis for a relationship audit should extend beyond recording sales volume or superficial "profit" achieved from each customer. The analysis should show the return achieved in the relationship by relating sales volume to the variable costs of purchased items, production, service delivery, sales effort and logistics. Fixed costs, or those which are incurred irrespective of sales volume, should also be assigned to particular relationships, such as those of developing or adapting an offering or investing in production facilities or providing dedicated logistics. Less significant relationships will have to be analysed

1 HISTORY AND CURRENT STATUS

- WHAT IS THE HISTORY OF THE RELATIONSHIP?

- WHAT IS THE CURRENT PURPOSE OF THE RELATIONSHIP FOR BOTH PARTIES?

- WHAT IS THE SUBSTANCE OF THE RELATIONSHIP: ACTOR BONDS, ACTIVITY LINKS AND RESOURCE TIES?

- WHAT IS ITS FINANCIAL PERFORMANCE?

2 ATMOSPHERE OF THE RELATIONSHIP

- HOW COMMITTED ARE BOTH COMPANIES TO THE RELATIONSHIP AND TO THAT INVESTMENT?

- WHAT IS THE DISTANCE BETWEEN THE TWO COMPANIES?

- WHAT IS THE POWER AND CONFLICT POSITION IN THE RELATIONSHIP?

3 POTENTIAL AND INVESTMENT

- WHAT IS THE POTENTIAL OF THE RELATIONSHIP FOR BOTH PARTIES?

- WHAT INVESTMENT IS REQUIRED FROM BOTH PARTIES TO FULFIL THAT POTENTIAL?

- WHAT ARE THE THREATS TO THE RELATIONSHIP?

4 NETWORK

- WHAT IS THE NETWORK POSTION OF THE RELATIONSHIP?

- WHAT IS ITS ROLE IN THE COMPANY'S PORTFOLIO?

5 CURRENT OPERATIONS

- IS CURRENT MANAGEMENT OF THE RELATIONSHIP IN LINE WITH OVERALL STRATEGY?

- IS THE CURRENT PATTERN OF INTERACTION APPROPRIATE?

Figure 5.7   The relationship audit.

in aggregate form. We will look at this issue in more detail in Chapter 8 on Prices and Costs.

Atmosphere

The questions in this section deal with the level of commitment of both companies to the relationship, which will be strongly affected by their previous experience and their assessment of its potential (see below). An assessment of the distance between the companies and the levels of power and conflict between them are important indicators of whether the supplier will be able to change the current state of the relationship. They may indicate that changes will be needed in the way that the supplier communicates with the customer or that it should seek to reduce its dependence on it.

Potential and investment

Questions in this section must examine the relationship from the perspective of both customer and supplier, as there are likely to be differences between their views. These views will affect their willingness to make the investments that are necessary to achieve the potential of the relationship. The potential of a relationship may include the generation of cash, or "profit" at various levels of cost allocation, or the acquisition of new technology or access to other relationships. It is common for a marketing company to fail to fulfil the potential of its relationships, either because it is unable to convince the customer of that potential, or because the marketer is unable to secure the necessary investment from the customer or from his own company. This emphasizes that skills of communication and influence are needed both *inside* the marketer's own company and with the customer.

Network

The potential of a relationship can never be assessed in isolation from the marketer's other relationships and the wider network position of both companies. By analysing the connected relationships of the customer the marketer can find out where his offering fits in with those of the customer's other suppliers (and its customers) to provide an offering to meet the needs of a final user. The problems, potential and investment prospects in any one relationship must be compared with the prospects of the other relationships in its portfolio. Also, each relationship within a portfolio must complement the others.

Current operations

It is important for marketers to check that their current operations in a relationship are related to their overall strategy for that relationship. All too often the actions of individual marketers, or others in the company, are out of line with that strategy or with each other. For example, a development department may fail to respond to a modification request from a customer because it is concerned about the costs involved. This may jeopardize the future of a high-potential relationship. The pattern of interaction with a customer refers to such issues as the frequency of sales calls on the customer and the seniority of those making the calls. Paradoxically, this is a relatively unimportant aspect of the overall management of a relationship, but in many companies it receives a disproportionate amount of attention. This is because these companies have failed to take a strategic approach to their relationships and instead are more concerned with short-term cost and revenue issues.

Conclusion

This chapter has built on the ideas presented in earlier chapters about the nature of business marketing and the context in which it operates. Business marketing can be expressed as a set of six tasks dealing with understanding and implementation. At the heart of business marketing is the *management* of each single relationship with customers.

Some of a company's customer relationships will be individually significant in terms of their current contribution of revenue, profit, learning, access to other networks or their potential for the future. Each of these will justify the effort of managing them individually. Others may have been significant in the past, but no longer justify the costs and efforts that are involved. The marketer may have to disinvest in those relationships to lower their operating costs, to use whatever power he has to increase the contribution to them by the customer in terms of effort, resources or finance. Other relationships will not be individually significant, but collectively may be of great importance. Each of these alone is unlikely to justify dedicated investment, adaptation or management time. Instead the marketer will need to seek ways to categorize these relationships according to their common characteristics and manage groups of relationships in a similar way.

This chapter has outlined a process for assessing or auditing each individual or group of the customer relationships of a company. This is not a one-off process, but one that will need to be repeated on a regular basis, to ensure that relationship management and operations coincide with company strategy and work towards the optimization of the rate of return on the company's prime assets.

Relationship management is not a linear process leading to some ideal state or "partnership" between customer and supplier. Both companies will try to manage a relationship for their own ends. Marketers must try to build and manage a relationship over time to achieve its potential for them, within the context of the customer's problems, its aims for the relationship and its wider portfolio of relationships. Relationship management has to take a realistic view of the value of each relationship. This may lead to greater investment, more intense interaction and reduced distance between the companies but it can also lead to the marketer reducing or stopping investment and increasing the distance between the supplier and the customer.

In this chapter we have emphasized that the development of an offering to solve the problems of a customer is an important business marketing task. In the next chapter we deal with this development process in more depth. This offering is the marketer's promise to his customer. It has no value unless that promise can be fulfilled. This critical issue of fulfilment is then addressed in Chapter 7.

Further Reading

James Anderson and Jim Narus (1991) Partnering as a Focused Market Strategy, *California Management Review*, Spring, pp. 95–113.

Barbara Bund-Jackson (1985) *Winning and Keeping Industrial Customers*, Lexington, MA, Lexington Books.

David Ford (ed.) (2001) *Understanding Business Marketing and Purchasing*, London, International Thomson, especially readings 4.1–4.9.

David Ford *et al.* (1998) *Managing Business Relationships*, Chichester, John Wiley.

N Kumar (1996) The Power of Trust in Manufacturer-Retailer Relationships, *Harvard Business Review*, November–December, pp. 92–106.

Glen de Souza (1992) Designing a Customer Retention Plan, *The Journal of Business Strategy*, March–April, pp. 24–8.

Frederick Webster (1992) The Changing Role of Marketing in the Corporation, *Journal of Marketing*, vol. 56, October, pp. 1–17.

BUILDING OFFERINGS: DEVELOPING THE PROMISE

6

Aims of this Chapter

The central theme of this chapter is the marketer's *problem-solving abilities*. The chapter is concerned with how marketers can develop and use these abilities to build offerings and make promises in business relationships. The overall aim of the chapter is to enable marketers to understand the complexity of offerings in business marketing and how these offerings can be developed to relate to customer problems. The chapter starts by explaining the different elements of an offering and how they are related to each other. When marketers talk about their offerings they often speak of their "quality". Quality is often a misused term in business (and consumer) marketing and another aim of this chapter is to bring some clarity to the term. Following this, the chapter shows how a company's offerings must relate to the abilities of both customer and supplier and to the relationship between them. We then go on to describe the strategic decisions that suppliers face in their offerings. Finally, we examine the process of developing offerings.

What is an Offering?

The problems of business customers are often complex and can rarely be solved simply by a physical product alone. For example as the complexity of software packages for ERP (Enterprise Resource Planning) has grown, so the customer demand for *advice* during both purchase and implementation rose accordingly. It is conservatively estimated that for each dollar spent on the purchase of this type of software, a further five dollars are spent on *service* and *consulting* in the choice and implementation of a system.

The offerings of business marketers consist of different combinations of the five elements shown in Figure 6.1, *together*.

- **Products:** These are the physical part of the offering. This is what the customer can see and feel after the purchase. An offering may consist of one product as in the case of a

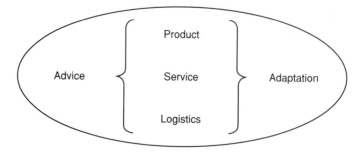

Figure 6.1 Elements of an offering.

single piece of machinery, or many different products as in the case of a catalogue supplier of office equipment. Just because they are the most obvious element of an offering, products are often wrongly considered by many customers and suppliers to be the most important element. However, as we will see, the product element is often relatively unimportant in solving a customer's problems when compared to others. Also, a product itself has no intrinsic value. Its only value is as a solution to a problem: *There is no market for quarter inch drills, but there is an enormous market for quarter inch holes.*

- **Services:** These can be a major part of the offering. This is for three reasons: first, the product element of many offerings has little value without the associated services. Common examples include the need for upgrades for software, maintenance service for equipment, or training. For example, Heidelberger Druckmaschinen, the maker of huge printing presses, has set up "print academies" in nine cities around the world to organize courses on printing techniques for customers and would-be customers of its equipment.[1] Second, many customers now purchase a service instead of purchasing a product. Examples include companies that lease rather than buy cars, or contract out the cleaning of their premises, rather than buying their own cleaning equipment and airlines that do not buy engines for their aircraft, but contract with a supplier for "power-by-the-hour". Finally, business services have increased in importance as companies depend more and more on "external" technologies, rather than retaining expensive skills in-house. Examples include contracting out design activities in the automotive and fashion industries; contract manufacture for electronic components; outsourcing maintenance as in the airline industry and accounting and data processing in a wide range of companies.

- **Logistics:** Logistics are not just the ways in which the other elements of an offering are delivered to the customer. In many cases logistics can be the most vital element of an offering for competitive success, particularly when the product and service elements of an offering are undifferentiated between different competitors. For example, a supplier of basic automotive component products such as hoses or radiators may seek to

[1] *The Financial Times*, 2 August 2001.

differentiate its offering from others by providing "just-in-time" or "zero-inventory" deliveries to the plants of car manufacturers in a number of countries. Similarly, a supplier of components for maintenance, repair and operations (MRO) may operate an in-plant store of parts for a high-volume producer of food products to eliminate production disruptions caused when parts fail. Logistics are also an important part of the offering for advertising agencies, accountants, trainers and consultants. These companies often establish relationships with companies with whom they normally compete, in order to offer advice and service to clients in other countries.

- **Advice** concerns all the activities of a supplier, which are aimed at increasing the customer's understanding. The importance of advice in an offering will depend on the customer's uncertainties. When customers have low *need uncertainty* and *market uncertainty*, a supplier can provide the necessary advice in its brochures and web-sites and during sales-calls. However, advice from the supplier is of greater importance when need and/or market uncertainty are high. In this situation the value to the customer of the advice of a trusted supplier can far outweigh the price of a subsequent purchase. Advice is not the same as the "hard sell", when a marketer tries to push the customer to buy her offering, irrespective of its problems and uncertainties. However, it is important for a supplier to have skills in communicating its offering and influencing its customers, as we discussed in the previous chapter. Advice is a two-way process in a business relationship. Customer advice is important for reducing the supplier's uncertainties. Customers can advise on the nature of their problems, on the way that an offering will be used and how it must relate to those of other suppliers and to the customer's own offering for its customers. Customers can also contribute their technologies to the interactive development of the supplier's offering.

- **Adaptation** occurs when a supplier makes a change to any element of its offering *that it would not normally do for other customers*. So it is not an adaptation if a supplier *always* modifies the product element of its offering to each customer's requirements but it would be an adaptation if it agreed to change a standard product, or its normal service or logistics package. We have seen in the previous chapter that adaptations are an important way for a supplier to demonstrate its commitment to a relationship. However, adaptations can also lead to considerable costs and disruption to the company's operations. It is important for business marketers to work closely with others in their company to translate their understanding of customer problems into offerings that can provide solutions for different customers with the maximum commonality. Marketers are still likely to come under pressure from customers to adapt their standard offerings and the control, management and correct pricing of adaptations are important aspects of business marketing and of the company's operations.

Inter-relationships between the elements of an offering

The five elements of an offering are distinct from each other, but at the same time they can influence or replace each other. The product and service elements of an offering are frequently interchangeable, for example, a supplier can provide an offering that consists largely of a product, such as a fleet of delivery trucks, that are purchased by the customer.

The customer is then responsible for hiring and managing drivers for the trucks, scheduling and using the trucks to make deliveries and maintaining the trucks during their life.

Alternatively, the supplier can provide an offering that does not involve purchase of the trucks. Instead it can provide the service of delivery trucks, available for the use of the customer, with guaranteed availability at a fixed mileage charge.

Or the supplier's offering could consist of the service of buying the customer's existing fleet and managing these vehicles and deliveries for the customer. Or the supplier could simply provide the service of delivering the customer's goods, in the supplier's own vehicles with a guaranteed speed and reliability level and charge per item delivered.

An example of product/service interchangeability within one company is provided by Fresenius, the world's biggest maker of artificial kidney machines. Also, through Fresenius Medical Care, they are the biggest provider of kidney dialysis services, using a chain of 1300 global clinics.[2]

The characteristics of both service and product elements are inter-related with the logistics element. For example, the ratio of the weight of the product element to the value of the offering is often critical to the logistics that can be used. Similarly, because services such as security or facilities management often have to be delivered to a wide range of locations for the same customer, then suppliers have to establish an extensive branch network to deliver their offering.

The advice element is also inter-related with product, service and logistics. For example, when the product element is a commodity, then the customer may know all it needs to know and advice might not play a role at all. In contrast, the products and services involved in establishing a complex communications network will require considerable advice from the supplier. But it is not the intrinsic complexity of the product or service elements that affect the role of advice. Instead it is the nature of the customer's problems and uncertainties that determine the need for advice. If the product/service is simple but the customer has no experience of it, then advice will be important. If the offering is complex, but the customer has no need uncertainty, then advice will not be valued by it.

A supplier may seek to simplify its products and services so as to minimize the advice that is needed and thus gain a cost advantage over its competitors that can be reflected in the price that it charges. This is commonly achieved by modularizing the offering or by simplifying the choice process. Both of these have been part of the strategy of Dell, whose competitors did not initially believe that customers would buy expensive computers by phone.

Adaptations can be made to any of the elements of product, service or logistics. Adaptations to the advice element are also important in many relationships. This would include having special consultants for particular customers or developing knowledge of a particular application to enhance advice to a customer. Minor adaptations in one or more elements are, if carefully controlled, a useful way for a marketer to tailor a standardized

---

[2] *The Financial Times*, 2 August 2001.

offering to the requirements of individual customers. The adaptations that are initially developed for a single customer can sometimes be applied to others. More often it is important for a marketer to set the costs of an adaptation against the value of the relationship in which they were made. The marketer should also be aware that using scarce resources of time and money to make an adaptation for one relationship can have a negative effect on others.

Box 6.1   Product/Service Inter-relationships in the IT Industry

Carly Fiorina, the Chief Executive of Hewlett-Packard asserted in 1999 that the end of the "pure product" was over. As computing and communication technologies converge, the value of a product becomes closely related to other elements of an offering. So HP re-invented itself as a provider of "information-technology services and solutions". The wish to add to the service and advice elements of its offerings was the rationale behind HP's bid for the consulting business of PricewaterhouseCoopers. The same thinking could also be seen in IBM's actions to build one of the largest IT consulting operations in the world and in Compaq's take-over of Digital, mainly to acquire its consulting arm and in Cisco's $1 billion stake in consultants KPMG. Of course these moves do not take place in isolation in the network. If a consulting company becomes allied with a hardware/software producer, then that may change the consultants' relationship with its customers. These customers may doubt the independence of the consultants' advice, especially when equipment purchase is involved.[3]

Sometimes the complex offerings demanded by business customers can only be provided by a number of suppliers working together. For example, SAP worked closely with its partners to develop the SAP Partner Value Net. This classifies partners into eight categories: software partners, service partners, technology partners, support partners, hosting partners, channel partners, content partners, and education partners. With these partners SAP is able to offer customized solutions to individual customer's problems, using the resources of all of the companies involved.[4]

Quality of Offerings

The quality of an offering is a measure of the extent to which it actually solves a particular problem for a particular customer.[5] This means that customers will have a different view of the quality of the same offering *depending on their problems and uncertainties*. Also, customers will consider that different elements of an offering are

---

[3] *The Economist*, 16 September 2000.

[4] Adapted from the SAP web-site www.sap.com

[5] This definition means that quality depends both on the characteristics of the offering and how well that offering is fulfilled in practice.

important to its quality, depending on their problems and uncertainties. For example:

- Some customers will not know the best way to solve their problem, or be able to evaluate different offerings. In this situation of high need or market uncertainty, the supplier's advice may be critical to how these companies assess the quality of an offering.
- In contrast, where the customer has little need or market uncertainty and is an experienced buyer, then its view of the quality of an offering is more likely to be based on exactly what each of the elements of product, service and logistics do to solve its problem.
- In other cases, it is the supplier's ability to adapt its offering to suit a particular requirement that is critical to "quality" for these customers.[6]

Matching offerings to problems

Because the fit between an offering and the problem it is intended to solve is the critical aspect of the quality of that offering, marketers need to continually assess how their offerings relate to each customer's problems. Offerings can fall into one of four categories, as follows:

- **Offering < Problem:** This is when only a part of the problem is solved by the offering. This may be because of technological, resource or cost problems in the supplier or because of poor diagnosis of the problem by customer or supplier. Customers often have to accept this inadequacy for a long period, if more complete solutions are not available, or try to find or develop a supplier to solve the problem.
- **Offering = Problem:** In this case, the customer gets a solution which exactly solves the problem – nothing more and nothing less. This may seem like optimal "quality". It is similar to the situation described by Mari Sako as "contractual trust", where a supplier does only what is specified precisely in the contract and fails to demonstrate commitment to a relationship or to achieve customer satisfaction.[7]
- **Offering > Problem:** In this situation, the supplier's offering does more than solve the original problem. This could be positive, if the offering also solves another problem. For example, the supplier of a production item that meets a customer specification may also provide just-in-time delivery so the item no longer has to be kept in inventory. Provided that this can be achieved within cost constraints, extra problem-solving may be an important way of demonstrating commitment and building a relationship. Marketers often refer to this as "customer delight". However, this situation could also be negative if an offering solves a problem, but also creates another one, for example, use of an offering may lead to problems of emissions or recycling.

---

[6] Operations managers often find it useful to distinguish between those elements of an offering that are unimportant as long as they meet a minimum standard, i.e., the "qualifiers" and those which are critical to customers' views of quality, i.e., the "order winners".

[7] Mari Sako, *Prices, Quality and Trust: Interfirm Relations in Britain and Japan*, Cambridge, Cambridge University Press, 1992.

- **Offering <> Problem:** The solution exceeds the problem in some aspects but fails to meet requirements in others. This situation indicates a mismatch between offering and problem, either because of over-standardization by the supplier, a badly designed offering or poor communication between the two companies.

Specifications

Customers are likely to require a detailed specification for complex offerings or for those that centre on important or difficult problems. Sometimes the specification is a detailed description of what the offering must do in order to solve the customer's problem – a *performance specification*. At other times the customer develops a *conformance specification*, of the characteristics the offering must have, or of how it will solve the problem. A customer will only be able to develop a performance specification if it has little or no need uncertainty. It will only be able to develop a conformance specification if it has the product technology to design the offering and also some knowledge of the process technology involved in its fulfilment.

Purchasing textbooks emphasize the importance for customers of clear and unambiguous specifications.[8] But customers do not have the knowledge, abilities or resources to develop specifications for all of the thousands of offerings that they buy. There is a growing tendency for customers to express specifications in more general performance terms and to seek the involvement of suppliers in their development. This tendency has been reinforced by the growing dependence of customers on external technologies in their suppliers.

Quality Function Deployment (QFD)

QFD, or the "House of Quality" is a technique that was developed in Mitsubishi's Kobe shipyard and used extensively by Toyota.[9] It is now widely used to make sense of the important connections between *what* is required by customers and *how* it should be achieved. It is important for business marketers to understand and be involved in the QFD process. They must provide the information on what is required and also assess the extent to which the offering characteristics actually provide a customer solution.[10]

Quality and fulfilment

An offering is a promise to the customer which, if accepted, needs to be fulfilled. Fulfilment depends on the transfer ability of the supplier and we will deal with this ability

---

[8] David Farmer and Arjan van Weele, *Gower Handbook of Purchasing Management*, second edition, Aldershot, Gower, 1995.

[9] J Hauser and D Clausing, "The House of Quality", *Harvard Business Review*, May–June, 1988, pp. 62–73.

[10] Examples of QFD may be found in Richard B Chase, Nicholas Aquino and Robert Jacobs, *Operations Management for Competitive Advantage*, ninth edition, Boston, McGraw Hill-Irwin, 2001.

fully in Chapter 7. Both the supplier as well as the customer will need to consider how an offering will be fulfilled when it is being developed. The quality of an offering depends both on the promise that it makes and the supplier's ability to fulfil that promise.

Price, costs and value

Price, costs and value are complex issues in business marketing and we will devote Chapter 8 to a full analysis of these. For the purposes of this chapter, it is important to emphasize that the price that a customer is prepared to pay for an offering is related to the extent to which an offering solves its problems and not to any intrinsic characteristics it might have, or the absolute "quality" of any of its elements. The price that a customer is prepared to pay is not necessarily related to the supplier's costs of developing or fulfilling its offering and the possibilities for change and substitution between different elements provide important profit opportunities for marketers. The costs of developing, adapting and fulfilling different elements of an offering also present marketers with important issues of management and control. Customers will value different elements of an offering in relation to their own problems and uncertainties. For some customers, enhanced logistics will be more valuable than improvements in the specification of a product that only fulfils a simple function for them. For others, advice may be more important than speed of delivery, while others may value a product adaptation more than a high level of service. They will also consider the value of their relationship with a supplier when considering the price of an offering, as well as any other costs that they may incur in receiving, learning about, integrating and using the offering. Marketers must also consider the value to them of each relationship as well as their own costs, when considering prices.

Offerings in Relationships

A relationship may start because a supplier already has an offering that solves a customer's problem. But in many cases, that offering will have been developed, or at least agreed through interaction between the customer and supplier. Some or all of the elements of the offering are also likely to evolve further as the relationship develops. The management of this development and the control of adaptations are central to business marketing and marketers have to manage a difficult balance with their offerings in a relationship, as follows:

- In order to control their costs, they must try to minimize the adaptations they make for individual customers and maximize the standardization between them. Customers often also try to standardize the offerings they receive from different suppliers to simplify their own operations.
- The more that a supplier standardizes its offering for different customers and the more that a customer standardizes the offerings of different suppliers, the less they will be dependent on each other and the less chance there will be that they build a strong relationship with each other.

Marketers must always keep in mind the different problems of their customers and accept that their offerings must accommodate them as far as possible. They must have good financial information to know exactly what the costs of different adaptations are. They must also work closely with operational departments responsible for fulfilling their offerings to build in standardization where it will be accepted and flexibility where it is needed. They must also understand that the different elements of an offering are inter-related so that, for example, a costly adaptation in the product element may be avoided by providing additional advice on how to use it or by changing the service element to improve the customer's processes.

Offerings and Abilities

We explained in Chapter 1 that both the customer and supplier bring their problems, uncertainties and abilities to their relationship. This means that the offering that is transferred between them depends on the abilities of *both* companies.

Supplier's problem-solving ability

A supplier's *problem-solving ability* is its ability to design and develop an offering that will provide a solution to a customer's problem. Problem-solving ability is built on the following:

- the supplier's resources: physical, financial and technological (see Chapter 2);
- the supplier's network position: its ability to use its relationships with other companies to access their resources and combine them with its own to build an offering.[11] This ability is becoming more important as technologies become more complex and interconnected and outsourcing increases.
- the supplier's ability to manage its relationship with the customer, to determine its problems and to build, adapt and fulfil its offering – its skills in relationship management.

A customer buys an offering from a supplier but that offering is based on all aspects of the supplier's problem-solving ability. Business marketers must expect that their customers will not only evaluate the "quality" of their offering and fulfilment, but also assess all aspects of their organization and problem-solving ability, before they will commit themselves to building a relationship with the supplier.[12] This means that business

[11] The ability to use and integrate the skills and resources of other companies is sometimes referred to as "Network Competence", Thomas Ritter, The Networking Company, *Industrial Marketing Management*, vol. 28, no. 5, 1999, pp. 497–506.

[12] For a discussion of supplier assessment see, for example, E Timmerman, An Approach to Vendor Performance Evaluation, *Journal of Purchasing and Materials Management*, vol. 22, Winter 1986, pp. 2–8 and LC Giunipero and DJ Brewer, Performance Based Evaluation Systems, *International Journal of Purchasing and Materials Management*, vol. 29, Winter 1993, pp. 35–41.

marketers cannot just concentrate on managing their relationships with their customers or on their current offerings. They must also be concerned with questions about developing their company's resources and their company's relationships with its own suppliers and the capabilities that they bring.

Customer's demand abilities

Business marketers cannot take all the credit for the excellence of their offerings! These offerings are likely to be developed and to evolve through interaction with customers and so they also depend on the customer's demand ability. Just like a supplier's problem-solving ability, a customer's demand ability is based on its physical, technological and financial resources, on its network position and on its relationship management skills. A customer's demand ability enables it to advise the supplier of the type of offering it should produce. This is likely to be particularly important to the supplier when it is unsure of how the offering will be used – its *application uncertainty* – or of the level of demand – its *demand uncertainty*.

We emphasized in Chapter 5 that business marketers must choose the customers with which to build a relationship, rather than seek business from everywhere, or simply accept that which is offered. This choice must obviously be based on the nature of the customer's problems and the potential of the relationship for profit. It must also be made on the basis of the customer's demand abilities. The marketer must assess how these can help her to develop her offerings and relationship management skills and apply these profitably in a number of relationships. In order to take advantage of customer demand abilities, a supplier might have to "pay for" business with a technologically advanced customer, either through extensive interaction or by charging a low price.

Strategic Decisions on Offerings

The development of a supplier's problem-solving ability requires an investment of resources and time. It must be based on the answers to two important questions, as follows.

What customer problems should the supplier seek to solve?

Managers are frequently told to ask themselves the question, "What business are we in?" Nowadays this is a difficult question because, as we have argued, there are no narrowly defined industries or neat business markets. So it is useful to redefine the question as, "What customer problems do we aim to solve?". The supplier must then analyse any gap that exists between these problems and its own problem-solving ability. This analysis may lead it to invest in developing the company's problem-solving ability or change the problems it attempts to solve or the customers it addresses.

When carrying out this analysis, the marketer should bear in mind the following:

- Business marketers are often preoccupied with trying to build and fulfil offerings to solve the problems of their customers. But it is often more important for them to find customers who have problems that relate to their existing and expensively acquired abilities.

- Not all the firms in the same industry or market will have the same problems and a supplier is only likely to be able to serve a subset of those that buy a particular "product".
- Careful definition of the problems that it aims to solve enables a company to separate the *real* competition that it faces, as opposed to those companies that simply have a similar product.
- Problem definition also overcomes the issue of market definition because customers with similar problems are not necessarily in the same (traditionally defined) market or industry.

What offering policy should we have?

The definition of a supplier's business in terms of the customer problems that it addresses is an important first step in developing a policy for its offerings. This policy can be focused on a particular customer problem, a range of offerings or the supplier's relationships.

Problem focus

This focus involves the supplier in concentrating on a single type of problem and developing a number of offerings which solve that problem in different ways. A simple example is a business travel agent who offers train tickets, rental cars and flight tickets as solutions to the problem of business travel. However, a focus on providing a wide range of different solutions is more difficult in the case of complex problems, such as those addressed by financial services companies or producers of production machinery. This is because these companies cannot afford the range of abilities and technologies necessary to develop and fulfil a variety of offerings effectively or economically. A recent example of this problem is Xerox, who refers to itself as "the document company", providing a full range of offerings for the reproduction of documents. However, it failed to match its successful offerings in analogue copiers with similar success in digital copiers. Many suppliers seek to get round the difficulty of sustaining a range of different offerings by acting as agents for the offerings of other suppliers and combining them with their own to provide a full range. Many customers also require suppliers to bring together the development and fulfilment of other suppliers' offerings when they operate a tiered supply network. Another difficulty with this problem focus is the heavy investment needed to develop a range of offerings. This may limit the supplier's ability to *adapt* different elements of these offerings to meet customer requirements and hence to build customer relationships.

Range focus

This focus can take two forms: the first form involves the company building a range of offerings for different problems, built on the company's abilities and its distinctive product and/or process technologies. This focus addresses the problems of over-extending the company's technology in a problem focus (above). It seeks to maximize the company's return on these technologies. For example, Rolls Royce markets a range of offerings all using its gas-turbine technologies, but suitable for powering military or civil aircraft, for propelling military ships, pumping oil or gas, or for generating electricity. In this focus, one element of the offering, typically the product or service, will have only minor variation. Thus, Rolls Royce uses the same basic designs of gas turbines, but modifies them to burn different fuels in different problem situations. This focus typically involves variation in other elements of the offering for each problem. For example, aerospace customers require Rolls Royce to be closely involved in joint studies of aircraft performance for many years (advice). In contrast, naval customers take responsibility themselves for the wider aspect of ship design and performance. The offerings for pumping and power generation must provide customers with a package, bought "off-the-shelf" and delivered to any location however remote (logistics), so that they can simply switch it on. This approach depends on the supplier having a well-developed knowledge of a wide range of different customer problems and the ability to manage many different types of relationships.

The second form of this focus is when a supplier provides a range of offerings, all using similar abilities and technologies, but intended for the *same* problem. This has a number of advantages: it requires only limited problem understanding and a narrower range of relationship management skills. It also has the advantage of allowing the supplier to invest heavily in a narrow range of skills or technologies and to develop a reputation for excellence in them. It also is likely to lead to lower costs of operations. But of course it restricts the supplier's ability to maximize the return on its technological assets. Also, even though the offering may be highly sophisticated in one element, it is unlikely to be a complete solution to a customer's problem. Customers will have to integrate the offering with those of other suppliers and use their own demand abilities to build a complete problem solution. Examples of this approach include suppliers of printers, drilling machines, air-freight, or advertising service agencies specializing in creativity or media buying, etc. The narrowness of this focus means that suppliers are vulnerable to technological obsolescence. They are also less likely to have a close relationship with customers that will enable them to monitor and react to changing requirements.

Relationship focus

This focus involves a supplier in seeking to capitalize on its important relationships and build the necessary offerings for each case. This approach has been successfully followed by Jack Welch at General Electric. Rather than try to sell existing products to more customers, Welch concentrated on broadening GE's offerings for its existing customers by adding new services. Similarly, Jorgen Centerman, Chief Executive of the electrical engineering company, ABB, faces the problem of a broad portfolio of offerings marketed to thousands of customers in many different ways with consequent limitations on efficiency. For this reason he is seeking to re-orientate the company's research and development towards a greater emphasis on its relationships with its customers, rather than simply with its own engineers, sales teams and suppliers.[13] A relationship focus is being followed by a number of large accounting companies that seek to provide profitable consulting and legal services in customer relationships that were initially based solely on auditing. For example, PricewaterhouseCoopers currently receives only 40 per cent of its revenues from traditional accounting and auditing services. This approach has led to major concerns by regulatory authorities about its effects on the nature of the traditional audit relationship. Similarly, a number of consulting companies are following the same strategy as that of Accenture, which aims to build a network of businesses to meet the full range of client needs – consulting, technology, outsourcing, alliances and venture capital. Of course this approach involves the danger that in order to acquire the necessary wide range of internal technologies, these consultants will have to build conglomerate businesses that are remarkably similar to those that they have so recently been advising their corporate clients against![14] More generally, a relationship focus increases a company's dependence on a limited portfolio of relationships and restricts its ability to learn from exposure to other customers and competitive activities.

Developing Offerings

Business marketers have the responsibility to work with a number of functional areas in both their own and customer companies to develop their offerings. This task will vary depending on whether it takes place in an existing or a new relationship and on the knowledge of the two companies. We can examine these variations as follows.

Developing offerings in different Buy-cycles

In Chapter 4 we suggested that a customer is likely to look first of all within its existing relationships for solutions to its problems. We referred to this as *Buy-cycle 1*. In Buy-cycle 1, growth for the supplier comes from growth of the customer (the cake is growing), or growth of the supplier's share of the customer's business (its slice of the cake is growing) or new business in the relationship (new cake). Although Buy-cycle 1 infers "business as usual", it still involves the marketer in development issues, as follows:

- Even if the relationship involves long-term exchange of a *similar* offering, it is still important for the supplier to develop and innovate in the *fulfilment* of that offering (see Chapter 7). This may involve investment in production or service facilities or automatic order processing, both to reduce costs and to enhance the quality of fulfilment.
- A customer's problems will change over time and competitive offerings will have to develop. This means that refined or new offerings may be required in an existing relationship. We saw in Chapter 3 how important it is for suppliers to capitalize on the resources of customers and work with them on these developments.

[13] *The Economist*, 20 January 2001.

[14] *The Economist*, 7 July 2001.

Buy-cycle 2 occurs when either the customer or supplier seeks a new relationship. It involves both more expense and more uncertainty than Buy-cycle 1, as the companies need to invest in learning about each other as well as developing and fulfilling an offering. New relationships are an obvious source of growth for the business marketer. They may provide the opportunity to exploit the offerings that have been developed in existing relationships or to develop new technologies or offerings that cannot be developed in existing ones. When considering the potential of a new relationship, business marketers must assess the extent to which they can use the same offerings that have already been developed for existing relationships. They must also assess the extent to which the costs of any development can be recouped in that relationship and in others.

Knowledge and offering development

It is important for business marketers to be aware of how the respective abilities of the two companies can affect the process of offering development, as well as determining which company is likely to lead it and the costs and revenue that will arise. This is shown in Figure 6.2.

Cell 1 is the case where neither supplier nor customer is able to define the nature of a customer's problem. This situation is common where a problem has its origin in the customer's customers. For example, companies in the mobile telephone industry are currently unsure as to exactly what requirements final customers, and hence their suppliers, are likely to have for mobile information, data transmission, voice or music. In Cell 2, the customer can define the problem, but neither company knows the solution. This may mean that the customer will lead the development of an offering even though technical work will take place in the supplier. Cell 4 is the opposite of this situation, where the supplier can diagnose the customer's problem and in this case the supplier is likely to lead the development. In Cell 3, the customer understands both the problem and the required solution and the supplier understands neither. This is likely to be a low-margin case for the supplier as the customer will have little *need uncertainty* and the supplier is likely to be fulfilling an offering based on the product and process technologies of the customer. In Cell 5, neither company has difficulty with problem definition, but neither knows the solution. Cell 7 is the opposite situation. Here the customer is dependent on the supplier to both define its problem and provide a solution. This situation is surprisingly common in business markets. For example, one CEO of a high-tech firm remarked: "Our customers have no idea what we can deliver next year. When we ask them what they want, they say that they want the old product." In Cell 6 the supplier understands the application (problem), but the solution is defined by the customer. This is a common situation where experienced producers work to the detailed design of a customer. Examples include both the fashion and automotive industries In Cell 8, the customer understands the problem and is able to specify its requirements, but the solution will be based on the supplier's technology. Finally, Cell 9 is a situation where both companies understand both problem and current solution and so are equipped to work together on innovation.

CUSTOMER SUPPLIER	DOES NOT KNOW THE PROBLEM	DOES NOT KNOW THE SOLUTION	KNOWS BOTH
DOES NOT KNOW THE PROBLEM	Cell 1 Collaborative Investigation	Cell 2 Collaborative Investigation	Cell 3 Supply to Customer Specification
DOES NOT KNOW THE SOLUTION	Cell 4 Collaborative Investigation	Cell 5 Collaborative Development	Cell 6 Customer Specified Fulfilment
KNOWS BOTH	Cell 7 Supply to Supplier Specification	Cell 8 Supplier Specified Fulfilment	Cell 9 Collaborative Innovation

Figure 6.2 Developing offerings.

Developing the elements of an offering

Until now we have only discussed development at the broad level of the offering as a whole. A number of particular issues arise when we examine the development of individual elements within the offering, as follows:

Product

Business marketers are often faced with a "product development procedure" in their companies. This outlines the *stages* that each development should go through as it progresses from idea generation to commercialized product.[15] However, as long ago as 1986 Takeuchi and Nonaka[16] suggested that these stage approaches were like a "relay race" where each department, such as research, engineering, production does their work on a new

[15] See, for example, Robert G Cooper, *Winning at New Products: Accelerating the Process from Idea to Launch*, 2nd edition, Reading, MA, Addison-Wesley, 1993, Steven Wheelwright and Kim Clarke, *Revolutionising Product Development*, New York, Free Press, 1992.

[16] Hirotaka Takeuchi and Ikujiro Nonaka, The New New Product Development Game, *Business Review*, January–February, 1986, pp. 137–46.

product and then hands this over to the next. Not only is this likely to lengthen the process, but the departments do not work effectively together and are likely to "drop the baton" at each hand-over. Instead they advocated a "rugby scrum" where representatives from each function within the supplier *and the customer* work together throughout the development process. This means that activities such as product and production design take place *concurrently*.[17] For this approach to work, business marketers cannot just simply specify a customer requirement and pass this on to a development department. Instead, they must be involved throughout the process in liaising with each department and the customer on the trade-offs between the product's performance – *what* it will do and the different ways of *how* it can be achieved and at what costs. Second, there is now greater emphasis on the process of continuous improvement. Product development is not seen as single one-off process to produce the product, but one that is continuously refined. This involves business marketers in a variety of techniques, including "benchmarking" their products (or other offering elements) against those of competitors and against customer priorities and translating these into offering improvements.[18]

Service

The same processes of simultaneous development and continuous improvement can be applied to the service element of an offering. But two additional issues arise for the business marketer. First, each service delivery is individual and the quality of fulfilment is likely to depend heavily on the personnel involved. This means that *consistency* of delivery is critical to success. For this reason, business marketers need to understand the limits that staffing issues place on service design and how service can be modified to cope with those limits. Continuous improvement programmes will also require them to be closely in touch with those responsible for service delivery.

Second, there is an increasing tendency for the product element in an offering to be replaced by a service as companies concentrate on fewer areas of distinctiveness and contract out major aspects of their business. This is often a difficult transition for many companies because responsibility for the successful use of an offering is often retained by the supplier. So instead of simply producing good products, the supplier must often manage a large staff to provide service provision to an agreed standard in remote locations. Common examples include the supply of major items like railway trains and commercial aircraft and also more mundane items, such as when a lubricating oil supplier switches from selling cans of oil to the planned servicing of its customers' vehicles.

Logistics

The development of the logistics element of an offering is likely to be relatively straightforward when serving customers that purchase infrequently or that are buying

[17] SC Wheelwright and KB Clarke, *Revolutionising Product Development*, New York, Free Press, 1992.

[18] Nigel Slack, Stuart Chambers and Robert Johnston, *Operations Management*, 3rd edition, Harlow, Essex, Pearson Education, 2001.

offerings that are not critical for their operations. But some customers may require complex and costly logistics arrangements, if these can reduce their overall costs or add to their competitiveness. Customers will also vary in the extent to which they require logistics that are *adapted* to their individual requirements. High levels of adaptation will mean that they are likely to have more interaction and involvement with their supplier. In contrast, other customers may prefer to avoid such involvement and be able to easily change between suppliers. They will make use of standardized solutions that entail lower immediate costs and retain the freedom associated with more arm's-length relationships.

The connection between logistics complexity and supplier adaptation presents the supplier with a number of choices when developing its logistics. These are illustrated in Figure 6.3 and we can discuss them using the simple example of the logistics for sheet steel.

Cell 1 is where the logistics arrangements are simple and low-cost and where customers see no benefit in involvement with the supplier for adaptation and advice. Examples would include the purchase of relatively simple offerings, based on commodity products such as standard mild steel sheets. Customers in this case are more likely to appreciate the benefits of being able to switch suppliers easily. In this case the marketer must ensure that logistics and relationship-management costs are as low as possible through efficient ordering and delivery systems. Large buyers will be serviced by a steel producer, delivering full truckloads of standardized products, small buyers will probably buy from a distributor. It is not only "established" companies in the steel business like manufacturers and distributors that can help users to solve their problems by operating in Cell 1. New types of suppliers have entered the network, such as E-steel Corp and MetalSite Corp in the USA and Steelscreen in Europe. These have relationships with producers of steel and deal with thousands of customers focusing on standardized products for customers whose main concerns are price and reducing the costs of ordering, administering and stocking. For steel producers, these new companies reduce commission costs as well as those of sales

Figure 6.3   Logistics and relationship involvement.

administration. These new suppliers both compete with established suppliers and support them. For example, they can make it possible for a steel producer to focus its own efforts on specialized products and use the traders as a cost-efficient operator for more standardized offerings.

Cell 2 also involves customers that prefer less complex or advanced logistics, but require logistical adaptations to their specific problems. This may involve the supplier guaranteeing availability by taking responsibility for the customer's inventories or providing a wider offering or customer-dedicated catalogue, with offerings from other companies, to reduce the customer's supply base. The need for technical advice is limited because of the low complexity of the logistics. But relationships in this cell can still be important and long-term, because without them companies would find that the paper-work costs of buying many items was greater than their price. An example of this would be cold-rolled steel for use in car production. When suppliers adopt strategy in Cell 2 they must have an ability to work closely with customers and develop and maintain a responsive relationship with them. Companies operating in Cell 2 may be producers, distributors or other firms that specialize in logistics.

Cell 3 involves complex and therefore expensive logistics, which are not adapted to the specific problems of individual customers. In this case efficient operations are provided by advanced warehousing and transport equipment. For example, a steel supplier may include steel-service operations such as cutting, bending or blasting. Information may be exchanged by complex systems such as EDI – electronic data interchange. The best known of this is "Odette", which was developed by European car manufacturers and has been applied to all their suppliers. This system is illustrated in Figure 6.4. In many cases customers are willing to adapt their own systems to fit those of suppliers in this cell. Suppliers taking this route thus generally invest more in developing advanced solutions for transfer than they invest in specific relationships.

Cell 4 involves considerable adaptations made for each customer and complex logistics. A typical example of this is the just-in-time deliveries from component and system suppliers to car manufacturers. For this type of integration to function well, there must be substantial integration of activities and communication in both companies. The planning and management of this investment lead to a high-involvement relationship including similar adaptations to those in Cell 2 and complex logistics as in Cell 3.

Advice

We have seen throughout this book that business relationships are based on customer problems. Very often suppliers are involved in identifying these problems as well as advising what would be a suitable solution. A supplier's advice is often as valuable to a customer as the subsequent delivery of an offering. But business marketers face two problems in managing and developing the advice element of their offerings. Traditionally advice was provided by a supplier's sales force, who called on technical assistance as needed. However, the operating costs of a business sales force have escalated and many companies have sought to standardize the advice element, increase

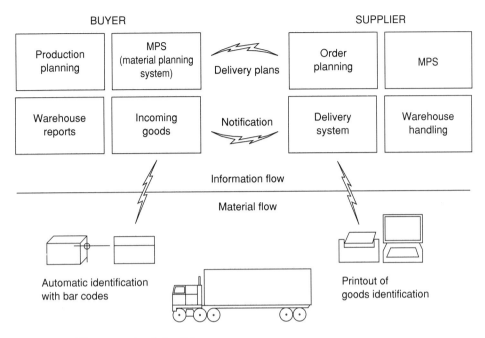

Figure 6.4 The principle of the Odette system.
Source: Gadde and Håkansson (1993) p. 162.

its quality and reduce their costs by providing web-based information and customer "hot-lines".

Second, the advice and adaptation elements of an offering are often closely related. Thus, advice on complex customer problems often leads to unplanned and uncontrolled adaptation by the supplier. This means that business marketers need systems to approve and monitor adaptations against their assessment of the overall value of each relationship.

Adaptations

Suppliers need to adapt different elements of their offerings to meet customer requirements and to demonstrate commitment to their relationships. At the same time they need to restrict the extent of these adaptations as a way of controlling their costs. Business marketers must balance these conflicting pressures. Success depends on two factors. First, the marketer must be able to identify real, widespread customer problems that can be solved within the constraints of the offerings the supplier can provide. This not only requires that the marketer is skilled in customer analysis, but also that she understands the product and process technologies of her company.

Second, the company's offerings must be developed so as to achieve a customized solution for each customer without individual adaptation.[19] This requires that each element of an offering should be designed to consist of independent modules that can be assembled into different forms, easily and inexpensively. It also requires that the elements of the offerings, such as service and product, can be substituted for each other where necessary. Finally, it requires that the company's relationships with its suppliers should be responsive to its requirement for flexibility. For example, Hewlett-Packard use a modular design for their DeskJet printers. Standard printers for the world market are produced at a factory in Singapore. The European distribution centre separately purchases the power suppliers, packaging and manuals needed to customize the printers to meet the power and instructional requirements of customers in different countries. As well as meeting a range of requirements, Hewlett-Packard have lowered their total manufacturing, shipping and inventory costs by 25 per cent.[20]

Conclusion

An offering is the supplier's promise to solve a customer's problem. It consists of five elements: product, service, logistics, advice and adaptation, each of which may be more or less important depending on the customer's problem. An offering provides the link between a supplier's abilities and a customer's problems.

An offering is based on the problem-solving ability of a supplier. This in turn is a function of its physical, financial and technological resources, its network of relationships with other companies and its relationship management skills. However, because offerings are developed and fulfilled interactively by both customer and supplier, offerings also depend on the customer's demand ability. This is based on the customer's physical, technological and financial resources, on its network position and on its relationship management skills.

Both business and consumer marketers must assess the requirements of their customers. Both are involved in developing offerings that will satisfy those requirements. But the business marketer faces a more challenging task:

- She must work with individual customers to assess their problems.
- She must develop offerings that are more complex and which involve adaptation to individual requirements.
- She must seek to minimize the costs of adaptations while at the same time demonstrating commitment to and developing customer relationships.
- She must consider how her company's offerings relate to its overall technological position and its technology strategy.

And then of course she has to fulfil the promise made in her offering and that is the subject of the next chapter.

---

[19] This section is based on Richard B Chase, Nicholas J Aquilano and F Robert Jacobs, *Operations Management for Competitive Advantage*, ninth edition, New York, McGraw-Hill Irwin, 2001.

[20] Ibid.

Further Reading

Kim B Clark and Steven C Wheelwright (1993) *Managing New Product and Process Development*, New York, Free Press.

LE Gadde and H Håkansson (2001) *Supply Network Strategies*, Chichester, John Wiley.

Theodore Levitt (1980) Marketing Success through Differentiation – of Anything, *Harvard Business Review*, January–February, pp. 83–91.

Theodore Levitt (1981) Marketing Intangible Products and Product Intangibles, *Harvard Business Review*, May–June, pp. 94–102.

T Michael Nevens, Gregory L Summe and Bro Uttal (1990) Commercializing Technology: What the Best Companies Do, *Harvard Business Review*, May–June, pp. 154–63.

Albert L Page (1993) Assessing New Product Development Practices and Performance: Establishing Crucial Norms, *Journal of Product Innovation Management*, vol. 10, September, pp. 273–90.

Steven C Wheelwright and Kim B Clark (1992) *Revolutionising Product Development: Quantum Leaps in Speed, Efficiency and Quality*, New York, Free Press.

TRANSFERRING THE OFFERING: FULFILLING THE PROMISE

Aims of this Chapter

- To help business marketers to understand the issues involved in developing transfer ability and in fulfilling offerings.
- To enable them to communicate effectively with those involved in fulfilment and to contribute to decisions on the company's operations that affect its marketing success.
- To enable them to assess whether their offerings are the promises that they *should* make, because they relate well to their company's problem-solving and transfer abilities, their operations, resources and technologies and their wider strategy.
- To help them assess whether their offerings are promises that their company *is able* to fulfil.
- To help them ensure that their company actually *does* fulfil the promises that it makes.

Throughout this book we have emphasized that the essence of business marketing is the development and management of customer relationships. It is within these relationships that customers can find a solution to one or more of their problems. The solution is provided by an offering supplied by the marketing company that has a number of elements: product, service, adaptation, advice and logistics. This offering, based on the company's *Problem-Solving Ability* amounts to a *promise* by the supplier that it will solve the customer's problem. But, like any promise, the offering has no real value to the customer unless the supplier *can* fulfil it and actually *does* fulfil it.

This chapter is about fulfilling the promise of an offering. Fulfilment is based on the company's *transfer ability*. The definition of transfer ability that we have been using in this book is as follows: transfer ability is a measure of how well a supplier can deliver its offering to the customer and *fulfil* its promise, so that the customer actually receives the anticipated solution to its problems at the time, in the place and at the price it was anticipating. The emphasis here is on consistency of supply, of conformity to the specification of the offering and cost control. These require investment in different organizational skills from the supplier to develop its production and service processes, its systems, its logistical sophistication, its efficiency and to reduce its costs. A supplier's transfer ability is particularly important to a customer with high transaction uncertainty. Fulfilling an offering for some customers will be straightforward and will involve few operational problems. For others, the requirements of cost, consistency, timing or location will place great demands on the supplier. It is particularly important for business marketers to understand precisely what their company's transfer abilities are and to contribute to decisions on developing them. This is because suppliers are likely to be an integral part of the operations of their customers for many transactions over a long period. Hence the precise fulfilment of the supplier's offering is likely to be critical to the customer's own operations and vital for the development of the supplier's relationship with it.

We start by examining some of the difficulties in fulfilment that companies face and then look at the decisions that a company must take to develop its operations and to build its transfer ability. We then examine areas that are critical for success in fulfilment such as the design of operations, the management of quality and inventory. Finally, we examine some of the particular issues that companies face in fulfilling the service and logistics elements of their offerings.

Introduction: Difficulties in Fulfilment

It is vital, but increasingly difficult for the business marketer to actually *do* what she *says* she will do. These difficulties in fulfilment are for a number of reasons:

- Fulfilment requires an increasingly complex set of resources, technologies and operations. Suppliers are more and more dependent for these on their own suppliers, distributors, development partners and even their customers.
- A large number of different people and functions inside and outside a supplier are involved in fulfilling an offering. These include buyers, development, service, sales, operations, logistics and finance staff.
- Business marketing is not just about making one promise and then fulfilling it. Instead, both the offering and its fulfilment evolve over time. Many different individuals and functions will be involved in this evolution.

Control or integration?

Marketing has to make sure that all those involved in fulfilment work towards the same aims, but it cannot *control* these other functions. Marketing people are unlikely to understand the technicalities of all of the issues involved or the strategic priorities of their colleagues. Nor can business marketing operate in isolation from these other functions. Its role is to *integrate* their work and to do this it must be aware of the pressures under which they operate, as well as the specific tasks they each have to carry out.

If there is cohesion between the strategies of marketing and operations and between the promises the company makes and the means for their fulfilment, then the chances of the company being able to deliver the promise to customers are enhanced. Figure 7.1 shows this link between some types of promises and the areas of operations that can assist in their fulfilment.

Understanding Transfer Ability

Every company has considerable investments in the facilities and operations on which its transfer ability is based and which enable it to fulfil its offerings. These investments take a long time to come to fruition and must be based on a clear understanding of evolving customer requirements. They must also be based on an analysis of the company's product and process technologies, as discussed in Chapter 3, and of its physical resources. It is vital that business marketers understand what is involved in these investments and the form they take in their own company and in its principal customers. These investments effectively determine a company's ability to fulfil its offerings and strongly affect the design of those offerings. Hence they are a strong influence on the company's marketing strategy.[1]

It is not enough for business marketers to provide information on current or future customer requirements and leave operations decisions to others. If the wrong operations decisions are taken, they can mean that a company is unable to fulfil its offerings in the way that its customers require. If marketing decisions are taken without an appreciation of operational issues, then failures in fulfilment are likely and operational costs will rise. Operations must also evolve as customer problems change and technology moves on. Business marketers and operations managers must not only be aware of issues in each other's areas, but must be involved in them on a continuing basis. Key areas for this co-operation include the design of offerings and capacity planning, quality and cost control and delivery management.

Managing Operations: Approaches and Problems

We will initially examine some of the issues that operations people face to manufacture the product element of an offering. Later in this chapter we will deal with service

---

[1] An interesting example of operations strategy affecting both a company's offerings and its marketing is provided by Black and Decker. This company has developed its process technologies so that it is one of the most sophisticated makers of small electric motors in the world. Their marketing strategy over the years can be interpreted as seeking to exploit this distinctive process technology by finding new offerings to wrap around these motors: drills, lawnmowers, hedge-cutters, power saws, etc.

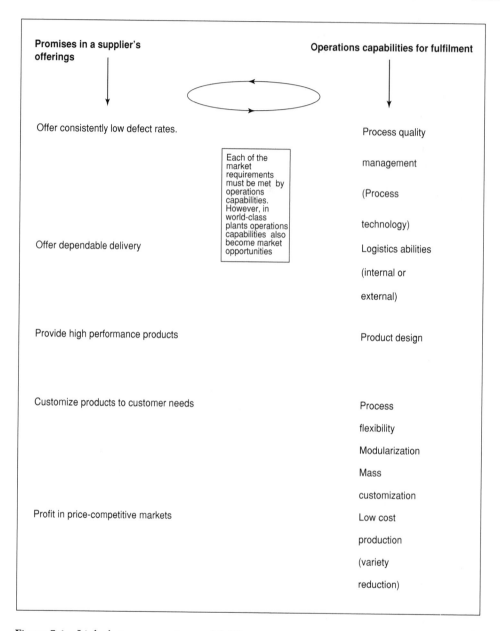

Figure 7.1   Links between promises and fulfilment.

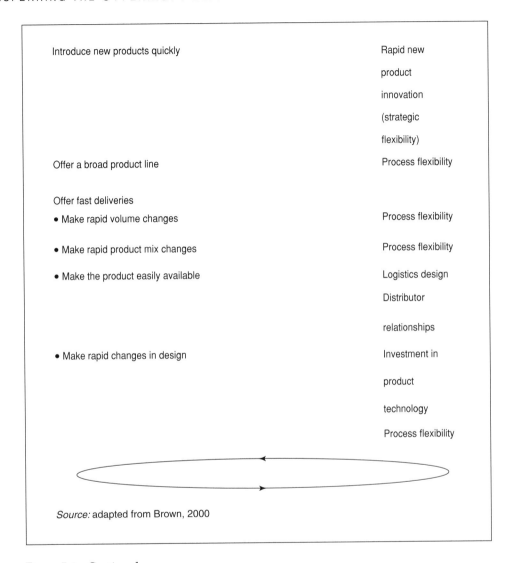

Figure 7.1 *Continued.*

operations. There are a number of different approaches to modern manufacturing operations and these are outlined in Table 7.1. Each of them is concerned with two critical issues:

- Optimizing a company's operations for maximum efficiency, while at the same time enabling it to fulfil offerings for diverse and changing customer requirements.
- Influencing the company's strategic and market direction to be in line with the company's current and evolving operational capabilities.

Table 7.1 Approaches to modern manufacturing operations.

Paradigm	Author	Description
Mass customization	Pine[2]	Concerned with how companies can balance the need for cost reduction through high volume with the need to design and fulfil offerings for customer's particular requirements
Flexible specialization	Piore and Sable[3]	Concerned with how individual companies can concentrate on limited activities and technologies, within networks to produce complete offerings
Lean production and lean supply	Womack et al.;[4] Lamming[5]	This concept was developed from the massively successful Toyota Production System (TPS), which focused on the removal of all forms of waste from operations
Agile manufacturing	Kidd[6]	This concept emphasizes the need for an organization to be able to switch frequently from one market-driven objective to another
Strategic manufacturing	Hill[7] (1995); Brown[8] (1996; 2000)	Here the authors emphasize the need for operations capabilities to be framed in a strategic context and brought to the fore

A company will have to put in place the transfer abilities to fulfil the offerings on which its network position is based. Underpinning these abilities will be decisions that will include *at least* the following:

- The amounts of capacity required by the organization to achieve volume targets and the need for flexibility to cope with adaptations.
- The range and locations of facilities.
- The technology investment to support process and product developments.

[2] BJ Pine, *Mass Customisation: The New Frontier in Business Competition*, Boston, Harvard Business School Press, 1993.

[3] MJ Piore and CF Sabel, *The Second Industrial Divide: Prospects for Prosperity*, New York, Basic Books, 1984.

[4] J Womack, D Jones and D Roos, *The Machine that Changed the World*, New York, Rawson Associates, 1990.

[5] R Lamming, *Beyond Partnerships: Strategies for Innovation and Lean Supply*, London, Prentice-Hall, 1993.

[6] P Kidd, *Agile Manufacturing: Forging New Frontiers*, New York, Addison-Wesley, 1994.

[7] T Hill, *Manufacturing Strategy*, London, Macmillan, 1995.

[8] S Brown, *Strategic Manufacturing for Competitive Advantage*, Hemel Hempstead, Prentice-Hall, 1996; S Brown, *Manufacturing the Future: Strategic Resonance for Enlightened Manufacturing*, London, Financial Times Books, 2000.

- The nature and structure of its supplier relationships. This is often referred to by operations people as its "extended enterprise".
- Its organizational structure and the activities it performs, to reflect its distinctive technologies, often outsourcing other activities.
- The extent and nature of alliances with competitors.
- Its relationships with distributors and sub-contractors.
- The rate of new offering introduction.
- The skills of its personnel to accommodate flexibility of volume, variety and other changes.

Specific Aspects of Operations and their Links to Fulfilment

Transfer ability is based on the operations capabilities of a company and these must be poised and ready to be utilized. Operations capabilities must also be enhanced over time to meet ever higher customer expectations. There are at least three critical factors that need to be developed in order for the promise contained within the offer to be fulfilled. These are the company's *process choice*, its *operations investment* and its *quality*.

Process choice

Process choice is concerned with the means by which a company transforms inputs into its offerings. It is a major strategic decision because no amount of reactive, tactical measures can hope to compensate for inappropriate investment in "wrong" processes that cannot fulfil offerings to match customer requirements. Process choice has to be based on current and future customer demands and hence requires an input from the company's marketers.

Process choice for products

We can outline the five types of processes for fulfilling the product element of an offering, as follows:[9]

- **Project:** This type of process can fulfil highly adapted offerings. It often takes a considerable time and requires dedicated resources for each project. Examples include construction, shipbuilding, large computer installations, etc.
- **Job shop:** This process can also fulfil high variety, low-volume offerings, but the company will produce a series of products, each of which is different, but which use the same operations, such as in precision engineering or printing, etc.
- **Batch:** This process has less variety than a job shop and uses the same operations until a batch is produced. Examples include the manufacture of component parts for the auto industry, most clothing and industrial equipment manufacture.

[9] For a full discussion of the issues in process choice see Steve Brown, Kate Blackmon, Paul Cousins and Harvey Maylor, *Operations Management*, Oxford, Butterworth-Heinemann, 2001, Chapter 3.

- **Line:** This process fulfils high volumes of offerings to a similar design, but with some variety, as in motor vehicle manufacture.
- **Continuous:** This is an even higher-volume process, with less variety and is used in the food industry, steel making and utilities.

The choice of process effectively determines the type of offering that a company can fulfil. The basic distinctions between them are illustrated in Figure 7.2.

Process choice for services

A useful distinction between the different processes through which the service element of an offering can be fulfilled can be made by comparing the amount of personal contact that is involved:

- **High contact operations:** These involve the use of large numbers of highly qualified "professional" staff, such as engineering and management consultants, accountants, lawyers, systems analysts. Companies using these operations often produce offerings with little or no physical product. Others may use them as the first stage of a complex offering involving a large-scale physical product, such as the planning studies for a mass-transit system or a new airport. This kind of operation is often valuable for customers that have high need uncertainty.
- **Mass service operations:** These are used by companies that have many customer transactions, requiring limited inter-personal contact and little customer adaptation. Personnel have little discretion in their interactions with customers in these operations. Examples include parcels services, airports, catalogue suppliers for maintenance or office items.
- **Service shop operations:** These involve high levels of contact, adaptation, volumes of customers and staff discretion between the customers and staff. Examples include hotels, rental companies and travel companies.[10]

Marketers must also be involved in decisions about the process choices that are made by their company for both the product and service elements of their offerings. These decisions will strongly affect the design of the company's overall offering and its ability to fulfil it.

Operations investment

There is often inter-departmental conflict about the investments that a company should make in its operations and this may cause problems in the fulfilment of the company's offerings. Two equally dangerous positions can be taken when it comes to investment in process technology. The first is to not invest and the second is to "throw money" at technology in the hope that somehow this will ensure success. If a firm does not invest, then it will become incapable of competing against other companies that do invest.

---

[10] Adapted from Nigel Slack, Stuart Chambers and Robert Johnston, *Operations Management*, Harlow, Essex, Pearson Education, third edition, 2001.

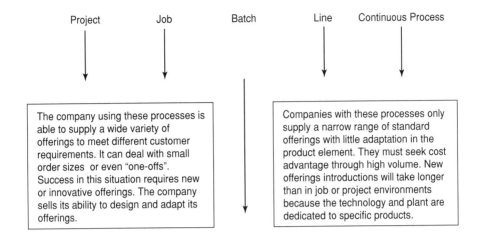

Figure 7.2   The link between process choice and marketing strategy.
Source: Steve Brown *et al. Operations Management*, Oxford, Butterworth-Heinemann, 2001.

It is difficult to make a worthwhile appraisal of potential operations investments because of the considerable time between an investment and its benefits and also because it is difficult to forecast the outcome of investments in unpredictable business networks. The accounting methods that may be used in these appraisals also have problems. For example, a company may wish to calculate the "pay-back time" of an investment in an automated inspection system for components or in a laptop-based diagnostic system for its service engineers. Such a calculation would require the company to make a very difficult, and almost certainly inaccurate estimate of the sales and profit increase that would result from greater consistency in component quality or better service provided to its customers. Similarly, if the company tried to calculate the Net Present Value (NPV) of these investments, then it would probably have to assume that customer requirements, achieved price and labour costs and competitive position would all remain constant. All these factors will change over time and, more importantly, they will degenerate if the company retains outdated operations methods.

Ultimately, the greatest cost is in not investing in operations. But if marketers are unaware of the issues involved and there is not a productive debate between them and operations management, then the right investment decisions are unlikely to be taken. Sometimes massive investments in operations technology have been made that have gained no benefit for the firm. For example, General Motors invested heavily in a highly automated plant in Hamtramck, Michigan, but the huge investments brought little benefit in terms of market share. In 1979 they had a domestic market share of around 61 per cent, but by the end of the 1990s it was around 32 per cent. In contrast, General Motors' rivals, particularly the Japanese car manufacturers, had invested in the right technology to fulfil customer requirements for cars to their individual specification with high "build-quality" and good reliability.

Strategic flexibility

Operations investment decisions are often large-scale, expensive and critical. They tend to steer a company down a particular direction, often for a long time. Wrong decisions can cripple the company's capability to meet customer requirements. Companies have difficulty in predicting overall future requirements. They also have to fulfil offerings despite rapid changes in demand and they often have to adapt their offerings to individual customer needs. Therefore, operations investments are increasingly oriented towards technologies such as Computer-Integrated Manufacture (CIM) and Advanced Manufacturing Technology (AMT):

> The fragmentation of markets, the development of new market segments or niches, as well as faster design ... all contribute to the need for strategic flexibility. Thus, flexible manufacturing technologies provide a real strategic option ... in which high levels of economies of scope and a "design for response" capability position the firm to enter a broader range of different markets at its own discretion".[11]

For example, Motorola initially made Advanced Manufacturing Technology investments in the flexible manufacture of components for cellular telephones but it was then able to successfully use these distinctive process technologies (see Chapter 3) for other electronic component applications. This is typical of the sort of flexibility that technology investment can offer to a supplier. AMT investments can enable the company to provide a range of products or components based on group technology or shared design characteristics. This in turn provides strategic options based on economies of scope, rather than economies of scale.

Quality

Quality is a major issue because there is now far greater competition than ever before in most markets. The number and capabilities of new entrants into markets have raised competition between new and existing players, all of whom have to compete to "world-class" standards. This intense competition has helped to redefine the term, *world class*, when applied to quality. World class now has less to do with being *better* than competitors, it merely denotes the ability to compete *at all* in global competition.

We have already pointed out that quality has two inter-related aspects for the business marketer. The first of these is a measure of the extent to which a supplier's offering

[11] D Lei, M Hitt and JD Goldhar, Advanced Manufacturing Technology: Organisational Design and Strategic Flexibility, *Organisational Studies*, vol. 17, no. 3, pp. 111–25.

provides a solution to the customer's problem, as discussed in Chapter 6. The second aspect of quality is perhaps even more important. This is as a measure of the extent to which the supplier fulfils the promise of its offering in practice and throughout the relationship. Quality of fulfilment means that the company must provide "right first time processes" and "conform to specification", of the customer. This task is made more difficult for the business marketer because the customer may not be the end-user and thus a marketer often must also have to interpret the requirements of her customer's customers. The importance of the fulfilment aspect of quality is apparent in a number of definitions. For example, according to Feigenbaum, quality is "the total composite product and service characteristics ... through which the product or service *in use* will meet the expectations of the customer" (1983. p. 7, emphasis added.[12]) Feigenbaum also emphasizes the importance of operational management and control to quality: "control must start with identification of customer quality requirements and end only when the product has been placed in the hands of a customer that remains satisfied" (ibid., p. 11).

The management and control of quality must be based both on "hard" measurement tools and "soft" issues such as leadership and commitment. A company may provide a "quality" offering which will fail if it is not supported by fulfilment quality in such aspects as responsiveness to the need to adapt, reliability in delivery and in conformance to specification, service availability and target cost. Conversely, a quality control system may well be in place using sophisticated process charts and other tools to ensure fulfilment quality but the offering itself may not meet a customer's requirements.

Total Quality Management (TQM)

TQM is an approach to the management of quality that has been widely adopted. It emphasizes:

- the need to integrate functions to achieve total quality;
- the importance of continuous improvement;
- the need to think in terms of product (offering) and process (fulfilment) quality;
- a focus on providing customer satisfaction;
- the issue of quality as a company-wide concern.[13]

In 1996 a survey in *Automotive Engineering* described a five-year study of the financial performance of 160 automobile-parts suppliers in Japan, Europe and the USA. The results showed that commitment to quality had a profound effect upon the profitability of suppliers. Companies that implemented quality management programmes were able to lower production costs, enhance productivity and innovate more effectively. All these factors are important to both the promise and the fulfilment of an offer.

However, quality of fulfilment is difficult to maintain for at least two reasons. First, if the company enjoys success with its quality efforts, then it may be tempted to sit back,

---

[12] A Feigenbaum, *Total Quality Control*, 3rd edition, Boston, McGraw-Hill, 1983.

[13] Brown *et al.* 2001, op cit.

convinced that "quality has been achieved". Second, if a firm does not enjoy instant results with its quality efforts, then there is a tendency to abandon the effort. Quality is neither easy to instil, nor to remain committed to over the long term. If quality were easy, then all companies would succeed in it!

ISO 9000 and quality

ISO 9000 is a standard that many firms have adhered to in order to demonstrate that they have quality systems in place. The ISO series standard is influential in many countries and ISO 9000 certification is used extensively by companies in the European Union. For example, firms that provide offerings for the health, safety, or environmental sectors often cannot be considered as suppliers without having ISO 9000 in place.

Quality in service fulfilment

Gronroos' Service Quality Management Programme highlights some of the issues in managing the fulfilment of the service element of an offering.[14] These can be summarized as follows:

- **Service Concept Development Programme:** This involves the development of the concepts that guide the investment of resources and activities to be used in the service element of an offering. These concepts must be expressed in terms of the customer problems that the supplier is addressing, or "What" the service element will do (performance specification). It is important to emphasize that the service element does not operate alone, but is combined with other offering elements. So the programme must also be concerned with how service combines with other elements to produce a coherent offering. For example, a fire insurance company may emphasize the totality of its offering so that it not only covers the costs of damage to equipment, but also provides advice on prevention, fire control and fighting equipment (product), arranges repair and covers for business losses during those repairs (service). This supplier may need to make its offering available to its customers' locations in different countries (logistics) and may also be called on to adapt its offering to the particular requirements of companies in high risk businesses, such as oil or chemicals.
- **Service-Outcome Management Programme:** This involves development of the supplier's ability to achieve a required conformance specification of service, or "How" it will solve the customer's problem. This is often agreed specifically with each customer. For example, the Body Shop has a close relationship with the Lane Group which is responsible for deliveries to the Body Shop's outlets. The relationship arranges that 99.7 per cent of deliveries take place within a two-hour "delivery window". This means that the service outcome is measurable and "tangible". As a result, adherence to standards, which is part of service quality, can be measured

---

[14] Christian Groonroos, *Service Management and Marketing: A Customer Relationship Management Approach*, 2nd edition, Chichester, John Wiley, 2000.

against agreed criteria – in the same way that the fulfilment of a product element is measured.

- **Customer Expectations Management Programme:** This concerns the management of the supplier's relationships with its customers. Customer expectations must be managed so that they relate to the offering that the supplier is *able* to deliver and to the offering that is *justified* by the potential of the relationship. Unless this is achieved, there will always be quality problems in the relationships. For example, a delivery company must make it clear that the service levels it is able to provide in most locations will be lower when those deliveries involve the use of ferries or are to remote parts of a country.

- **Internal Marketing Programme:** The quality of the service element of an offering is heavily dependent on the skills and orientation of those involved in its fulfilment. This programme aims to educate staff in the supplier's service concept and to train and motivate them to fulfil it. There is often an important role for marketers in this programme, both in explaining the concepts behind the company's offering and in the education task itself.

- **Physical Environment and Resources Management Programme:** The supplier's physical resources, technology, information and computing systems form the technology base for service production and the physical environment for service consumption. It is important that they are not developed to some *internal* criteria of efficiency. Instead, they must be able to support customer interaction and information and facilitate delivery of the service element to the standard required to solve customer problems.

- **Customer Interaction Management Programme:** Of course a supplier cannot "manage" its interaction with customers completely, as any relationship is the outcome of the managerial efforts of both companies. Nevertheless, it is important for a supplier to educate customers on how they can contribute to making service interactions as productive as possible. For example, adjustments in the timing of service interactions can reduce queues and their costs for both customer and supplier.

Managing inventory

The fulfilment of a supplier's offering and the management of its customer relationships are closely linked to the management of its inventory and materials. Inventory management has been one of the greatest areas of contrast between much of Western and Japanese manufacturing. In recent years, many Western firms have tried to emulate some of the practices that have underpinned Japan's success in many industries. But many Western manufacturing companies have tended to view materials management as a tactical activity and have relegated purchasing and materials management to a reactive function, rather like manufacturing itself. Purchasing has been viewed by some customers as the "buying function", that responds to production requirements, after they in turn, have been determined in isolation by marketing. In Japan, by contrast, inventory management has been seen as *strategic* and as an essential part of the complete range of capabilities that will enable the firm to out-perform other players in the market. This approach requires that business marketers are closely aware of the issues faced in inventory management, so that they can both contribute to its efficiency and use it as a tool within their relationship management.

A number of approaches to managing inventory emerged from the 1960s onwards, particularly Materials Requirement Planning (MRP), Manufacturing Resource Planning (MRP II), and more recently, Enterprise Resource Planning (ERP). However, these approaches depend heavily on proprietary software packages as some sort of panacea for manufacturing, rather than representing a genuine change of approach. In contrast, many Japanese companies have taken the approach of insisting that there should not be any idle time, waiting, or buffers in their manufacturing operations. The Japanese terms for these are:

Muda: waste
Mura: inconsistency by machines or workers
Muri: excessive demands upon workers or machines.

These three factors have to be dealt with when a plant tries to implement Just-in-Time. The opposite of Just-in-Time is *Just-in-Case* in which a plant's problems and poor operating performance are hidden by holding large amounts of inventory. However, when there is little "buffer" inventory, *Muda*, *Mura*, and *Muri* become prominent. Reducing inventory will initially cause problems to surface that have previously been covered by excess inventory. Management then has the simple decision of whether to stay with excess inventory, hide the problems and incur the costs, or to deal with problems as they arise in the name of continuous improvement.

Well-managed inventory is essential for all companies if they are to fulfil their promises for product quality and delivery timing. However, there are particular dangers with certain types of inventory, due to factors such as price reductions, obsolescence and seasonal demands. For example, around 80 per cent of the cost of a personal computer is made up of components such as the processor chip. During the 1990s these components fell in price by an average of 30 per cent per annum. The danger of obsolete inventory increases each day that these parts are stored as inventory. Even more extreme problems emerge when a producer is caught in the middle of a big step-change in technology, such as the introduction of the Pentium processor. This can mean that a producer and its distributors can be left with millions of dollars of out-dated products. Dell provides an example of the value of good inventory management: it is able to turn its inventory around 50 times in a year, in contrast to others who boast of stock turns of 6–10 times. This enabled it to fulfil an order for 2,000 PCs and 4,000 servers loaded with proprietary and multimedia software to 2,000 Wal-Mart stores in six weeks – just in time for the Christmas season. Dell does not see any conflict between market demands and operations capabilities and measures success not only in financial terms but also in strategic operations terms:

[Michael Dell] … now wants to measure parts inventory in hours instead of days. Seven days doesn't sound like much inventory, but 168 hours does … In a business where inventory depreciates by 1 per cent per week, inventory is risk. A few years ago no one in this business realized what an incredible opportunity managing inventory was.[15]

---

[15] *Fortune*, 11 May 1998.

BOX 7.1 Promise and Fulfilment in Operations

The gap between promise and fulfilment has cost many Chief Executives their jobs. It was one of the key reasons why Compaq ousted Eckhard Pfeiffer at the end of the 1990s. He promised in 1994 that Compaq would "build to customer order", but the company's operations were unable to fulfil that promise. By 1996 only 5 per cent of its PCs were built to order and Compaq had not improved dramatically on this by the end of the decade. Compaq had concentrated on the *low-cost* production of standardized PCs. It did not have the capability to fulfil the offerings it had promised and which met customer requirements.

A gap between promise and fulfilment is rarely caused by one factor. Compaq also had problems with inventory management – its annual rate of inventory turns. The number of machines shipped in a year, divided by the number on hand in current inventory, was around seven turns in the late 1990s, far behind that of its competitors. In 1998–99, the inventory in Compaq's distributors increased to an estimated eight to ten weeks' worth of sales. This meant that Compaq could not launch new the products that its promised innovativeness required, until its distributors sold existing models. According to a Compaq vice president: "A computer is like fruit or fish ... You have to sell it before you smell it" (*Fortune*, 16 August, 1999).

Fulfilment and Third Parties

A company's problem-solving abilities are based in part on the abilities of its own suppliers. In the same way, its transfer abilities are also based partly on those of others. Often, important aspects of the fulfilment of a company's offering are carried out by other companies such as sub-contractors, transport companies, distributors and systems integrators. This poses particular problems for the business marketer. Not only must she be in touch with the transfer abilities and problems of her own company, but also with those of companies on which she depends. We can examine the issue of third-party fulfilment for each element of an offering:

- **Product:** Sub-contractors often design and/or fulfil all or part of the product element of a supplier's offering. In this case, success in the fulfilment of the company's offering will depend on the transfer abilities of these other companies.
- **Service:** The service element of a company's offering may be developed and fulfilled by an external contract-service organization.
- **Advice:** The advice that a supplier offers may be based on research or information supplied to it by others. The advice element may be fulfilled by independent experts, who are contracted to the supplier or who work independently.
- **Adaptation:** Adaptation frequently requires equipment, staffing and materials supplied by others. Often it is fulfilled by others, such as when a large-volume supplier contracts out "specials" to other, more flexible suppliers.

- **Logistics:** This is the element of an offering where third-party fulfilment is most commonly involved. Hence it must be an important focus of attention for business marketers.

Third party logistics

Business marketers commonly face choices about when to develop and fulfil the logistics element of their offering themselves and when to allow others to carry them out, either independently or on a contract basis for them. In some cases a supplier will wish to be in direct contact with the users of its offerings. But in many cases, a supplier delivers to other companies, which in turn deal with the final user. It is not unusual for two or more intermediaries to be involved in these transfer operations. Marketers face a number of issues involved in these choices:

- **Costs and information exchange:** A typical producer relies on both direct and indirect logistics. SKF, the world's largest manufacturer of rolling bearings is one example. Around two-thirds of its turnover is direct sales to industrial users handled by its own sales force and subsidiaries. SKF is in direct contact with customers who buy large volumes of bearings, or where the exchange of technical information is important. Other customers buy only small volumes of bearings, usually of standard types. Cost considerations mean that SKF uses distributors who have a portfolio of offerings from different suppliers. This makes sales visits and delivery economically feasible. Independent distributors account for about one-third of the total sales of SKF and an even greater proportion of its profits.
- **Market complexity:** Very often business is obtained from a large-volume customer, such as a car producer, on the basis of a promise of efficient logistics for its after-sales customers. Distributors are important in fulfilling these promises, such as in the case of replacement bearings for cars serviced either by repair workshops or do-it-yourself motorists.
- **Globalization and fragmentation:** The ability of a supplier to fulfil the logistics element of its offering has become increasingly important as companies need to supply customers on a global basis. Additionally, logistics fulfilment has become more important as business has fragmented with the growth of outsourcing and specialization.

Networks of companies and fulfilment

The traditional view of business in the marketing textbooks has been to see it from the perspective of a *manufacturer*, who designs and produces a product that is then transferred, more or less untouched through a number of intermediaries to the end-customer. This view of business involves the manufacturer in designing an appropriate *distribution channel* for its products. However, the perspective of business marketing that we have used in this book widens this focus in three ways:

- We have widened the focus from that of a simple product to that of an offering with a number of elements.

- We have shown that the design of an offering is increasingly carried out in different companies from those that fulfil it. Also, the offering that is finally fulfilled for an end-consumer is the outcome of the efforts of many companies and of interactions between them. So business marketers have to be concerned with both design and fulfilment in their own company and in others in the network.
- We have taken the focus away from business marketing in an easily defined manufacturer to that of a wide range of potential suppliers in the network.

These suppliers will have different types of offerings. They will vary in their dependence on other companies for the elements of these offerings and may or may not design or fulfil all of the elements of their offering themselves. Different parts of their offering may be created in a number of different companies and merged in others. They may then be inventoried in a separate company and installed by another. Sometimes separate companies are involved in transportation or after-sales service. Very often the companies in the network may be distributors who seek to design the offerings of their suppliers and also influence how those offerings are fulfilled. For example, they may wish to control the logistics *from* their suppliers as well as *to* their customers. This means that some or all of the elements of a supplier's offering may actually be determined or fulfilled by either the company itself, or a customer, or a third party.

This means that the business marketer will have to examine the design and fulfilment of her offering within this wider focus. Marketers cannot restrict their role to finding out what customers want and then communicating these requirements to designers and to operations staff and then assume that an offering will be designed and fulfilment will take place. Instead, business marketers must work closely with be operations to relate customer requirements to the company's technologies and resources and to its existing and emerging operations capabilities.

Marketers also have to accept that the successful development and fulfilment of their offerings must relate to the current and evolving problem-solving and transfer abilities of many different companies in the network. All of these will have a stake in the fulfilment of the supplier's offering and a view of their respective roles in it.

[Successful companies] view their distribution channels as webs of capabilities embedded in an extended enterprise. They have realised that by sharing their resources and capabilities in novel ways and new situations they can take advantage of profit-making opportunities that they could not exploit on their own.[16]

Conclusion

In this book we have described how the boundaries between companies in business networks have become blurred as they jointly develop offerings and merge their technologies, operations and information. We have also shown that companies

[16] James Narus and James Anderson, Rethinking Distribution: Adaptive Channels, *Harvard Business Review*, July–August, 1996, pp. 112–120, quote from p. 112.

themselves can no longer be separated into neat categories of manufacturer, wholesaler or retailer so that now we simply see a great diversity of "suppliers". Both this and the previous chapter have shown that it is not just companies that cannot be isolated from each other. The staff in these companies cannot work in isolated functional areas, or "silos", such as marketing, purchasing or production. Instead, all staff have to be aware of how their expertise is integrated into the totality of the company's work and each member of staff has to contribute to decision-making in other areas in addition to their own.

Operations management and the fulfilment of a company's offerings involve issues that are not normally considered part of the responsibilities of a business marketer. Operational fulfilment has a number of impacts on business marketers as follows:

- A company's transfer ability is based on its operational capability. The actual transfer of an offering is carried out by staff other than those in marketing. So marketing must understand the operational issues in their companies, the problems that operations staff face and the broader technological and operational strategy within which they are working.
- Marketing must be involved in the inevitable trade-offs and compromises between current customer requirements, the potential of different relationships and the existing and developing capabilities of the supplier.
- Business relationships involve a continuing cycle of offering and fulfilment and problems of quality in either aspect can ruin those relationships. Marketing must be involved in avoiding failures and in building capabilities. It is not enough for them to simply apologize to customers and blame operations when things go wrong!
- A supplier's offering must evolve over time as customers face different problems and as the supplier's own operations evolve. Business marketing must be involved in planning the direction of that evolution and be aware of the constraints and opportunities it represents for the company's offering and its fulfilment.

The development of a supplier's operations may lead to cost savings and more effective problem solving for customers. On the other hand, the design of an offering and the promises that a marketer makes may severely hamper current and future operations. Business marketing is about working with colleagues in all functional areas to bring the company's operational skills to bear to promise a solution to a customer's problem and to fulfil that promise. This cannot be achieved if marketers are figuratively and literally outside the company and its operations.

Further Reading

RB Chase and DA Garvin (1989) The Service Factory, *Harvard Business Review*, July–August, pp. 61–9.
A Feigenbaum (1991) *Total Quality Management*, New York, McGraw-Hill.
Christian Gronroos (2000) *Service Management and Marketing*, 2nd edition, Chichester, John Wiley.

YP Gupta, SC Lonial and WG Mangold, An Examination of the Relationship between Manufacturing Strategy and Marketing Operations, *International Journal of Operations and Production Management*, vol. 11, no. 10, pp. 33–44.

TJ Hill (2000) *Manufacturing Strategy: Text and Cases*, Burr Ridge, Ill: Irwin/McGraw-Hill.

J Womack, D Jones and D Roos (1990) *The Machine that Changed the World*, New York, Rawston Associates.

PRICE, COSTS AND VALUE

8

Aims of this Chapter

Pricing for the business marketer is an important but complex issue. If all other aspects of marketing strategy and implementation are sound, but pricing policy is flawed, then a company may fail. Many pricing decisions are made without thinking through all the issues involved, or they are based on a hunch, or are simply whatever emerges from a bargaining session with a customer. There have been many attempts to provide guidance on pricing for the business marketer but many of these fail because each marketer finds that he faces very particular conditions. These may make any general techniques difficult to apply or even seem irrelevant.

Because of the complexity of the pricing task and the importance of relating closely to particular conditions, this chapter does not provide a procedure or a set of steps to determine the "best price". Instead the chapter aims to highlight some of the important issues and considerations that the marketer must bear in mind when taking pricing decisions.

The chapter explains the relations between price and customer problems and then shows how the price that a customer is prepared to pay may involve trade-offs between different elements of the offering.

We then examine the issues of value, cost and quality in pricing and how questions of relationships and network position affect pricing. Finally, we explore the problems of controlling price and show how marketers need to manage their prices over time.

The Problems of Pricing

Pricing decisions are difficult enough in consumer markets, but the business marketer also faces a number of extra issues. For example:

- Some business marketers charge the same price to all their customers, but others have to negotiate individually with each one. This is often because the marketer supplies an

adapted offering to each customer and thus has to forecast costs and consider profit targets in each case.
- Other marketers have to work to a fixed specification of requirements from a customer that includes what the price *must* be. These marketers must then manage their costs within this limit.
- Some marketers have to operate under long-term contracts that specify that the price paid will reduce each year of the contract.
- Some marketers find that they cannot identify all the costs that their company will actually incur when it supplies an offering. This is either because the information is not available in their company, or because a new offering must be developed and it is difficult to forecast what this will cost.
- Business marketers have to calculate their own costs of supplying an offering. They also have to work out the extra costs that the customer will have to incur in addition to the price it pays, to gain the benefits of the supplier's offering.
- Finally, business sales and purchases take place within a relationship. The marketer must also think about the value of that relationship to his own company and to the customer and how this might affect the price he wants to charge and the price that the customer is prepared to pay.

Fundamentals of Business Pricing

Business marketing is about making a profit by providing a solution for a customer to one or more of its problems at a price that exceeds the supplier's costs. However, customers and their problems and the purchase situations they face vary enormously:

- It is very important for some customers to solve a particular problem. So the *value* of a solution to them will be high and they will be prepared to pay a much higher price than other customers. For example, keeping a factory clean is much more important for a customer in the food industry than it is for one in engineering.
- Customers are often *uncertain* about what is the best solution to a problem. So they sometimes find it hard to judge the value of different offerings for them and hence the price that they should be prepared to pay for them.
- Some problems are intrinsically more difficult to solve than others and the costs of providing a suitable offering may vary accordingly, but customers may not understand either the difficulty of the problem, or the supplier's costs. Thus they may be unwilling to pay a price that reflects these costs. The difficulty of solving a customer's problem will also vary depending on the experience, skills and resources of that customer. Also, minor changes in a supplier's offering to meet a customer's particular requirements may have a dramatic effect on the supplier's costs.
- Some customers may have relationships with many suppliers, each of which offers a suitable solution for a particular problem. These customers may value some of these relationships differently from others. Other customers find that when a particular problem arises, they do not have a relationship with a suitable supplier.

The price that the customer is prepared to pay

There is no right price for an offering under all circumstances. Nor is there an objective value for any offering. Instead we can say that the price that an *individual* customer is prepared to pay for a particular offering from a *particular* supplier will depend on the *customer's perception* of:

- the importance of the problem;
- the extent to which it believes that this offering provides a solution to its problem;
- the value to the customer of its relationship with the supplier as a source of future solutions;
- the total costs that the customer must incur in order to obtain the solution; As well as the price it must pay for the offering, these may also include the costs of adapting its own operations to accommodate the solution, the costs that will be incurred in using the solution throughout its life and the effects of taking a solution from one supplier on the customer's relationships with its other suppliers.
- The number and characteristics of alternative suppliers and offerings that are available to the customer.

A supplier makes a profit when it provides a solution to a customer's problem at a *total* cost to the supplier that is less than the price that the particular customer is prepared to pay for it. The costs to the supplier will depend in part on the difficulties of developing and fulfilling an offering for each customer. However, the profit from transactions with a customer are only part of the value that a supplier can receive. The supplier must also bear in mind the value of the relationship with the customer as a source of future profit, learning or access to other companies in the network.

Although a supplier's difficulties will affect the price that it is willing to charge each particular customer, the customer may or may not accept a price based on all of the supplier's costs or difficulties. The issue of which of a supplier's costs should concern the customer and be a factor in the price that is paid is likely to be an important topic in the negotiations between the supplier and customer.[1]

Pricing skills for the business marketer

A business marketer needs a number of skills in pricing. Specifically, he must be able to:

- identify the problems of different customers, whether or not he currently has a relationship with them;
- assess the price and other costs that each customer is prepared to incur to have these problems solved;

---

[1] The debate about the supplier's costs and difficulties is likely to centre on the issue of whose problem they are. A customer may well say that they are the supplier's problem and nothing to do with them. An interesting example of this was provided when Boeing was developing the 777 airliner, United Airlines was the lead customer, who cooperated in the development process. At one meeting between the senior management of the two companies the Boeing representative announced that they had suffered some cost increases. To this, the response from United was reported as being brief and to the point: "Tough."

- choose which customers and which of their problems he will attempt to solve. This choice must be based on his own skills, resources and costs. The choice must also relate to the value of each of the relationships in his portfolio, to the customer's other relationships and to the wider network situation.
- develop an offering for the customer within the constraints of his own cost structure and the price the customer is prepared to pay. He must communicate the value of that offering as a solution to the customer's problem, when compared with other solutions.
- manage the process of fulfilling the offering so as to ensure that the price received generates enough revenue to exceed his costs.

The business customer also requires very similar skills. It also has to identify its problems and work out what it is prepared to pay to have them solved. It must evaluate potential suppliers and assess the value to it of their offerings and of its relationships with them. The customer also has a role in managing the fulfilment process and it also has a stake in making sure that the supplier does not incur unmanageable sacrifices. It is no good for a customer to receive a promise of an offering from a supplier that the supplier cannot fulfil, or can only fulfil by bankrupting itself!

We now turn to an analysis of the issues that a business marketer must address in developing these skills. As always, we start our analysis with the customer and its problems.

Price and Customer Problems

Sometimes a business customer can state clearly what its problem is and readily compare the offerings of different suppliers. In other words, it has no *need uncertainty*. Examples would include the delivery of packages to a range of addresses by a certain time, or of sheet steel to a certain specification. The customer may have relationships with a number of suppliers, each with a suitable offering, so the customer has no *market uncertainty*. In these cases the customer's main concerns are likely to be to avoid paying more than is necessary. It has *transaction uncertainty*. In this situation, it is relatively easy, but time-consuming and costly for the customer to check each offering and choose the one at the lowest price.

If a supplier accepts this situation, then it must compete by reliably providing a fixed offering at the lowest price. Its profit will depend on achieving lower costs than its competitors in both the development and fulfilment of its offering. In other words, it is the supplier's *transfer abilities* that are critical in this case.

Many of a customer's less important purchases fall into the situation we have described. But in this case, the total costs for the customer of making a purchase are often far greater than the price of each product or service involved. For example, many companies acknowledge that the average administrative costs of placing and receiving an order can exceed $100. In this situation the real problem for the customer is not about the price or "quality" of each item required, but about choosing, ordering and receiving a range of reliable individual offerings with minimum trouble, evaluation, time, disruption or managerial involvement.

There are a number of potential solutions to this problem. For example, a supplier could provide a credit card service for the customer to issue to each of its staff involved in buying, to simplify and reduce the costs of placing and paying for orders. Another supplier could offer a wide range of product and service items from a single catalogue, pre-approved by the customer, thus reducing the customer's costs of searching and ordering. This is often done for so-called MRO (maintenance, repair and operating) items.

Thus, it is important for the business marketer, when considering price, to identify the *real* problems of each customer, rather than work on the basis of either the customer's initial view of what it wants or see the problem simply in terms of the supplier's own offerings. Customers pay a price because of the value to them of the solution to their problem that they receive, not because of any intrinsic value or cost to supplier products or services.

Box 8.1   Pricing for Customers' Problems

One large distributor of many small low-value products knows that its customers have problems when they urgently need items to cope with breakdowns or for new developments, and they are unable to stock all of these. It solves the customers' problems by providing speedy, reliable deliveries of guaranteed products either by courier, from trade counters or by next-day surface mail or in an emergency by helicopter. Customers are prepared to pay a price for these problems to be solved which is much more than the "normal" price for each item from conventional distributors. Hence they are able to have a pricing policy expressed (internally!) as "Never knowingly oversold"!

The Canadian aerospace company, Bombardier, discovered that many small companies might benefit from private business travel, but could not afford to buy an aircraft at current prices. It launched a fractional-ownership programme with American Airlines. This allows companies to buy as little as one-eighth of an aircraft, thus dramatically lowering the price of entry into business-jet aviation. The offering also gives security and convenience by providing pilots trained by American Airlines and planes that are maintained by the original maker. Over 75 per cent of the customers for this offering have never owned a business jet before.

Source, The Growth Philosophy of Bombardier, *McKinsey Quarterly*, 1997, no. 2, pp. 4–29.

Pricing for complex problems

Sometimes it is difficult for a customer to make sense of a complex problem or identify a suitable solution. It may also be difficult for a potential supplier to immediately provide an offering that meets the customer's requirements or guarantee efficient fulfilment. Some potential solutions may also require both the customer and supplier to make adaptations in their operations or in their offerings. Both customer and potential supplier may also find it difficult to identify the costs of solving the problem in advance. A solution in these cases is only likely to be obtained within a complex relationship.

Hence the task of solving complex problems for a customer will depend on whether or not the supplier already has a relationship with the customer.

If there is no relationship, then the supplier will have to develop one if it is to solve the customer's problem. The supplier will need to include the costs of building this relationship and of the adaptations it has made in its pricing calculations. The supplier will also have to evaluate the risks involved in making substantial initial investments against the likely future revenue *after* the initial problem solving.

If there is already an established relationship, then the supplier must audit that relationship to assess its potential and determine whether it wants to solve the problem for the customer. Does it want the work? Factors affecting this decision are likely to be:

- the costs and problems of developing and fulfilling an offering to solve the problem;
- the likely revenue from doing so;
- the effects of solving it on this and the supplier's other relationships (see below);
- the effects on the relationship of *not* agreeing to solve it, or of trying and *failing* to solve it. The customer may view the relationship as an important way of solving difficult problems. If supplier declines to do this, then it will affect the customer's perceptions of the value of the relationship.

A supplier's problem-solving ability to correctly identify the appropriate solution for a customer's problem and to develop an offering that will meet its requirements is often critical in complex problem solving. In this case, a customer will often accept inadequacies in the supplier's transfer ability and hence in the actual fulfilment of the offering. For example, a large retailer may have a complex problem in using data on its customers' purchase habits. It may accept some hassles over delays in delivery of the necessary software or minor glitches in its operation, as long as the software has the ability to ultimately solve its problem.

In other cases, the complexity of the problem for customer may be because of difficulties in fulfilling the offering. In this case it is the supplier's transfer ability that is crucial. For example, a newspaper publisher or a producer of fresh flowers is likely to be far more concerned with a carrier's reliability of delivery of their offerings against schedule, rather than whether the scheduled delivery time is an hour faster or slower. Pricing in complex problem solving requires the supplier to estimate the value to the customer of its problem-solving abilities and/or transfer abilities.

The difference between complex and simple problem solving has important *strategic* implications for the business marketer. If the supplier chooses those relationships based on only limited problem-solving, then it will require a tightly controlled cost structure and operations and its pricing will have to reflect this. If the supplier chooses to develop relationships based on its ability to solve complex problems, then it will have to make long-term investments in its technologies and in its problem-solving ability or transfer ability. This must be reflected in its pricing policy. It will also restrict the supplier's relationship portfolio to those customers that are prepared to pay for these expensively acquired skills.

Customers faced with a complex problem are likely to look to existing relationships first because of their previous experience of problem solving. We referred to this situation in Chapter 4 as *Buy-cycle 1*. Because it has already made an investment in a relationship, a supplier is more likely to be selected to solve a particular problem. Also because some of the costs of its investment have already been recovered, it is more likely to make profit on supplying a solution, unless of course the customer insists on taking into account that this investment has been previously made and recouped.

Price and the Offering

The price that a supplier charges a customer should be based on the value to that customer of the solution provided by all elements of an offering: product, service, advice, adaptation and logistics. Price should not be based on the supplier's own assessment of the "quality" of the offering or the specification of the product or service elements. Nor should price be determined solely by the costs of providing these elements, although costs are an important element of pricing as we will see below. A supplier can often increase the value of its offering to a particular customer by adapting one or more elements to suit the customer's particular requirements. For example, a particular customer may be willing to pay more for the same product element if it can get improved delivery or modified service.

Trade-offs

A marketer must be able to find out the particular trade-offs that a customer would prefer between different elements of an offering. An example of trade-off analysis is shown in Box 8.2.

Box 8.2 Trade-off Analysis

Suppose that a company is considering an offering based on the following differences in specification for each of the five elements:

- **Product:** A microchip with the speed of either a 386 or 486 version 1 or 486 version 2.
- **Service:** Service calls provided on the day of request or the following day.
- **Advice:** Provided either through a help-line or a call-out service.
- **Adaptation:** Either no adaptation or a willingness to adapt the product or the service only, or adaptation to both product and service.
- **Logistics:** Either next day or same day delivery.

If customers are asked to indicate their preferences between these different levels, a clear picture can emerge of the value that they place on the different elements and their levels. A hypothetical example of trade-off analysis is given in Figure 8.1.[2] The

---

[2] The statistics for this method are explained in P Green and G Wind, New Way to Measure Consumer's Judgments, *Harvard Business Review*, 53 (July–August), 1974, pp. 107–17 and P Naudé and F Buttle, Assessing Relationship Quality, in D. Ford (ed.) *Understanding Business Marketing and Purchasing*, London, International Thomson, 2001.

analysis indicates that product speed (44 per cent of total importance) and the level of adaptation offered (25 per cent of total importance) are clearly the two most significant elements of the total offering.

More importantly, conjoint analysis also indicates the trade-offs that buyers will make between different product offerings, based on the utility values of the different attribute levels. In this case, for example, we would argue that the buyer definitely wants a product based on a 486 version 2 chip, given its high utility value (4.3) over the version 1 chip (−0.3).

Conjoint analysis also enables a marketer to analyse the value to customers of different combinations of elements of an offering. For example, one question is whether customers would prefer this offering to include help-line advice, next day delivery and possible adaptation to both product and service, or whether they would prefer call-out advice, same-day delivery, and only service adaptation. We can see from Figure 8.1 that the second offering is the most preferred, given the various utility levels, below:

Help-line advice, next day delivery and possible adaptation to both product and service: $-1.4 - 1.4 + 2.8 = 0.0$.

Call-out advice, same day delivery, and only service adaptation: $1.4 + 1.4 + 0.8 = 3.6$.

Through this analysis a marketer can determine which offering provides the greatest value and charge for that accordingly. Also, when used carefully, variations in price itself can be incorporated as one of the variables in the analysis.

Variations in offerings

Complex customer problems can often be solved by different combinations of the elements in an offering. For example, one supplier could offer a standardized product, with minimal service, at a low price. Another could offer a product that was more closely adapted to the customer's specific requirements with advice on integrating it into the customer's operations, but at a much higher price. Because each supplier's offering is a unique combination of elements, customers have to compare a wide range of different offerings at different prices and this may lead to *market uncertainty*. The marketer must be sensitive to this and be able to explain the actual value to a customer of different offerings for a specific problem, when compared to other offerings He must also be able to say precisely what the price and other costs each competing offering involves. It is also important to re-iterate that when solving complex customer problems, the marketer must choose a combination of product and service specification, advice, adaptation, logistics and price that is not only acceptable to the customer, but that also relates to his own overall cost structure, operations, his ability to fulfil the offer and his strategy for the relationship.

Price and Costs

It is essential when considering pricing questions for a supplier to make a realistic assessment of all the costs incurred both by itself and its customer and of the value to each

PRICE, COSTS AND VALUE

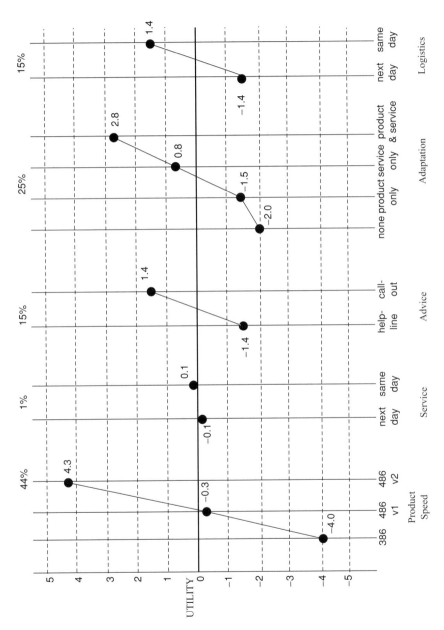

Figure 8.1 Trade-off analysis.

of them of an individual transaction and the relationship of which it is part. Some aspects of these assessments can be easily quantified. Others will depend on the marketer's judgement and his ideas for the future development of a relationship.

The marketer needs to examine his own company's costs and also consider how the customer is likely to evaluate its own costs. For the customer, the most easily recognizable cost is the price it pays to the supplier. For the supplier, the most obvious costs are the variable costs of fulfilling an offering: the costs of labour, materials advice, adaptation and logistics. However, a supplier (and a customer) may also incur additional costs.

Fixed costs

Business marketers incur two types of fixed costs that must be paid for irrespective of the volume of business. The first type of fixed costs are the *general* costs of running the entire business, which are incurred almost irrespective of the overall level of business. These include the rental of premises, the maintenance of operations and accounting and management costs. Also included are the costs of operating the marketing function and the costs of developing the company's technologies, offerings and operations.

The second type of fixed costs are those that are *specific* to a particular relationship and are of two kinds:

- *Initial costs* of a relationship are incurred before any transactions have taken place. They include the costs of finding out about the customer and communicating, influencing and negotiating about the offering and its suitability for the customer's problem. There may also be the costs of initial adaptations to an existing offering. Some companies, such as those supplying the aerospace industry often have to develop a completely new offering, based on existing or new technologies, for each new aircraft, before they can expect any orders. Often the supplier has to bear the risks of these developments and it will only be able to recover them if the customer is able to sell its aircraft. These costs are *investments* based on an assessment of the *initial potential* of a relationship.
- *Recurrent costs* are incurred regularly throughout a relationship. The supplier and the customer both may have to continuously develop the offering. The customer may also incur costs of changing its operations to accommodate the offering. Both incur the costs of developing and managing their relationship with each other. The supplier may also have the costs of maintenance and service to ensure that the offering provides a guaranteed solution and actually solves the customer's problem. These costs are *investments* in the *continuing potential* of the relationships. Without them, transactions may not continue.

The customer and supplier will have other relationships, other offerings and other problems. Devoting resources and attention to this offering and this relationship may involve giving up some of the benefits from these others, with associated costs.

Some companies have large general overheads, such as the costs of operating a major factory. Professional services companies, such as accountants or consultants often have the high-fixed costs of employing large numbers of expensive personnel. These costs can only be reduced through expensive redundancy schemes. These fixed costs must be recovered by all the company's relationships as a whole.

Other companies have relatively low general overheads and most of their fixed costs are specific to each single relationship. This is common in many service-dominated business, such as banking, or research. Many advertising agencies also often employ account management and creative staff to work solely on each of their major accounts. If an account is lost, then the staff concerned have to go elsewhere. Similarly, major retail chains often have a continuing relationship with a particular firm of architects. These architects are also likely to invest in staff members solely for this relationship.

If a supplier does not cover all its fixed costs, at least in the long term, then the company's survival is at risk. On the other hand, if too much of the company's general fixed costs is allocated to a particular relationship or transaction, then this can lead to an unrealistic price quotation and a failure to get business. Companies must also be flexible, for example, if a company has high fixed costs, then it is important to cover these when pricing each transaction. However, once these fixed costs have been covered, it can then consider further business, or build new relationships on the basis of only the variable costs involved. On the other hand, marketers must keep in mind the costs of their investment in a relationship. They cannot make an investment and sell at prices that do not reflect costs on the basis of some vague promise of future revenue. All relationship investments must be fully costed and relate to the strategy for that relationship and the potential of that relationship for future revenue, profit or any other benefit.[3]

Variable costs

Variable costs are the actual costs of fulfilling the offering in a particular transaction. They include the costs of labour and materials in fulfilling the product and service elements, in providing any advice, in making adaptations and in providing logistics for that transaction. It is important for a supplier to cover these variable costs. This is particularly so when the company has relatively low fixed costs, both general and relationship-specific, but high variable costs. For example, many construction companies have very few permanent staff or amounts of equipment. The also work on large projects for customers that buy new offices or plants very infrequently and so there is no continuing relationship with them. These contractors have high variable costs which include paying for their sub-contractors and renting equipment for each project they undertake.

Assessing costs

In all cases it is important that the marketer has good information on both his overall cost structure and the specific costs of each relationship and transaction. However, often

---

[3] This is often referred to as the "myth of the follow-on order", in which a customer asks for a special deal on a small order on the basis that a big one is to follow. He repeats this a few times and then the big order does come, but for a competitor, leaving the first supplier to count his losses!

companies do not know the real costs of each of their relationships. Many accounts departments provide cost and revenue information about products and production units rather than about adaptations or relationships, so many companies continue to sell to some customers at prices that do not reflect either their real current costs or the potential of the relationship. On the other hand, suppliers can sometimes incur costs of development in one relationship and then use this development in others, without further investment. They must then take the decision of whether to charge the new customer a lower price, based only on variable costs, as a way of building that relationship, or charge a higher price to take short-term advantage of the situation. In some cases a supplier will be prepared to make at least some transactions at below their variable cost, if these losses can be outweighed by the potential value to the supplier of a continuing or developing relationship.

Some of the costs of suppliers and customers are easy to measure and others are much more difficult. For example, it is common for customers to work out their additional costs of receiving and using an offering in their more important relationships. Figure 8.2 shows how a customer's total costs are substantially increased if it takes into account the costs of preventing, detecting and correcting defects, as well as the costs to the customer of complaints from its customers relating to these problems. The figure also shows how differences in quality of fulfilment between three suppliers also dramatically affect their relative competitiveness. The figure emphasizes how important it is for marketers to understand customer's costs when considering their prices. It also emphasizes that

Cost of defect prevention $'s	Supplier		
	A	B	C
Qualifying visits	250	250	250
Laboratory tests	200	200	200
Specification revision	300	—	—
Cost of defect detection			
Incoming inspection	600	600	600
Processing inspection reports	1,200	1,200	1,200
Cost of defect correction			
Manufacturing losses	1,590	150	200
Handling and packing rejects	1,500	280	600
Cost of complaints and lost sales	13,200	—	2,043
Total	18,840	2,680	5,093
Total value of purchases	63,820	67,947	84,896
Ratio of additional costs (%)	29.5	3.9	5.9

Figure 8.2   Analysis of some customer costs of fulfilment failure.
Source: David Ford, The Handbook of Purchasing Management, Aldershot, Gower, 1985.

marketers must be involved in their company's fulfilment activities as discussed in the previous chapter.

As well as thinking about customer costs, marketers also need to be able to allocate their own fixed and variable costs to each relationship and the transactions within it. This will involve considerable determination by the marketer, even if his company has invested in so-called Customer Relationship Management (CRM) software. This software may well provide good information on revenue and achieved price and some or all of the variable costs of a relationship but it is unlikely to provide the necessary data on the important fixed costs of each relationship.

Price and Value

A customer pays a price to receive value and it can receive value in two ways:

- **The value of the offering:** This is a measure of the extent to which the offering solves a problem for the customer. This value depends on the quality of both the offering itself and of its fulfilment, as we discussed in Chapters 6 and 7. The value of an offering also depends on how important it is for the customer to solve that problem. The marketer must make a careful assessment of this value. Sometimes the value can be calculated in monetary terms, for example, a customer may currently do all its own testing of the instruments that it uses in its production but it may consider buying a testing service from an outside supplier. A potential supplier will need to estimate the current costs to the customer of employing staff to do the work for itself and also its costs of replacing any outdated equipment to continue to do so. The supplier should also try to assess the current costs to the customer of any disruption in its current operations and complaints from its own customers that these lead to. The supplier can then compare these costs with its own costs of providing the service. The price that it then decides on must be low enough to give a significant saving to the customer, when compared to current costs, but be above the supplier's costs. The actual level within this range will depend on the importance to the supplier of the order and the potential value of its relationship with this customer.
- **The value of the relationship:** A relationship itself has value for a customer in two ways: first, *currently*: because customer and supplier will have learned about each other's operations, transactions between them will be more predictable and reassuring. Adaptations to suit each other's operations mean that the supplier's current offering may be enhanced or more effectively or efficiently fulfilled. Second, *potentially*: learning and adaptation in the relationship may provide the potential for new solutions to evolve to solve future problems.

The relationship also has present and future value for the supplier. These values need to be assessed by the marketer through a relationship audit *and communicated to the customer*. If the marketer does not consider relationship value when setting prices, then he may set a price that is too high and harm the relationship. If this happens, he will lose the benefits of previous investments in the relationship and fail to gain the advantages of future benefits.

Sources of relationship value

For both companies, there are three aspects of a relationship that provide this value:

- **Activity links:** These co-ordinate the activities of the two companies, such as in the case of a Just-In-Time production system.
- **Resource ties:** These adapt the resources of each company to the requirements of both of them. For example, both companies might provide a joint development team to work on a new security system for remote sites.
- **Actor bonds:** These provide the basis of the social exchange between individuals for mutual learning and joint problem solving.

Together, these three aspects of a relationship can provide value to customer and supplier in a number of ways, including the following:

- Lower operational costs because the supplier or customer has modified their offering so that it "fits" more easily with that of the counterpart.
- Reduced development expenses for both companies based on information from each other about the capabilities or use of the offering.
- Improved material flow for both companies brought about by reduced inventories due to changes in delivery frequency and lot sizes.
- Quicker and cheaper problem solving through familiarity with each other's ways of working and through trust in each other.
- Reduced administration costs through more integrated information systems and because of experience of each other's ways of working.
- Both customer and supplier may be able to apply what they have learned in any one relationship to their other relationships.
- They may be able to gain access to other parts of a network through their relationship with particular customers and suppliers.

Each of these ways of providing value involves costs and investment that must be recovered through prices charged and revenue generated. The supplier must assess the value of these investments to the customer and hence to itself as a source of future profit. The price the supplier charges must relate to its current fixed and variable costs, the current value of the offering to the customer, the wider costs that the customer incurs and the future value of the relationship to the customer and to the supplier.

Price and Quality

We have said that the word "quality" only makes sense in relation to a specific problem of a specific customer. So marketers must be very careful when making generalized statements about the quality or value of their offerings. Customers do form ideas of the quality of offerings and it is important for marketers to be clear about them in both their own pricing deliberations and in discussions with customers.

We have already seen that for each customer, "quality" has two aspects: The first is the customer's evaluation of the extent to which the supplier's offering is a solution to its problem. This is the *quality of the offering*; and the second aspect is their assessment of the likely or actual *quality of the fulfilment of the offering*. Obviously, a marketer must relate the price of what he provides to a customer to this "quality", when compared with other potential suppliers. But each aspect of quality will vary in importance depending on the customer's problem, Some customers with a complex or difficult problem or with high need uncertainty about different solutions will be more concerned with the quality of the promise. Quality for these customers will be about the relevance of the supplier's offering to its problem. They will be mainly concerned with the supplier's problem-solving skills and may be prepared to, or may have to, accept lower "quality" in the fulfilment of the offering. In this case the supplier may be able to charge a high price for a "high-quality" offering, even when its fulfilment is of lower "quality". Conversely, even if its fulfilment was of superb quality, it could only command a lower price if its offering was of low quality.

On other occasions, a customer may be solving a simpler problem, or buying a simpler or more easily specified offering. In this case, the more important aspect of quality will be how effectively different suppliers fulfil their offering. In this case the supplier may not be able to charge a high price even if the quality of its offering had an excellent specification, if its fulfilment was of lower quality. Conversely, the supplier may be able to charge a high price, even for an offering that was not of particularly "high quality", if its fulfilment was "high quality".

In other cases, both offering and fulfilment are important. However, some customers may not understand that the fulfilment of different suppliers varies, even if their offering is of similar quality. It is then important for the marketer to explain the value of high quality fulfilment to the customer and that other, cheaper offerings may cause later problems for the customer.

Price and Relationships

Solving a problem for a customer is not usually an isolated transaction, but one of many episodes that take place within a continuing relationship. This causes two pricing problems for the marketer: first, it is often difficult for the marketer to separate out each individual problem that is being solved in a relationship and the value to the customer of each single offering, especially because that value may change over time. Second, because there may be many episodes in a relationship it is difficult for the marketer to control what is being done for the customer and keep a clear view of costs, revenue, profit, price and value for each relationship.

Pricing for transactions

The marketer has to fix the price charged for each transaction within each of his relationships. But in many cases it will not be practical to review price on every occasion. In this case the marketer will have to develop a list price for all customers or negotiate a standard price for each unit of the offering as a whole that is delivered, or for each element individually. For example, some companies will provide a certain number of days of advice after a sale and then charge separately for each one after this. But even this approach may not be flexible enough to cope with individual requirements or face local competition. So the marketer may have to provide flexibility either by giving discounts for volume or prompt payment or allowing sales-people to have some discretion over the price to be charged. These can easily get out of hand and the marketer must then face the issue of how to control the price that is actually achieved in individual transactions, as opposed to the notional or list price. We will examine this issue of price control below.

Pricing in a relationship

Pricing for the business marketer is not about making a profit on each transaction with its customers. Because the marketing company's relationships with its customers are prime assets, the pricing task is to maximize the rate of return on each over the life of that relationship – the "lifetime value" of the customer. Marketers invest in their relationships and their transactions are the way in which they generate a return on those investments. However, in seeking a return on their investment it is equally important that they do not jeopardize the long-term value of the relationship to themselves and to the customer.

Like any investment in tangible assets there will be a pay-back period for relationship investments. This is illustrated in Figure 8.3. In the early days of a relationship the

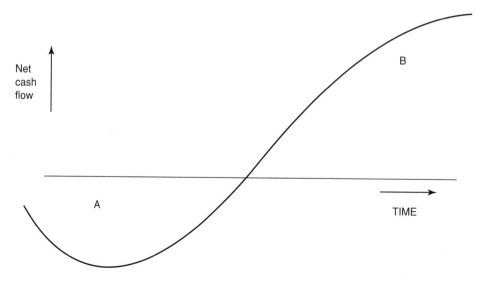

Figure 8.3   Relationship profit.

supplier is likely to incur considerable costs in building a relationship. Some of these costs will be the fixed costs of its sales-force, or marketing communication that must be spread across all relationships and are often referred to as "customer acquisition costs". There may be other costs of developing or adapting an offering for a customer. The costs of managing a relationship are likely to be lower after the supplier starts to fulfil the offering. These costs are often referred to as customer retention costs. However, overall profit on the relationship is not achieved until the area under the positive side of the curve "B" is greater than that on the negative side "A". This is likely to be quite long time, even in professional service companies that charge for the time of their staff on a daily basis. For example, one IT consulting company only charges at half its normal daily rate for its consultants when they are working on a new account and therefore does not generate its normal profits in the early stages. It also calculates that many of the non-chargeable days of its consultants are actually spent developing ideas for new customers and so these delay the time at which the relationship becomes profitable. Another professional services company calculates that on average it is 18 months before it starts to make a profit on its relationships. This is because of all of the extra tasks of adaptation and sorting out difficulties for which it is unable to charge the customer fully.

The marketer's relationship strategy and pricing policy must reflect the fact that the costs of keeping a customer are far less than gaining a new one. This has a number of aspects:

- The supplier must be careful not to take its long-term relationships for granted. It must continue to invest in them at a level that relates to their potential and resist the temptation to "milk" them for short-term profit.
- It must also adjust its prices to give its customer a share of the benefits of its lower costs, especially because the relationship may have already solved some of the customer's most difficult problems and therefore the customer is likely to be less "excited" by the marketer's offering.
- On the other hand, the marketer must also bear in mind when pricing that a customer will also have lower costs of relationship management in established relationships and would have to incur "switching costs" in developing a relationship with a new supplier.

One way of managing price in established relationships is through so-called "open book" agreements where the supplier agrees to disclose its costs of supply and to price at an agreed margin on top of these. This transparency provides the customer with reassurance that the marketer is trying to achieve cost improvements, but not taking advantage of the customer. Many marketers are apprehensive about these agreements but they do provide the supplier with an opportunity to be open about a relationship and its value to them and to demonstrate commitment to its future.

Price and loyalty

Very often business (and consumer) marketers will seek new or additional orders by lowering their prices. However, it is important for the marketer to realize that the customers who are likely to respond to a low-price offering from one company may equally respond to price reductions from other suppliers. These customers are likely to have little loyalty to any supplier. Instead they may be customers that are mainly concerned with low initial price and less concerned with building a relationship which would provide them with long-term value.

Price and the Relationship Portfolio

Some relationships may have the potential for growth in sales; some may be an important source of learning; some may provide access to different parts of the network but others may only be considered as a source of *current* revenue, with no longer-term potential. Those relationships with high potential will require investment to realize that potential, while others will not justify it. A marketer may use some of the revenue generated from one low-potential relationship to invest in others with a greater potential, so as to maximize the return on the portfolio as a whole.

This means that the marketer cannot fix prices or assess the value of a relationship in isolation. Instead, he must bear in mind its contribution to the portfolio. Examples of this may include the following approaches:

- Charging a high price to maximize revenue from a relationship with a low potential.
- Charging a lower price to encourage a customer to develop the relationship. The marketer would then be pricing on the basis of the potential of the relationship, not its current value or immediate costs.
- Assessing the wider portfolio benefits of a relationship, such as the access it provided to other parts of the network, or the learning from the relationship that could then be applied elsewhere. The marketer may then set a price in the relationship that generates a lower margin, but that could be set against value in other relationships.

Common pricing

Ideally, a business marketer should develop an individual offering to relate to the problems of each customer. But many companies have a large number of relationships and it may not be possible to find out the precise requirements of each one. It may also be too costly to adapt the company's offering in each case. Companies can reduce their costs by seeking to standardize their offerings across their current portfolio, as far as possible and seeking new relationships with similar requirements to their existing ones. Sometimes companies can achieve the benefits of both standardization and adaptation by providing a modular offering that each customer can choose from.

Pricing decisions involve similar considerations. There are obvious benefits for the marketer from pricing for each relationship separately. However, it would be costly and impractical for companies with a large number of relationships to find out what each customer was prepared to pay, or to administer individual price decisions. It may also be illegal to charge a different price for an identical offering to different customers. So marketers must often work with standard prices across a number of relationships. This is simpler, cheaper and allows pricing decisions to be centralized and more carefully controlled. It can sometimes be achieved by pricing on a modular basis (see Chapter 7).

Price and the Network

Business marketing takes place in a complex network of many companies of different sorts. Hence it is important for the marketer to be aware of the way that the surrounding network affects pricing decisions. There are a number of aspects to this:

- The marketer must not just consider the problems and volume of demand from his immediate customers. The nature of these problems and the level of demand for its offerings will be derived from the demand of the final end-user in the network. Demand for the business marketer's offering will not increase or decrease by the same amount as this final demand and there will often by significant multipliers. For example, if a producer of consumer durables finds that demand from its consumers has declined slightly, it may postpone many of its purchases of production equipment.
- When setting price, it is important for the marketer to appreciate that a sale has not been made until the final customer has made a purchase and received the offering. The revenue from this customer is shared between all those in the network who have contributed to the offering. The actions of any of the companies in the network can affect that sale and the viability of all of the companies involved. Similarly, if a supplier cuts the price of its offering to a final customer he will automatically devalue the inventory of any intermediary supplier.
- It is important for the marketer to examine the different ways that prices are set across the network, rather than simply consider how his current competitors set their prices for similar solutions to the same customers. If new companies enter the business, they may apply technologies that are either new or that have not previously been used in particular applications.
- In some networks one company will be the price leader. In this case, other suppliers and customers will compare prices and offerings with those of the leader. The price leader may be the company with the highest sales volume, or it may be the technology leader. Because of its position, the leader is likely to act to preserve stability in the network. Price leaders are therefore only likely to be an important influence during periods of relative technological stability in a network.
- A supplier must realize that its own network position and the network position of its customers will affect their view of their problems, their knowledge of alternatives and the prices that they believe are appropriate for a particular offering. A supplier must assess the relative importance of its offering and the problem that it solves *when compared to a customer's other suppliers*. A customer's network position is likely to be more important as a determinant of the price that it is prepared to pay than the marketer's costs of producing the offering.

- As well as its relationship with its customer, the marketer may have a relationship with the customer's customer or with other connected companies. These may influence the customer's attitude to the supplier, its freedom to choose others and hence the price that it is prepared to pay.
- A price decision by one company may lead others to make changes, elsewhere in the network, whether they are customers, suppliers or competitors. These changes could precipitate a price war between companies. This means that the marketer must examine his pricing decisions on the basis of whether he wishes to achieve network change or stability.

Price and Competition

Price is an important, but dangerous competitive weapon for the business marketer. It must be managed with regard to the "quality" of the offering, the overall competition that the company faces and the situation in specific relationships:

Price competition in specific relationships

The price that a supplier is able to charge in a relationship will depend on its position in that customer's portfolio of suppliers. Late entrants to the portfolio will often have to "buy" into a relationship with a combination of price and/or an enhanced offering. They may have to charge a low price because the total costs to the customer of using a current supplier are low, because it has already incurred the costs of adaptation to that supplier. A supplier is unlikely to replace a current supplier with a price that is only marginally lower than a competitor's. This is because the customer will not only compare prices between offerings, but also take into account the value of its existing relationship, the "switching costs" of building a new one and the uncertainties that it will face.

The current supplier in a relationship may lower its own price to fight off competitors that offer lower prices. However, there can be dangers in this. If a current supplier dramatically reduces price to counter a new offering, then the customer may well ask, if it is able to charge such a low price now, why was it charging a higher price before!

Customers are likely to have different expectations of the suppliers in their portfolio. It may see one as the supplier of standardized offerings at a low price, another as a provider of solutions to difficult problems, but at a high price and another as an emergency provider, again at a high price. Relationship strategy involves working within these customer perceptions, but attempting to change them over time.

Overall price competition

Although price is an important element of strategy for the business marketer, it is customer problem solving that must remain at the core of strategy. There are dangers for the marketer if it relies too much on low prices to gain business, because there will be little else to sustain its relationship with the customer other than that price. It is much easier for a customer to compare prices than other elements of an offering and the supplier is vulnerable to any other offering at a lower price. Price reductions can be implemented quickly and so marketers often use them instead of investing in their offerings and their relationships. Competitors can easily follow a price reduction and this may lead to a damaging downward spiral.[4]

Controlling Price

It is important for a supplier to control the actual price to a customer in each transaction and relationship. Price control has a number of dimensions.

Controlling adaptations

Business marketing often involves continuous adaptations to an offering to suit a customer's specific requirements. All adaptations involve costs. If these costs are not passed on to the customer, then profits will decline. If they are passed on, then the company may become uncompetitive, despite the "quality" of the offering as a problem solution. The marketer, in conjunction with the customer, must balance the costs of improving an offering against the extra value to the customer and the customer's willingness to pay for that improvement. *Real* customer orientation sometimes means not giving customers what they ask for, but instead suggesting a more "standardized" offering that can be delivered at an overall lower cost. This again points to the value to a supplier of building relationships with customers with similar requirements and spreading costs over different relationships.

Price, profit and the salesforce

Price control is often reduced when a salesforce is given discretion to negotiate a price in a specific relationship. For example, if a company has a profit margin on its list price of 20 per cent, and a salesperson negotiates a price reduction of "only" 5 per cent, then the company loses 25 per cent of its profit. Sales people often do not appreciate the real effects of price erosion on profits and this is made worse because they are often rewarded for achieving sales volume, rather than profit.

Price lists, invoiced price and achieved price

Salesforce negotiations are only one of the reasons for erosion of achieved price. It is common for business marketers to give discounts for many things:

- for early payment (which are often taken by customers even if they pay late!);

---

[4] A Diamantopoulos, Pricing, in Mike Baker (ed.), *The Marketing Book*, 4th edition, Oxford, Heinemann, 1999, pp. 337–52.

- for volume (which customers often try to insist on even for a small order because, "a big order is following");
- retrospectively for all orders given over a previous year;
- for the customer's freight costs;
- as a contribution towards the customer's advertising to its customers.

Often marketers do not fully understand what their actual "achieved-price" is because their accounting systems do not provide the information. A number of items must be deducted from the notional price charged in addition to the company's standard costs of an offering. These include special payment terms, customer-specific rebates, extra packaging, order handling costs, dedicated stockholding costs, freight costs and the costs of unusable material left over after production. Often a full calculation of these costs will highlight that the company is making a negative real profit on many orders.[5]

Costs are also often poorly controlled over a portfolio of relationships. In one study, Marn and Rosiello showed that one marketer had an average achieved price of $20/unit[6] but only 16 per cent of its customers actually paid this price. The price variation was between $14 and $26 – plus or minus 25 per cent. The lower prices were often given irrespective of the importance of the relationship to "old favourite" accounts who knew who to call in the supplier to get an extra discount. This case shows that price control can only be achieved on the basis of a clear relationship and portfolio strategy and good accounting information.

Price and Time

Pricing in business markets is not carried out just once for each offering or each relationship. Price has to be modified as both offerings and relationships evolve. Companies often develop new offerings in co-operation with one or more customers. However, even in this case the same or similar offering may be made available to other customers. The marketer has to make a decision about the list price for the *generic offering* and for any *adaptations* of that for particular customers.

Generic pricing of a new offering

This is the case when a single offering is being introduced into a number of existing or potential relationships. At this time the supplier will not have recovered any of the costs of developing the offering and both customer and supplier will have little experience of using the offering. It is also likely that the offering is still being developed and the supplier may need help from the customers to achieve this.

---

[5] For a full discussion of this issue see, Johan Ahlberg, William E Hoover, Hanne de Mora and Tomas Naucler, Pricing Commodities: What You See is not What You Get, *The McKinsey Quarterly*, 1995, no. 3, pp. 67–77.

[6] Michael Marn and Robert Rosiello, Managing Price, Gaining Profit, *Harvard Business Review*, September–October 1992, pp. 84–94.

The standard approaches to pricing of new products refer to the choice between a skimming and a penetration approach. The business marketer can use these as a starting point, but will need to modify them to cope with the realities of complex business networks:

- **Skimming pricing:** This is when the supplier charges a high initial price. It may be appropriate when the new offering gives the supplier a technological advantage over other suppliers, or where it has well-developed relationships with the customers. Skimming pricing may help the supplier to recoup the costs of developing the offering within a relatively small number of relationships. Skimming pricing involves taking advantage of a technological opportunity and the supplier must be quite sure of the extent of his technological advantage and of how long it is likely to last. This is particularly important in the pharmaceutical industry, where suppliers seek to maximize their profits on new drugs by skimming within the period of patent protection. Marketers should also be aware that skimming may be resented by a customer, particularly if that customer believes that it had a role in identifying a problem or developing a solution, or if the marketer needs its help for further development.
- **Penetration pricing**, or low initial pricing may be appropriate in a number of situations:

  - when the supplier has few technological or relationship advantages;
  - where the offering has wide application in a number of relationships;
  - where there is a need to generate high sales to recoup development costs;
  - Where close interaction with the customer is not needed to explain the offering or to integrate it into the customer's operations.

Penetration pricing may also mean that the marketer shares the benefits of the new offering more fully with customers and this may assist the development of the company's relationships.

Re-pricing offerings

The business marketer will need to consider re-pricing an offering when the offering is further developed, or if the company wishes to change its relationship with a customer, or if the relative value of the offering changes for the customer. The customer will be prepared to pay only a lower price if the relationship is based on a customer problem that has become less important, or if newer offerings are available that provide a better solution. The supplier will have to respond to this either by changing the basis of the relationship to extend the problems it deals with, or lower its relationship management costs and its price, or end the relationship. The supplier's costs are also likely to reduce with experience and the customer is likely to expect a supplier to pass on some of the benefits of this. It will be important for the business marketer to anticipate and plan for these changes through regular audit, rather than to assume that its offerings and its relationships will continue in the same way indefinitely.

Conclusion

This chapter has not produced a list of the steps that a business marketer should follow in order to arrive at the "right price". There is no right price for an offering in all situations and if there were, it would soon need to be changed as the situation evolved! Instead, the chapter has outlined some of the factors that the marketer needs to bear in mind when considering prices. Through all of these, there are some fundamental considerations. Price is but one of the costs that a customer incurs when it seeks to solve a problem by buying an offering. Some of these costs relate to the acquisition and use of the offering and some concern its wider relationship with the supplier. Both the offering and the relationship in which it is acquired have value to the customer. The marketer must consider this wider cost and value structure for the customer when considering individual transactions. Similarly, the revenue from its sales is not the limit of the value of a transaction to the supplier. Nor are the supplier's costs limited to those of producing and delivering its offering. Business marketers need to relate the costs of the development and fulfilment of their offering to the revenue received, the costs of developing and managing their customer relationships and to the wider benefits they receive through those relationships.

Marketers are responsible for maximizing a supplier's long-term rate of return on its investments in a portfolio of relationships. A strategic approach to pricing is essential for this. But pricing in business markets produces both accounting and administrative problems:

- A marketer cannot manage prices properly unless he has accurate and timely information on costs and revenue. Cost information must include the fixed costs of investing in a relationship as well as the cost of managing that relationship and the costs and achieved price for transactions in it. All too frequently, however, business marketers attempt to manage their relationships without a clear idea of their profitability.
- A marketer cannot manage prices properly if he cannot control the discretion given to individuals to negotiate price or the effects of complex discount structures on the actually achieved prices.

Both of these are problems of information. They mean that marketers must work closely with financial staff to help them appreciate what information they need and why they need it.

Business pricing shares many features with consumer pricing. But the business marketer is less able to set price for the whole of a market or segment. Instead the business marketer must deal with much greater complexity. The marketer must be able to tailor price to wide variations in customers' views of their problems and the value to them of potential solutions. At the same time he must seek the administrative convenience of standardization wherever possible. He must also balance short-term revenue against the long-term value of relationships and relate the price he charges in an individual relationship to the wider portfolio and the network in which he operates.

Further Reading

Robin Cooper and Robert S Kaplan (1991) Profit Priorities from Activity Based Costing, *Harvard Business Review*, May–June, pp. 130–7.

GD Kortge and PA Okonkwo (1993) Perceived Value Approach to Pricing, *Industrial Marketing Management*, May, pp. 133–40.

A Marshall (1979) *More Profitable Pricing*, London, McGraw-Hill.

K B Monroe (1990) *Pricing, Making Profitable Decisions*, 3rd edition, New York, McGraw-Hill.

MH Morris and G Morris (1990) *Market Oriented Pricing: Strategies for Management*, New York, Quorum.

H Simon (1992) Pricing Opportunities and How to Exploit Them, *Sloan Management Review*, Winter, pp. 55–65.

DEVELOPMENTS IN BUSINESS MARKETING

Aims of this Chapter

- To show how the nature of customer relationships and the whole field of business marketing is changing fundamentally. Business marketers need to understand the dynamics of these changes and consider how to capitalize on them.
- To examine some of the factors in customers and in the wider network that are forcing marketers to review how they manage their customer relationships. We then explore one of the most important of these factors, that of *information technology*, in more depth.
- To show how the Web opens up a range of new possibilities for both customers and suppliers and changes the way in which they manage their external relationships.

How Marketing is Changing

The first IMP work[1] established the idea that business marketers could not just launch a "marketing mix" at a set of passive customers, each of which they imagined to be similar to the others and individually insignificant. Instead the work showed that suppliers in business markets tend to have long-term and complex relationships with relatively small numbers of individually significant customers, each of which is different from the others and all of which are active participants in those relationships. Sales and purchases are made within those relationships.

Since then, the idea of business marketing as a relationship management task has become widely accepted. But the nature of that task has changed considerably since the original IMP studies, and it is continuing to change. Figure 9.1 shows some of the factors

[1] Håkan Håkansson (ed.), *International Marketing and Purchasing of Industrial Goods: An Interaction Approach*, Chichester, John Wiley, 1982.

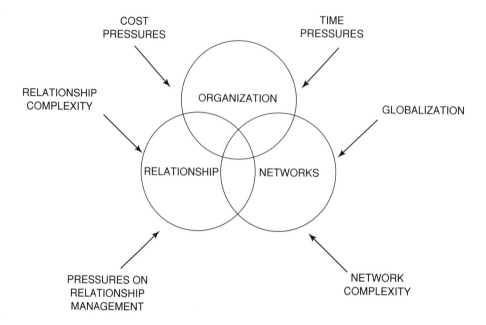

Figure 9.1 Changes in business marketing.

that are forcing change in three inter-locking areas: company organization; the nature of relationships and the nature of networks. Business marketing is in the middle of these three areas and is affected by all of these factors together.

Organizational changes

Many of the changes in business marketing stem from changes in organizations themselves. Increased competition has meant that companies are extremely concerned to lower both the purchase price that they pay for an offering and the total life-time costs of using the offering. They are also keen to reduce the costs of their purchasing organization and the wider costs of their operations. This leads them to reduce the number of their suppliers and require some suppliers to take on the role of managing others. This puts pressure on suppliers to lower their own costs and hence their prices and to extend their offerings to take more activities and costs away from their customers. Cost pressures may also lead customers to sacrifice the long-term value of many supplier relationships in order to achieve short-term price reductions from other suppliers.

Customers are also under greater pressure to achieve shorter time-to-market. This may mean that they will be more dependent on their relationships with the suppliers that help them to develop their offerings. But time pressures may also lead customers to abandon some relationships that were previously important and search for other suppliers offering quicker, cheaper, but less adapted solutions.

Relationship changes

Business relationships are extremely varied, but nevertheless there are some common changes that are affecting many of them, such as relationship complexity and pressures on relationship management.

Relationship complexity

Business relationships have generally become more complex. This is because customers concentrate on fewer of the technologies which they need to produce their own offerings. They are then dependent on suppliers to do more for them and their expectations of suppliers have increased. For example, it is now common for suppliers of equipment to provide a package of product and service, with a guaranteed usage level, cost-saving and re-purchase value at the end of its life. Frequently, customers require their suppliers to carry the risks involved in developing an offering, so that the supplier can only recoup its investment if the customer's own offering is successful. Because suppliers are more involved with customers in developing the offerings of both companies, then more people from different functional areas are likely to be involved in the relationship. An extreme example of this in one of our studies was a relationship in which 600 people in the customer were in regular, significant contact with 200 people in the supplier.[2] Relationships have also become more complex with the development of the technology to effectively integrate the operations of supplier and customer and to reduce their *combined* cost base. Examples include inter-company CAD/CAM systems, inter-organizational information systems and inter-company enterprise resource planning systems.

Pressures on relationship management

The increased complexity of business relationships adds to the problems of the business marketer and her customer in co-ordinating all of the interactions between them. For example, the purchasing manager at a large mechanical engineering company admitted that he had been in his job for a whole year before he found out that two large meetings were held annually at which the technicians from his own firm met with those from a supplier and discussed technical issues. They had not seen any reason to tell the purchasing manager about the meetings as they thought that "no commercial issues were discussed"![3] Relationship complexity also means that the traditional role of the business salesperson is being reduced in many cases. This is because there are now far more ways for customers and suppliers to communicate with each other but it is also because many sales people have neither the technological knowledge or organizational power to undertake a major role in some relationships. It is far more likely to be other, more highly technically skilled staff that negotiate the

[2] Håkan Håkansson and Lars Erik Gadde, *Professional Purchasing*, London, Routledge, 1992.

[3] Ibid.

details of an offering and how it needs to be adapted. Sales and even marketing people are reduced to a service function in many companies, where they smooth any ruffled feathers and keep a relationship on track, rather than being responsible for frontline selling or relationship management.

Many business customers are also aware of the issues of relationship management and network issues and have devoted considerable efforts to developing their own processes of supplier and relationship assessment.[4] This places increasing pressure on business marketers to develop their relationship and portfolio strategies and their skills at managing relationships inside their own company. If not, they are likely to become a passive player in the portfolio management processes of their customers and to lose the ability to decide and control the direction of their own company's marketing strategy.

Finally, business marketers increasingly have to manage relationships with a number of different companies who are involved in a project for a particular customer. For example, the sale of a traffic-charging scheme for a city would involve liaison between the producers of the smart cards for drivers to use; the producers of the chips that hold data on the cards; the software company that programmes the chips; the maker of the roadside card-readers; the providers of the customer billing services; the overall system operator and the city itself, as final customer.

Network changes

Although the idea of business networks as a way of understanding business marketing is relatively recent, major changes are occurring in networks themselves which affect business marketing. Two of the most significant are globalization and network complexity.

Globalization

The globalization of networks means that business marketers are now subject to competitive pressures from a much wider range of companies, each of which has rapid access to similar technologies. It also means that the development and fulfilment of offerings can now take place on a global basis using facilities in many different countries. For example, GE Capital Services opened India's first international call-centre in the mid-1990s. It now employs more than 5000 people there on jobs ranging from collecting money from delinquent credit-card users to data-mining. Similarly, it has been estimated that a typical Western bank could outsource 17–24 per cent of its cost base to India, reducing its cost to income ratio by 6–9 per cent and in many cases doubling its profits.[5]

---

[4] R Lamming, *Beyond Partnerships: Strategies for Innovation and Lean Supply*, London, Prentice-Hall, 1993, PD Cousins, Supply Base Rationalisation: Myth or Reality, *European Journal of Purchasing and Supply Management*, vol. 3, no. 4, 2000, pp. 199–207.

[5] *The Economist*, 5 May 2001.

Network complexity

Analysis of an "industry" used to be relatively straightforward. There would be a number of "manufacturers" that each competed with the others in a similar way and sold a clearly defined type of product to a set of "wholesalers" and on to a larger number of "retailers" and so to final consumers. But nowadays things are different:

- Many competing manufacturers actually co-operate with each other to develop and deliver their offerings *together*.
- Some of these manufacturers buy products from and sell products to their "competitors".
- Some of these manufacturers will supply directly to customers, as well as selling to wholesalers or retailers.
- Other "manufacturers" do not produce products themselves, but outsource them all from other suppliers.
- Many retailers sell products under their own brand-name and design and arrange production. They are "manufacturers without factories".
- Some suppliers have no design ability. Instead they produce offerings solely to the design of retailers or for "manufacturers" who only design, but do not produce their products.
- Companies exist in the network solely to be intermediaries between these producers and manufacturers or retailers.
- Some companies do not sell products to customers, but instead provide services based on those products.
- And finally, customers themselves now deal with a wide range of "suppliers", some of which may be manufacturers and others which are retailers of many different types.

Box 9.1 Network Complexity

Octel Network Services is a firm in Dallas that operates more than one million electronic voice "mailboxes". One of its major clients is EDS. EDS, in turn, has a $3.2 billion contract to run the computer and telecoms networks for Xerox. This deal involves 1,700 employees of Xerox transferring to EDS. Xerox itself provides invoicing and billing services for Motorola, which in turn designs and makes parts of Octel's voice-messaging systems and thus the circle is completed!

Source: Brown *et al.* (2000)

Change and information

All these changes in organization, relationships and networks are possible because companies have access to much greater information on the world around them. The flow of information between companies means that they are drawn closer together. At the same time companies need to look more widely outside their existing relationships and are now more able to do so and this leads to change and instability in companies, relationships and networks.

Business marketers need to understand how information flows within their own company and how the information flow *between* companies can be used for competitive advantage. With this in mind we turn now to the Internet, and explore some of the ways in which this technological development is fundamentally altering the way in which companies are able to interact.

The Internet, the Web and Business Marketing

The Internet is an electronic medium based on broadcasting and publishing that facilitates two-way communication. This communication is not physically face-to-face, nor time-bound. Interaction between buyers and sellers is through computers on networks, so that individuals and organizations can communicate directly with one another regardless of location or time. The development of the Web means that the network in which a company operates is extended far beyond the companies in its immediate vicinity, or its current suppliers and customers, to a global network of real and virtual companies and relationships.

For business customers, the most obvious function of the Web is to facilitate *search* and thus immediately to revolutionize a customer's knowledge of this global network. Excite, Yahoo!, Lycos, and other search engines allow the surfer to seek offerings by different suppliers or different characteristics from a multitude of companies and web-sites all over the world. They are also able to hunt for information on solutions to problems from a profusion of sites, and access the opinions and experiences of their peers in different parts of the world by logging on to bulletin boards and chat rooms. The use of intelligent agents, i.e. software that will search, shop, and compare prices and features on a surfer's behalf reduces business buyers' search costs across standard online storefronts, specialized online retailers, and on-line mega-stores. They are also able to transform a diverse set of offerings in a diversity of locations into an easily comparable form. In one sense this will increase a customer's market uncertainty, because of the diversity of offerings available, but it gives the customer additional power in its existing relationships because of information on what is available elsewhere and what is possible. In a similar way the Web empowers the business supplier by enabling it to communicate with a dramatically larger group of potential customers that may be acquiring greater skills and willingness to use non-traditional sources.

The Internet encourages customer search, which is costly and time-consuming in the real world, but at reduced time and expense in the virtual world of the Web. Dickson's theory of competitive rationality predicts that an abundance of choice leads to buyer sophistication – buyers become smarter and exercise this choice by shopping around, making price comparisons, and seeking greatest value in a more assertive way.[6] This is a

---

[6] PR Dickson, Toward a general theory of competitive rationality, *Journal of Marketing* vol. 56, no. 1, 1992, pp. 69–83.

radical change from the idea of business customers constrained in existing relationships by virtue of inertia and lack of knowledge.

The Web: mechanisms and enablers

To date, many companies have focused attention on establishing a foothold in the "marketspace"[7] of the Web but have yet to capitalize on the medium's potential. Despite certain limitations, the medium has the ability to dramatically enhance the range of market interactions, rather than just be a source of information. How does the Web achieve this? The answer lies in its five properties:

- **Search** is the process by which questions are *matched* with answers: customer problems with solutions: customers with suppliers. The Web facilitates efficient information markets, linking and matching companies at a level that was previously unattainable.
- **Connect** is the process of *linking*, the process whereby one-to-one, one-to-many, many-to-one, and many-to-many interactions are possible between customers and suppliers across time, 24 hours a day, 365 days per year and in space with a global reach.
- **Quantization** is the process whereby offerings are broken down into their smallest constituent elements. This deconstruction of offerings is a critical step in facilitating mass customization, a process of recombination of quantized service elements into configurations to suit individual customers. The ability to quantize and automate the production of matter-intensive products and services requires highly flexible manufacturing capabilities, involving many different companies. The Web can facilitate these.
- **Automation** is the process by which previously human actions are replaced by machine. It allows service bottlenecks to be bypassed, thereby increasing supplier efficiency, giving power and choice to the customer, and it also overcomes the traditional limitations of time and space.
- **Interactivity** is the outcome of two-way communication and the basis of business relationships. The Web facilitates this and allows customers to become *customizers* and co-producers and improves communication, co-ordination, community and creativity.

Box 9.2   An Illustration of Web Properties

Speech Machine's "CyberTranscriber" promises professionals another way to conduct business around the world. The Web-based voice-recognition service allows a manager to dictate a message or report by telephone, 24 hours a day, anywhere with telephone or Web access in the world. The manager simply dials a toll-free number, punches in an account number and starts talking (via phone or computer). The epistle is then encrypted, compressed and sent via the Web to the company's service centre in England. There, speech-recognition engines pioneered by the British military turn voice

[7] JF Rayport and JJ Sviokla, Managing in the Marketspace, *Harvard Business Review*, November–December 1994, pp. 141–50.

into text. On conversion, the transcript is sent once again via the Web, to proofreaders around the world with appropriate linguistic skills. The whole process takes approximately three hours, and operates 24 hours a day, year round, world-wide.

This service takes a secretarial service and breaks (quantization) it down into its constituent elements of shorthand (voice recognition and encoding), typing (transfer to document), proofreading, and iterative changes. It then distributes these elements globally and recombines them into a unique service. It automates the voice recognition, encoding and typing, searches and connects globally for appropriate proofreaders, and allows one to interactively change, modify or enhance one's original verbal monologue.

The Web in relationships

The Web can facilitate relationships between companies in a way that transcends national boundaries, encompassing elements of informing, investigating, interacting, distributing, transacting, eliciting feedback and supporting. These elements are summarized and illustrated for compactness in Figure 9.2. The horizontal axis of the figure shows the process of a single transaction through time – pre-purchase to post-purchase. The vertical axis relates to the direction of information flow between the companies:

- In the pre-purchase, pre-relationship stage, the Web can be used by a supplier to *investigate* by researching customer requirements and the offerings of competitors. In this the flow of information is primarily towards the supplier. The Web can also be used to *inform* customers of the supplier's problem-solving ability. In this situation, information flows towards the customer.

  As Figure 9.2 shows, the position of these two elements in the diagram can also be reversed when the *customer* investigates potential suppliers and informs them of its requirements and information flows from supplier to customer.
- The Web can be used in *interaction*, at the heart of business marketing, where the customer and supplier co-create a unique customized offering. Information obviously flows both ways in interaction, for example, by using the Web for joint design.
- The Web can facilitate the *order* process, where the customer provides the supplier with its delivery requirements and payment details.
- The Web can also co-ordinate *fulfilment* of an offering, involving information on specifications, production timing and logistics. This is particularly important where an offering is to be provided to a number of different locations and timing is critical to reduce inventories or to eliminate stoppages. Also, in the case of many heavily service-based offerings, such as those involving data-management, then fulfilment actually takes place via the Web.
- Finally, in the post-purchase stage, the Web can be used to gather *feedback* on the offering and its fulfilment, including customer satisfaction and commitment to the relationship. In this, information flows from the customer to the supplier. The web can

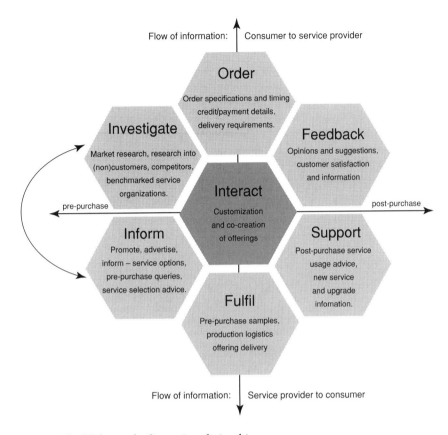

Figure 9.2 The Web as a facilitator in relationships.

also be used to provide continuing *support* through advice and information and to co-ordinate service back-up.

The Web and Cost Reduction

The marketspace of the Web is far more transparent than the traditional marketplace. Indeed, the economist Dillon Read suggests that the new economy should be called the "nude economy". This transparency makes it easier for buyers and sellers to search, meet, compare prices, and negotiate. *The Web reduces the costs of individual transactions* and the gap between buyers and sellers and because of this, barriers to entry are reduced so that smaller companies can operate within a complex network. We will use some of the ideas from transaction cost theory to examine the Web's impact on the costs of doing business.

Transaction cost theory argues that companies will adopt the way of working that optimizes their transaction costs. Two main types of transaction costs can be identified:

co-ordination costs and motivation costs:[8]

- **Co-ordination costs:** These costs are associated with the co-ordination of producers and customers. They comprise the costs of identifying and articulating problems and solutions and the subsequent costs of matching of customers and suppliers. These costs are those associated with need and market uncertainty for customers and demand and application uncertainty for suppliers. These include the costs of searching for buyers and sellers, learning about each other, interacting, developing, adapting, building a relationship, negotiating, comparing and deciding.
- **Motivation costs:** These costs are associated with managing a relationship. They include the continuing costs of informing, interacting and building commitment in a counterpart and also the costs of monitoring, policing and remedying problems in relationships.

Table 9.1 shows how the Web can reduce these various transaction costs.

Information and Learning

We have already emphasized that many of the changes in business marketing require marketers to search for more information and be able to manage and learn from that information. The Web can contribute to these requirements through a variety of mechanisms that range from familiar search engines, through comparison sites to various forms of electronic agents or "bots". Some examples of this are set out in Table 9.2.

Another example of how the Web can help reduce learning costs can be found in intelligent online catalogues such as that offered by GE Plastics. The GE Plastics' website supplies detailed product information augmented by an online downloadable database. The site provides a general introduction to GE Plastics and its range of manufactured products. Value is added through "Tech Tip of the Week" (tips and helpful hints for working with GE's engineering thermoplastics) and a summary of GE's latest press releases and announcements. A detailed online guide to their family of engineering thermoplastics is provided, complemented by a "Properties Guide" which gives detailed profiles of the typical property values for each material. To help the buyer select the best material for a particular job, GE Plastics offers an information resource called GE Select – a comprehensive database software covering the family of GE polymers. This database, available in different formats (Mac and Windows), provides complete properties and engineering data on all commercially available resin grades. Using the GE Engineering Design Database, the buyer simply determines the mechanical, thermal, electrical and other performance criteria they require and the most appropriate material/compound is selected. These features are augmented by a Design Guide (General guidance and recommendations for designing applications using GE Engineering Materials) and a Processing Guide (General guidance and recommendations for injection moulding

---

[8] P Milgrom and J Roberts, *Economics, Organisation and Management*, Englewood Cliffs, New Jersey, Prentice-Hall, 1992.

Table 9.1 How the Web can reduce transaction costs

Type of transaction costs	How the World Wide Web can reduce the transaction cost
Search costs (finding customers or suppliers)	Reduce time and effort in finding potential solutions, suppliers and customers. For example, search engines and comparison sites allow customers (suppliers) to find suppliers (customers) of specified offerings such as "Linux operating systems" or "environmental auditing".
Information costs (learning)	Customer wishes to learn more about thermoplastics and what is available before purchasing. Previously would have had to read magazines, talk to knowledgeable individuals and visit stores. Can now access company and offering information easily and at no cost and access potential suppliers on the Web.
Bargaining costs (interacting, communicating, negotiating)	Time normally taken by customer to negotiate can now be used for other purposes as intelligent agents transact and negotiate on the customer's behalf. Online bidding systems can achieve similar results. For example, GE in 1996 purchased $1Bn from 1400 suppliers over the Internet and there is evidence of a substantial increase since. Significantly, the bidding process for the firm has been cut from 21 days to 10. In the advertising auction site, "Adauction", buyers can automate bidding through a virtual agent called "proxy man".
Decision costs	The cost of deciding between supplier A vs. supplier B, or offering A vs. offering B. Web makes information available on suppliers (off proprietary and/or comparative web sites) and products and services. e.g. travel web sites allow customers to compare hotels and destinations online.
Policing costs (monitoring cheating)	Previously customers had to wait to receive statements and accounts, and then to check on paper for correctness. Online banking easily allows customers to check statements in real time. Chatlines frequently alert participants to good and bad buys, and potential product and supplier problems, e.g. the flaw in Intel's Pentium chip was communicated extensively over the Internet.
Enforcement costs (remedying)	When a problem exists with a supplier, how does the customer enforce contractual rights? In the real world this would require legal assistance. Publicizing the infringement of rights would be difficult and expensive. Chatlines and bulletin boards offer easy and inexpensive revenge, if not monetary reimbursement!

Table 9.2 **Mechanisms that facilitate search on the Internet**

Mechanism	Functions	Examples
Search engine	Searches by key word(s) and Boolean operators on the World Wide Web	Google, Alta Vista, Yahoo!
Comparison site	Web-sites that enable comparisons of offering category by attributes and price	Compare.Net (www.compare.net) a web-site that lists comparative product information and prices
True bot	A piece of software that combs sites for prices each time a request is made	RUSure and bots used by search engines such as Lycos and Excite
Intelligent agent	A piece of software which acts as a smart agent that will automatically seek out prices and features and negotiate on price for a purchase	Kasbah, a bot being developed by MIT can negotiate based on the price and time constraints that it is given

applications). Finally, using a Technical Support Resource the industrial buyer can get answers to any questions about GE materials they may have.

Links and Nodes: Direct Linking and the New Nodes

The Internet dramatically facilitates direct, unmediated *links* between companies but it has simultaneously encouraged the development of new more efficient intermediaries or *nodes*, as follows:

- **Links:** These are direct connections between buyers and sellers, i.e. companies who interact directly with customers without any intermediary. Direct linking has led to what has become known as Web-enabled *disintermediation*.
- **Nodes:** These are Internet companies that bring buyers and sellers together, by providing various distribution *intermediation* roles. The rise of these new nodes has led to what has become known as Web-enabled *reintermediation*.

Links and nodes can focus either vertically, between companies that trade with each other and/or horizontally between different industries.

In addition to these changes in transactions between companies (B2B), the Web has also facilitated changes in transactions within companies (B1B) involving *disaggregation* and its complement, *reaggregation*. These changes are defined in more detail below:

- **Disaggregation:** The division of a company's functions and/or its offerings into constituent parts (quantization).

- **Reaggregation:** The collecting together of functions or offerings into a whole, typically through customized (re)integration.
- **Disintermediation:** The cutting out of traditional links in the network between supplier and ultimate customer.
- **Reintermediation:** The creation of new intermediaries or market makers.

Astute firms have combined these processes into four distinct Web strategies: (1) disaggregated disintermediation; (2) disaggregated reintermediation; (3) reaggregated disintermediation; (4) reaggregated reintermediation. These are set out in Figure 9.3.

- **Disaggregated disintermediation:** This comprises the strategy where a company breaks or specializes its offerings into discrete and at times generic functions (embodying the process of quantization mentioned earlier) and delivers these direct to the buyer bypassing traditional intermediaries. For example, Etrust (etrust.com) provides the single function of "trust" in cyberspace. In the conventional marketplace trust was one of the functions provided by a well-known and respected brand-name. On the Web,

Inter-company **B2B (business to business)**

		Disintermediation	Reintermediation
Intra-company **B1B** (business within business)	Disaggregation	Vertical/horizontal-functional links (direct sale of discrete, functional offerings)	Vertical/horizontal-functional nodes (intermediary of discrete, functional offerings)
	Reaggregation	Vertical/horizontal-integrated links (direct sale of integrated, customized solutions)	Vertical/horizontal-integrated nodes (intermediary of integrated, customized offerings)

Figure 9.3 Web strategies – B2B and B1B.

many brands are unknown and "trustworthiness" is one of the primary stumbling blocks to Internet trade. Thus the function of trust has been disaggregated and embodied by Etrust, which acts as an inspector and validator of a web-site's level of security and use of data.

- **Disaggregated reintermediation:** This is the strategy where a company acts as a new intermediary for the exchange of discrete offerings. This is essentially the strategy pursued by some online auctions, such as the National Transport Exchange (nte.com) that have sprung up on the Web. NTE uses the Web to form a mediating spot-market of miscellaneous shippers who have loads in need of transport and a diversity of fleet managers who have cargo space to fill.

- **Reaggregated disintermediation:** This is where a company re-integrates discrete offerings often into one-to-one customer customized configurations and delivers these direct to the buyer. An innovative example of this strategy is Ernst and Young's online virtual consultant Ernie (ernie.ey.com). Ernie provides direct, customized consulting advice to other businesses, by providing a virtual interface for the integration of brainpower (Ernst and Young specialized consultants), information (monitoring of trends, news clipping service, benchmarking data, etc.), and online tools (supply chain diagnostic, software selection advisor, Web store front end management, and customer feedback programs).

- **Reaggregated reintermediation:** This is the strategy where a company acts as a new intermediary that provides integrated, customized offerings of previously disparate, disaggregated offerings. Most online exchanges simply link buyers and sellers, but others have gone beyond this to provide value-added customized integration. One such example is Esteel (e-steel.com) which integrates information sharing, credit facilities, supply-chain management and transaction execution into a complete one-stop Internet venue.

Ways of Interacting on the Web

The Internet makes some business models or configurations function more effectively, while at the same time enabling new virtual forms of organization to be set up. In this section we present a simple model to make sense of the wide variety of business-to-business interactions on the Web, and the processes that underlie them. We then explore the various factors that influence which type of interaction is likely to emerge.

Business-to-business interactions on the Web can be mapped on two dimensions, that relate closely to the ideas on business markets that we have developed throughout this book. These are illustrated in Figure 9.4.

- **Co-ordination:** The first dimension concerns how the interaction between companies is co-ordinated. Co-ordination can range from *directed* to *emergent*.[9] At the extreme,

---

[9] The issue of control and co-ordination has long been a concern of Transaction Economics. For a discussion of this, see OE Williamson, Transaction-cost Economics: The Governance of Contractual Relations, *Journal of Law and Economics*, vol. 22, no. 2, 1979, pp. 232–62.

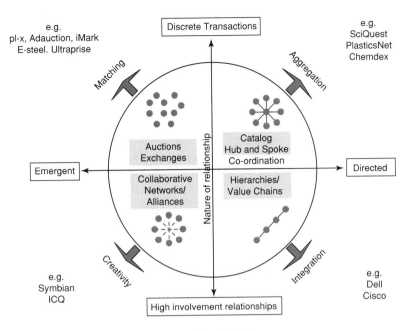

Figure 9.4   Alternative forms of interaction for the Web.

directed co-ordination occurs when one company assumes command and control of the interactions within a group of companies. This is a rare occurrence in practice, but examples among conventional companies include large retailers such as Benetton or Ikea that control many aspects of the development, production and distribution of merchandise. Emergent co-ordination is the opposite of this and occurs where control varies with the characteristics of the specific interaction, such as when one of the companies has technological superiority or is dependent on the other for a large proportion of its sales or purchases.

• **Nature of relationship:** Many businesses have a *high involvement relationship* with each other based on continuing commitment over a long time, with adaptations and learning by both companies. At the other extreme, many relationships consist of only one or more *discrete transactions* involving no adaptation between the parties and little in the way of investment, commitment or learning.

These two dimensions delineate four ideal types of interaction processes that are illustrated in the four quadrants of Figure 9.4. These are now discussed in turn.

Matching

This is where no single company exercises control over interactions and business takes the form of discrete transactions. Large numbers of buyers and sellers are brought together either to trade through the intermediary of credit/currency, or by direct exchange. Auctions are useful for trade in perishable goods and services, while online exchanges promote liquidity in hitherto fragmented markets. Auctions and exchanges can offer vertical (within industry) specialization and/or horizontal (across industries) functionality. The range of products traded range from traditional highly tangible products such as wheat or steel to the highly intangible services such as ideas and gene sequences.

An example is the Patent and License Exchange (pl-x.com), which offers an electronic market for the valuation and sale of intellectual property and patents. It is simply an auction for patents and licences, whereby organizations auction their intellectual property to the highest bidder. Other auction examples include Adauction (adauction.com) where advertising space is auctioned and Freemarkets (freemarkets.com) where a wide range of industrial products and services are auctioned. Exchange examples include E-steel (esteel.com) where steel is traded and Ultraprise (ultraprise.com) where business-to-business mortgages are traded.

Aggregation

This is also transactional, but involves the collection by one central buyer of products and services from a disparate range of sellers. The buyer adds incremental value by offering customers convenient access to a wide selection of offerings at current prices. This is often coupled with extensive product information to reduce the costs of search and transaction for the customer, combined with a more diverse supply base. The powerful central organization is the interface between producers and buyers, and thus has a measure of control over the interactions. The mode of interaction between the buyer and the multiplicity of suppliers is transactional, with prices pre-negotiated, varying according to pre-specified volume orders.

An aggregator acts as an intermediary between buyers and producers, adding value by offering services such as selection, breaking, bundling, distribution, pricing, and market segmentation. The mechanisms of this process are catalogues and hub-and-spoke configurations, which essentially underpin the classic business-to-consumer model of retailing. Web examples of this business-to-business model include SciQuest (sciquest.com) which focuses on the aggregation of scientific equipment, PlasticsNet (plasticsnet.com) which specializes in plastics, and Chemdex (chemdex.com) which focuses on the handling and supply of chemicals. These models excel with pre-planned purchases and fragmented supplier bases.

Integration

This involves the directive co-ordination of high involvement relationships between companies. One firm leads or manages the relationships with the objective of maximizing value for an end-user through operational effectiveness, employing Just-in-Time techniques to manage flows of materials and information between the parties involved.

The mechanisms of this process are seen in vertically integrated business, such as the oil industry. Web examples of this business-to-business model include Dell (dell.com) which produces PCs and servers to order and Cisco (cisco.com) which produces computer-networking products. Both integrate components from a diversity of suppliers.

Creativity

Creativity comprises the process whereby a disparate group of organizations come together in some form of long-term or close relationship to produce innovations which would be difficult to achieve on their own. All the parties invest in the relationship, but as each one brings unique skills or resources to the venture, there is typically no one controlling firm. Indeed, as the projects are often open-ended, it is often unclear at the outset exactly how to achieve the specified goal, or even if it is achievable.[10]

The mechanisms that embody this creative process include collaborative networks, alliances and joint ventures. Web examples of this process include Symbian (symbain.com), a joint venture between Ericsson, Nokia, Motorola and Psion to develop Web-enabled mobile computing devices), and Linux (Linux.com), a generic, open-source computer operating system that is developed by a loosely knit team of talented programmers working from all over the world.

The Factors that Determine the Way Companies Interact on the Web

The factors that determine the way that businesses are organized on the Web have been added to the two dimensions that we used to map interactions on the Web. These are shown in Figure 9.5 and can be outlined as follows:

- **Nature of relationship:** High involvement relationships, rather than discrete transactions tend to occur when:

  - the relationship requires a significant investment by the two companies in order to succeed, leading to so-called asset specificity:
  - the transactions between companies are frequent or take a long time to fulfil;
  - the offering involved is complex and its development and fulfilment are uncertain, so it is difficult to measure outcomes;
  - the relationship is connected or *embedded* with others in the network.

- **Co-ordination:** Directive rather than emergent interactions between companies are more likely when there is an asymmetry between the companies in information, technology, expertise or other bases of power. Directive interaction is also more likely when there is a need for speed in decision-making or in fulfilment.

---

[10] One reader of this chapter, suggested that a good example of this process would be the IMP Group itself, but that's probably more than a bit pretentious!

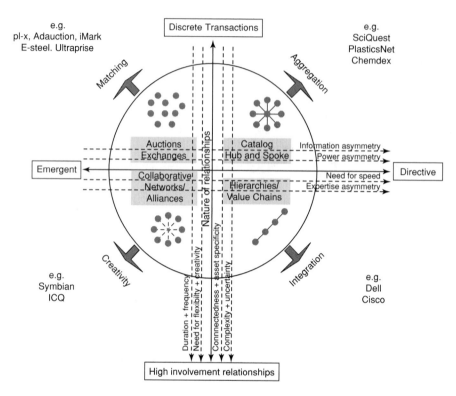

Figure 9.5 Determinants of interaction characteristics on the Web.

Changes in Interaction

The Web can be used to move interactions either way along the two dimensions of the model. However, initially one direction of movement predominates, producing more interaction based on discrete transactions, rather than close relationships and moving from directive control to emergent. However, marketers can and will increasingly use the Web in new creative ways to change emergent control to directive, and transactions to close relationships.

Take, for example, information asymmetry. Web-enabled search mechanisms provide price-related information in commodity markets and price and product-related information in the case of more differentiated offerings. This reduces the ability of sellers to direct the terms of their relationship, based on customer's need or market uncertainty. Thus, the ability to search tends to (re)establish information symmetry between customer and supplier. The practice of bundling a range of goods, service, advice, adaptation and logistics that is costly in conventional business in the "matter-intensive world" is rendered very simple in the marketspace. This may also provide advantages for customers prepared to search for and build their own offerings, but it may also mean that suppliers can achieve cost reductions in their own bundling or provide enhanced offerings at higher prices.

Another example can be found in asset specificity. As the cost of participating in Web-enabled electronic interactions is reduced by emerging public and proprietary standards for accessing and exchange of information in a secure and reliable way, thus the level of specific investments is in many instances reduced. For example, a dedicated order system installed by a supplier or buyer can be replaced by a simple non-specific Web-based system at a fraction of the cost. In contrast, the Web can also be used to increase asset specificity and thus barriers to exit. It can enable suppliers to learn more from their relationships and to use this to provide an increasingly customized offering for each customer. If the customer subsequently switches to a new supplier, it will have to invest a significant amount of time in "teaching" (if it can) the new supplier (if it is willing to learn) exactly how to optimally serve it! An example of this information-leveraging strategy can be found in Pacific Pride (pacificpride.com) that provides diesel fuel to commercial transport companies. The company retains and indeed expands its customer base (while charging above market prices for its fuel) because it offers information on the whereabouts of each truck and its fuel consumption, etc. This information enables better monitoring and control of a fleet by its management, while at the same time enabling Pacific Price to manage its inventory of fuel more precisely.

Conclusion

This chapter started by pointing out some of the wider changes that are occurring in business marketing. Many of these depend on a greater availability of information, but also require marketers to use that information more effectively. The importance of information naturally leads to an interest in the Web as a device for accessing and transmitting information. The chapter has highlighted the dimensions and extent of information flow on the Web.

However, a closer examination of the Web quickly takes us beyond a view of it simply as a source and exchange of information. The Web revolutionizes business networks. It enables the creation and development of companies with an almost infinite range of network positions and relationship behaviour, without the constraints of fixed assets or fixed ways of thinking:

- Disintermediation can lead to the breakdown of traditional relationships that "get in the way" of contact between those with problems and those with problem-solving abilities.
- Reintermediation means that companies with a wide network of real or virtual relationships can assemble offerings and save time and money for companies that previously had to manage relationships themselves or cope with inadequate solutions to their problems.
- Disaggregation means that activities that were previously inadequately or inefficiently performed in one company can be separately located for optimal efficiency in several, on a global basis.

- Reaggregation means that suppliers can optimize their offerings for efficiency and build relationships with a wide range of customers with fewer of the conventional constraints of fulfilment.

We have seen in this chapter that a seemingly obvious effect of the Web is to encourage a move away from closer, longer-term relationships towards a less stable focus on the short-term advantages of discrete transactions. However, the Web is far more complex than a device that allows companies to do quick, cheap deals. Rather than constraining companies to a single model, the freedom that the Web provides will enable them to maximize their advantage in a wide variety of relationship forms and will increase the diversity of relationship portfolios and the complexity of the relationship management task.

Further Reading

JY Bakos (1997) Reducing Buyer Search Costs: Implications for Electronic Marketplaces, *Management Science*, vol. 43, no. 12, pp. 1676–92.

S Brown, R Lamming, J Bessant and P Jones (2000) *Strategic Operations Management*, Oxford, Butterworth-Heinemann.

PR Dickson (1992) Toward a General Theory of Competitive Rationality, *Journal of Marketing*, vol. 56, no. 1, pp. 69–83.

L Downes and M Chunka (1998) The End of Strategy, *Strategy & Leadership*, vol. 26, no. 5, pp. 4–9.

JF Rayport and JJ Sviokla (1994) Managing in the Marketspace. *Harvard Business Review*, November–December, pp. 141–50.

The Economist (1999) Special supplement – *Business and the Internet: The Net Imperative*, 26 June.

DEVELOPING MARKET STRATEGY

10

Aims of this Chapter

- To discuss the idea of strategy in business markets and the need for strategic market management of market involvement.
- To explore how the market strategy of a company develops and discuss the role of management in the strategy development process. This will provide an insight into the complex issues of strategy development and a realistic perspective of the role of management in developing market strategy.
- To outline a framework that identifies and assesses the main choices and market strategy options open to a manager operating in a complex business network. This framework allows a manager to focus on key dimensions of strategy and devise and evaluate the alternative market strategies for companies in business markets.

In this final chapter we turn our attention to the issue of strategy development in business markets. Here we are concerned with how the overall position of a company in a network of market relationships changes and evolves over time. In particular, we discuss the main issues facing a manager in attempts to systematically review and manage the market strategy of a company.

The Concept of Strategy

The term "strategy" is used frequently in management and in marketing, but it remains a rather elusive concept. It hinges on the conviction that taking a holistic view of a problem, that is both broad and long-term, can help to distinguish what is trivial from what matters most in achieving desired goals. Being able to make this distinction should help a manager to generally operate more effectively and provide valuable guidance for how to act under different circumstances. Few would question the value of "strategic thinking". However, when people talk about a company's strategy they often mean different things and the notion of strategy is used frequently with different connotations and emphases. Attempts to reach agreement on what strategy is and what it is not can be a disappointing exercise and different definitions of business or market strategy co-exist, often in the same company. One such difference is between the view that strategy refers to an *idea* or *plan*, or that it refers to what is *actually being done* by the company.

There are a number of problems with the view of "strategy-as-plans". One is that the ideas and plans of particular individuals in a company tend to differ. So it is by no means obvious whose ideas and whose plans should be taken for the strategy of the company. In practice, the problem is often whether we should consider the plans of the board as *the* strategy of the company, or those of some member of the top management team and therefore disregard the ideas and plans of others.

Because of these problems, this chapter will refer to market strategy as what a company *actually does* or *will be doing*. We will consider strategy to be the actual market conduct of a company, rather than the plans or ideas of its managers. The reason is, broadly speaking, that results are achieved and can best be explained from what is being done with respect to the company's customers.

However, defining a company's strategy as its actual conduct does not resolve the ambivalence in the idea of strategy, which is illustrated in Figure 10.1. Strategy implies intent and change in what is being done and strategy always has a time dimension. Analysis and planning play an important role in how market strategy develops. Ideas and plans are important because they have the power to shape what is and what will be done. The pattern of conduct of the company towards customers reflects the ideas and interpretations of the individuals in the organization.

Defining strategy as *pattern* in the actual conduct of the company has some consequences that may appear startling.[1] It implies that every company has a strategy. Indeed, all existing companies have their own approach to business. It also implies that the strategy pursued by a company can be the outcome of unintended, unconscious and

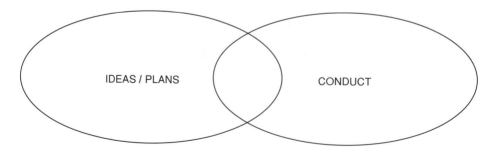

Figure 10.1   The two faces of strategy.

[1] L Araujo, and G Easton, Strategy: Where is the Pattern?, *Organisation*, vol. 3, no. 3, 1996, pp. 361–83.

uncontrolled behaviours.[2] Startling as it may be, defining strategy in this way offers some advantages. The main one is that it permits us to distinguish analytically the strategy content; what is being done, from the process by which the strategy is formed. Consequently, it also allows us to assess and evaluate different strategies and the way in which they are managed as effective or ineffective, managed or unconscious, good or bad.

The Content of Strategy

The idea of strategy implies that we can single out the important from less important things to be done in order to achieve desired results and goals. In business this means that we have to answer the question "What makes a difference to the performance of a company?" That, of course, is not a simple question to answer. Yet, if a company is to manage its strategy, then this question cannot be avoided, no matter how tentative the answer may be.

A common way to approach this issue is to assume that certain choices in what a company does affect its business performance and thus that the content of strategy can be characterized in terms of *choices*. Since market strategy, in principle, is about generating revenues and entails certain costs, our question becomes, "What is the impact of a choice on the amount of revenues generated and what are the costs incurred?"

A simple choice framework is illustrated in Figure 10.2 and is based on the profit and loss statement of a company. This can help us to focus on the choices or decisions that have major impact on results.

COST	REVENUES
	Who?
	(The set of customers served)
How?	
(Organizational and technical solutions adopted)	
	What?
	(The value to the customer provided by the supplier and its offering)

Figure 10.2   Choices in business market strategy.

[2] H Mintzberg, Of Strategies, Deliberate and Emerging, *Strategic Management Journal*, 1985, pp. 257–72. H Mintzberg, Crafting Strategy, *Harvard Business Review*, July–August, 1987, pp. 66–75.

Who and What

Figure 10.2 suggests that the current and future revenues of a company depend on:

- *Who* its customers are.
- *What* the company and its offerings do for its customers, when compared to available alternative solutions.

Companies can exercise some degree of choice, even if limited, in the "*who*" or scope of their customer base and in the "*what*" or type and range of offerings that they supply. All other things being equal, then broadening the actual customer base or the range of offerings leads to increased revenues while reducing the customer base or the range of offerings leads to decreased revenues. Both the customer base and the offerings of the company change over time and differ between companies. How the two change over time is an important descriptor of a company's strategy profile:

- Is the company acquiring new customers, or losing existing ones and at what rate?
- Are it and its offering valued better or worse with respect to alternative suppliers?

Traditionally, the scope of a customer base is referred to in marketing as the "market served" and the link between the change in this and the company's performance is relatively straightforward. Single customer relationships are important in business markets and the scope of a customer base corresponds to the company's relationship portfolio and its performance over time must be expressed in terms of changes in that portfolio. What happens in even one of these relationships can have a major effect on overall performance.

The link between *what* the company offers to its various customers and its performance is more complex. The difference between a supplier's offering and those of its competitors is traditionally referred to as its *market differential*. Customers use suppliers that they find better suited for their purpose than others. What matters for a single customer is not simply the content of an offering in terms of the elements of product, service, adaptation, advice and logistics at a particular price, but also other elements such as:

- How that offering compares with other known and available alternatives *as a solution to its specific problem(s)*.
- How the fulfilment of the offering to *actually* provide a solution compares with competing alternatives.

It is this differential in offering and fulfilment that explains whether and how much the customer buys from a supplier. The extent and nature of this differential are likely to change over time and impact on company's performance.

How

There is a third dimension of the company activities that has a bearing on its performance. This is "*how*" the company goes about its business, how it organizes in order to approach customers and how it fulfils a particular offering for customers. A single quality of offering and fulfilment for a particular customer can be achieved through a variety of offering designs, design processes and operational approaches. These different technical and organisational approaches require different resources and different activity patterns and therefore entail different costs and have different performance effects. Both the amount of costs and their structure follow from the operational approach that the company adopts.[3]

The importance of relationships in business markets means that customers value those relationships themselves, as well as any offerings that are transferred within them. In fact, it is no exaggeration to say that customers actually "buy" suppliers themselves and their skills and resources, rather than any single offering that they may produce. So a vital part of the "How" question in business markets consists of how a supplier manages its relationships with customers and uses those relationships to solve customer problems.

But the complexity of business relationships and the investments, adaptations and complex offerings that are involved means that these relationships cannot be developed in isolation from the operations of the company. A particular market or relationship strategy will affect all aspects of a company's operation. This makes it difficult to draw a clear distinction between market and overall business strategy. The two are closely interwoven and market strategy becomes the central part of business strategy.

The content of a company's marketing strategy, or what it does in order to achieve results can be described in three dimensions, as follows:

- Who – the customer scope;
- What – the differential of the offering;
- How – the technical and organizational arrangements that it adopts.

Choices in the three dimensions, and in particular how they are to change, impact on actual and expected results. Each of the three dimensions emerges over time in a series of decisions taken by managers as they cope with the operation of the company. It is the task of top management to monitor how the company's strategy develops.

The Strategy Process

Once we have defined the market strategy choices that characterize the conduct of a company, the next question we have to ask is: "How are the choices that affect the content of strategy actually made?" However successful a given strategy is at a point in time, it is not likely to remain effective indefinitely. Customers and their relationships in the network and the ways of operating and the available technologies are constantly changing. In such a context companies act, react and re-react. Managing the market

---

[3] The distinction between "what" and "how" is an important ingredient of operations strategy (see Chapter 7), particularly in such techniques as QFD (Quality Function Deployment) that map the relationship between customer requirements and the design characteristics of the offering (Nigel Slack, Stuart Chambers and Robert Johnston, *Operations Management*, 3rd edition, Harlow, Essex, Pearson Education, 2001.

strategy of a company means inducing change in the content of strategy and adapting to change. The need to manage strategy is greatest when a radical change becomes necessary. The question is, how can that be done?

There are a number of misconceptions about strategy management. One is that the content of market strategy is the result of a few major decisions taken from time to time by a few people at the top of the company who have the information and wisdom to make the "right" choices that will secure the market standing of the company for years to come. Unfortunately, that is seldom, if ever true. In practice, the strategy of a company results from a large number of decisions and commitments taken by middle management as they solve day-by-day problems as they arise. Another misconception is that strategic decisions come first and the nitty-gritty of tactics follows afterwards. That too is hardly ever the case for two very good reasons: first, there are always limits on what management does, or can know at any one time and thus companies need to adapt continuously to changing conditions both inside and outside the company. Second, market-related decisions are taken under time constraints and it is only possible to carry out a limited search for possible alternative solutions. These decisions tend to affect either the customer base or the company's differential or its technical or organizational arrangements.

Rather than being the outcome of single discrete decisions, the strategy content of a company results from a *flow* of decisions taken by different parts of the organization.[4] Choices about customer scope, the differential of the offering and the technical and organizational arrangements result from a series of decisions and reflect how problems of different magnitude are perceived and solved continuously throughout the organization. Market strategy is thus developed and changed by contributions of many who take part in the strategy development process.

The role of top management

The top management of a company is accountable for the performance of the company and for developing an effective market strategy. However, management cannot be reduced to decisions about the content of strategy taken somewhere at the top of the company. The role of top management is not a simple one. It is to manage the *process* of strategy development. Strategy management is about creating and maintaining the conditions necessary for effective changes in the content of strategy to occur. We will explore the strategy management process in more detail in the next section.

Strategy Development Process

Some of the misconceptions about strategy management that we have touched upon depend on a tradition in business education and consulting which approaches the task of strategic market management by focusing on strategic *decisions* rather than on the strategy development *process*. The differences between these approaches are now discussed:

[4] H Mintzberg, 1985, op. cit.

The rationalist approach

For a long time a view of the strategy development process that emphasizes strategic decisions has been taught in business schools and has become accepted among practitioners. The essence of the approach can be described as "think before you leap". It is based on an assumption that there are some major marketing decisions that deserve thorough analysis, attentive evaluation, careful choice among alternatives and well thought-out implementation. The logic of this approach can be labelled "rationalistic". Applied to strategic management, it results in strategic planning that broadly follows the steps illustrated in Figure 10.3.

The rationalistic model is appealing, and effective when feasible. But business markets have features that make it difficult to apply the sequential approach of the rationalistic model:

- **Genuine uncertainty:** Many of the factors that have a critical effect on the outcomes of strategy are unknown and effectively unknowable. This partly reflects the

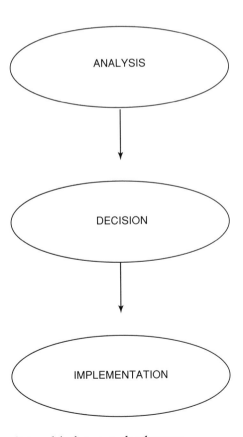

Figure 10.3 **The rationalist model of strategy development.**

complexity of business networks, that makes them difficult to map. It also reflects genuine uncertainty. For example, the future reactions of competitors and customers to technologies and ways of doing business can never be known in advance. The plans of different companies in the network are continuously "in-process". How they will unfold is thus genuinely unknowable and this means that even a thorough analysis will yield incomplete information.

> Strategy deals not just with the unpredictable, but the unknowable. No analyst could predict the precise ways in which all impinging forces could interact with each other, be distorted by nature or human emotions, or be modified by the imaginations and purposeful counteractions *of intelligent opponents*. (Our emphasis)[5]

- **Inter-dependencies:** Choices in the various dimensions of strategy entail a series of activities, investments and different individuals, functions and companies and these cannot be disconnected from each other. Any single strategic choice in practice entails a *set* of choices that cannot be well identified and specified in advance. The complexity of this can never be fully captured. Outcomes depend on a series of actions and counteractions. This makes it difficult both to define precisely, at a given time, what decisions are strategic and to identify all the existing alternatives to be taken into account.
- **Interactive choices:** Conventional definitions of business strategy emphasize the company's *own* resources and skills and its *internal* competencies and shortcomings.[6] But no company has sufficient resources itself to satisfy the requirements of any customer and so is dependent on the skills, resources and actions and intentions of suppliers, distributors, customers and even competitors to satisfy those requirements. Similarly, no company can exploit its own resources except in conjunction with those of others. So managers choose and adopt alternatives depending on the expected reactions of others. Once these reactions become known, they tend to correct their choices and adapt them to the changed situation. Whatever choice any one actor adopts reflects the choices of a counterpart. Coping with problems in a business relationship leads to solving problems jointly, in interaction. This produces continuous adaptations to the actions and reactions of others. These occur under time constraints and with incomplete information, involve continuous reading and interpreting of a situational context and adapting to and influencing each other. Interactive choices make it difficult to programme a course of action and to insist on its implementation.

Inter-dependence between companies means that in reality the strategy process is interactive, evolutionary and responsive, even if those involved believe themselves to be masters of their own destiny.

[5] JB Quinn, Strategies for Change, in JB Quinn and H Mintzberg, *The Strategy Process*, New York, Prentice-Hall, 1988.

[6] For example, "A strategy is the pattern or plan that integrates an *organisation's* major goals, policies, and action sequences into a cohesive whole. A well formulated strategy helps to marshal and allocate an *organisation's* resources into a unique and viable posture based on its relative *internal* competencies and shortcomings, anticipated changes in the *environment* and contingent moves by intelligent opponents' (author's emphasis), (Ibid.).

These features make the sequential logic of the rationalistic approach problematic in business markets. The emphasis on analysis, decisions and implementation as distinct steps to be managed and executed does not fit well in the context of business networks. Companies may appear to adopt this rationalistic approach in their strategic planning activity. In reality few companies follow it in their strategy management and elaboration of periodical strategic plans is often met with scepticism by line management. When the rationalistic model is followed, it produces, at best, sophisticated documents but often fails to produce effective results.

The organic approach

A different approach to strategy management is needed and indeed adopted in companies operating in complex business networks. We will call such a model of strategy development "organic" and it is illustrated in Figure 10.4.

The essence of the approach is that the content of market strategy (choices regarding its customer base, the differential of the offering and technical and organizational solutions), emerges from a continuous interplay of three processes:

- gaining understanding of the context;
- formulating intent;
- sustaining action and commitment.

The three processes occur in parallel and are closely intermeshed and inter-dependent. They embrace the rationalistic activities of analysis, decision-making and implementation but the emphasis shifts, as follows.

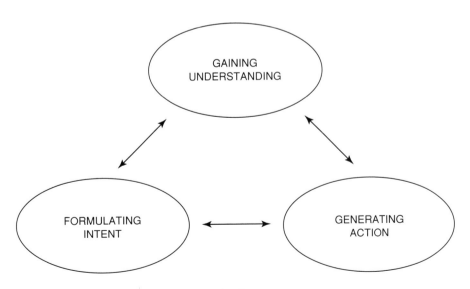

Figure 10.4　The organic view of strategy development.

Gaining understanding

Systematic market analysis is important, but the nature of business markets makes it necessary to reconsider the purpose and scope of market analysis. No amount of data and information on the state of the market can resolve the "genuine uncertainty", to which we have referred. The primary purpose of analysis in business markets is to achieve an understanding of how the network operates, how it develops and how companies in it react. In these circumstances being able to recognize patterns of behaviour offers guidance for how the company should act and react. To gain understanding requires more than analysis in the traditional sense of gathering and interpreting of the available data on patterns of sales and market shares. It means capitalizing on the *tacit knowledge* inside the company.

Box 10.1   Japanese success

"Their success, as any Japanese automotive executive will tell, did not result from a bold insight by a few big brains at the top. On the contrary, success was achieved by senior managers humble enough not to take their initial strategic positions too seriously. What saved Japan's near failures was the cumulative impact of 'little brains' in the form of salesmen and dealers and production workers, all contributing incrementally to the quality and market position these companies enjoy today" Middle and upper management saw their primary tasks as guiding and orchestrating this input from below rather than steering the organization from above along a predetermined strategic course.

Source: Pascale (1994)

Gaining understanding involves formulating assumptions about how customers react, what they value, what needs to be done to develop problem-solving and transfer abilities and how it can be done. This task is continuous and not linked to particular moments in which decisions are taken.

Gaining understanding is linked to action but action sometimes cannot wait for understanding. The traditional emphasis on analysis before decisions rests on assumption that the company has an analytical frame in place that is simply to be filled in with relevant information. When genuine uncertainty is present, then working on understanding requires continuous development of the analytical frame. In most situations, it is one of the consequences of interaction in business relationships that companies must decide and act on partial and incomplete information. That understanding, or set of actionable assumptions about how others will behave and the consequences of that behaviour, is the only guidance available to managers. This understanding often follows action by a company and its experience of the outcomes of it. Gaining understanding involves evaluating the outcome of actions against a purpose or intent. This amounts to "learning-by-doing" or trying out different approaches and being ready to correct them when needed. Acting in this way may lead to new goals as well as to new ways of reaching them. Recurrent evaluation and interpretation of experience are critical for understanding how the business network works.

Formulating intent

It is important to spell out in which direction the strategy of a company should develop along the three dimensions of content: Who, What and How. This is necessary in order to co-ordinate, in the direction of that intent, the complex activities of the company, such as its operations, purchasing, R&D. Establishing clarity of intent is also important so as to have something to relate to when reacting to events, such as to changes in the demands or requirements of customers.

Companies in business markets face a complex set of choices underlying market strategy and no-one in the company will have a full picture of what is or will be needed. What appears as a strategic decision is but an indication of a direction to be tried out. The company will also need to allow for adjustments and re-formulation. The formulation of a desired strategy content is thus at best an expression of intent about direction of change.

Formulating intent identifies a *preferred* future state, rather than the most likely future. This preferred state cannot be fully decided or specified. At the same time, formulating intent is more than setting quantitative goals or targets, or extrapolations from a current situation. To serve the purpose of co-ordination and criteria for taking decisions, a formulation of intent has to convey meaning, be understood, throughout the organization, to be "what everybody knows".[7]

Many companies attempt to achieve this through vision or mission statements, which are only effective if they relate closely to the reality that the company faces, express an intent that is achievable, are communicated and understood throughout the company and are followed through by action. A good example of this is provided by Honda, after it was overtaken by Yamaha as Japan's number one motor-cycle producer. Honda responded with the formulation of intent:

> *Yamaha so tsubu su!*
> We will crush, squash and slaughter Yamaha!

Honda implemented this by launching 81 new products in 18 months. This massive effort nearly bankrupted the company, but it did regain market leadership.[8]

Sustaining action and commitment

In business markets where relationship interaction becomes central to marketing, it is obvious that "effective ways to behave" cannot be entirely pre-programmed or prescribed.

---

[7] I Nonaka, The Knowledge Creating Company, *Harvard Business Review*, November–December, 1991, pp. 96–104.

[8] Steve Brown, Kate Blackmon, Paul Cousins and Harvey Maylor, *Operations Management*, Oxford, Butterworth-Heinemann, 2001, p. 41.

Interacting with customers entails purposeful and planned acts but also and most importantly, it involves reacting to the signals from and requirements of customers.

The uncertain and interactive nature of business relationships means that the way that the individuals involved react reflects how they frame, assess and interpret the situation. Their reactions are based to a large extent on convictions rooted in their past experiences that have been translated into their own rules of behaviour. Consistency in behaviour is important in relationships because it makes that behaviour intelligible to the customer.

Generating action and commitment cannot be reduced to prescription and control of behaviours. It is not taken care of by taking strategic decisions or attempts to implement a formulaic program. Instead, it is the outcome of the organizational culture of those who interact in market relationships and of criteria that stem from strategic intent and ideas that have emerged from previous actions.

If we are to summarize the implications of the "organic" model for strategy management, they are far-reaching:

- When considering the strategy process, it means changing focus from discrete strategic decisions and it points to a process through which the choices with respect to strategy content *emerge*.
- It offers a different perspective on the role of market planning in the reality of strategy.
- Finally, it suggests a different way to conceive of the role and task of top management in strategy development.

Management's Role in Strategy Development

The task of managing strategy is properly that of senior management and involves responsibility for the three processes we have outlined in the organic model above. In this view, the role of senior management is less about making the decisions about choices involved in strategy. Instead, it is more about ensuring that the choices being made by middle management produce the desired performance and add up to an effective strategy. The critical role for senior management is thus to support the three processes and to ensure consistent conditions for those making the operative choices.

The behaviour of individuals in a company is guided by how the situations they meet are framed and interpreted. These individual interpretations can be inconsistent and conflicting. Directing the behaviour of individuals involves working towards consistency in the way that the context and the situations that arise in a business network are framed. Much of the responsibility of market strategy management is organizational, in the sense of directing attention and action through various tools of organizing. Management studies has identified several "tools" that management can use to direct attention and interpretation of the context. These ultimately represent ways to manage strategy. A common framework is the one illustrated in Figure 10.5:

- Formulating a desired *strategy* offers criteria against which to evaluate the alternatives met in operations.

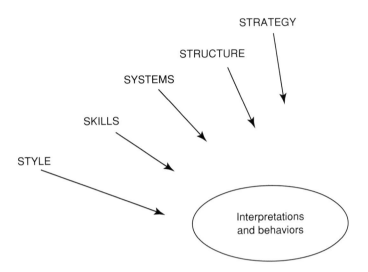

Figure 10.5 Tools of management.
Source: T.J. Peters and R.H. Waterman, *In Search of Excellence: Lessons from America's Best Run Companies*, New York, Harper and Row, 1982.

- Organizational *structure* specifies accountability and directs attention of different roles.
- Management control and support *systems* impact on what is measured, believed and thus taken into account in making choices.
- The individual *skills* and abilities of those in the company affect the way to frame situations and devise solutions.
- The *style* of management or management culture offers norms and values that, especially in an uncertain context, offer guidance on how to act.

The Role of Strategic Market Planning

Strategic planning has an important role to play in strategy development. It is important beyond the plans it produces.

- **Plans:** Plans have two functions: First, they are a way to express and to communicate the company's strategic intent, more or less explicitly. Second, they serve as a co-ordinating mechanism. Quantifiable plans are needed in order to co-ordinate the activities of different parts of the company, such as marketing and sales with production, research and development, purchasing and human resource management, etc.

  Plans are thus a base on which to co-ordinate various activities throughout the company but not the road map to desired performance. They cannot be a blueprint for strategy. The dynamics of business networks will make any blueprint obsolete in a short time and subject to adaptations and change.

- **Planning:** The value of strategic market planning lies primarily in the very activity of planning, that is, learning about how the context works and identifying alternative solutions for coping with it. Planning serves two purposes: the first purpose of planning is learning, i.e. gaining understanding. Planning is valuable in order to make the company's understanding of the market more systematic and diffused in the company. The second purpose of planning is attention arousal. It helps the company to focus on issues that cannot be solved for the moment but that need to be monitored and dealt with in the future. What is often overlooked is that one of the main outcomes of the planning is the listing of unresolved problems for which effective solutions are not in place.

Strategy Content and Options

We will now return to the ways in which companies act with respect to their customers and how these actions can be related to results. There is no one best strategy that can be linked to economic success for a company and quite different market strategies can be successful in business networks in terms of choices in the three dimensions of Who, What and How (customer base, offering differential and organizational and technical arrangements). The economic consequences of a given strategy will always depend on the features of the business network within which the company operates. In this section we review some of the options that a company has in the three dimensions of strategy content: who, what and how.

The scope of the customer base – *who*

Every company can at a point in time be characterized by the set of customers it serve and the offerings that it provides for them. Many business companies have a large number of customers, but it is common for a relatively few important customer relationships to account for a major portion of total sales. Research shows that 10 major customers often account for more than two-thirds of the sales and that in many companies 80 per cent of sales is often to no more than 20–30 major customers. Of course, exceptions do exist, dependent on the size of the company and how the customers are defined, but a business company's customer base is typically rather skewed or concentrated. Examples of this include suppliers to the automotive industry and to retailers, in advertising agencies, aerospace, accounting, steel producers, consultants and electronics suppliers.

Few companies in business markets constantly renew their customer base and sell all the time to new customers. Most companies serve relatively few customers with whom they maintain continuous business relationships. Only a minor portion of their sales in any one year is to "new" customers, with which they have never done business with before. Again, research shows that new customers seldom represent more than 5–10 per cent of the total business for established companies.

The customer base in most businesses tends to be heterogeneous. It consists of companies with different characteristics, varying from large to small, old to new, innovative to conservative and also ranging widely in their profitability, management style and growth potential. This heterogeneity of customers results in them having different requirements from suppliers and different relationships with them.

Few companies offer their customers only a standard offering. Companies can differentiate their offerings from those of other suppliers by changing one or more of its elements, even in the case of commodities such as chemicals, steel or coal. Companies also tend to vary one or more elements of their offering to the requirements of the different customers. For example, even suppliers of iron ore or coal may sort the material (product) differently for different customers, vary service, offer advice on economy in use, alter logistics or provide adaptations in their relationship that go far beyond these normal variations.

Any company has thus a portfolio of customers and a portfolio of offerings that change over time. Strategic options with respect to these can be illustrated in Figure 10.6. The framework is commonly used in marketing in order to assess the direction of change in the customer-offering scope of the company in the past and to sort out main future options. In principle it suggests that a company can do the following:

- **Cell 1** – Essentially maintain its current customer base and product-service range. Revenues can be increased by increasing the share of a customer's requirements that

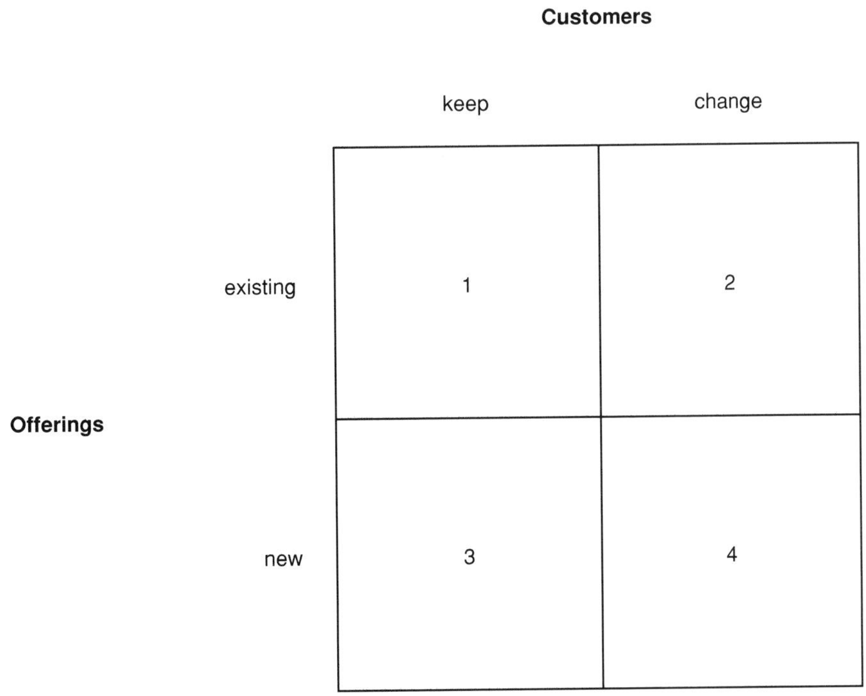

Customers

	keep	change
existing	1	2
new	3	4

Offerings

Figure 10.6   Strategy options in customer and offering scope.

the company supplies, or when customers grow and increase the use of the offerings provided by the supplier.

- **Cell 2** – Develop new customer relationships and/or withdraw from others while largely maintaining the existing range of offerings.
- **Cell 3** – Extend or change the content of the offering to the existing customers. This amounts to increasing revenues by broadening the content of existing customer relationships.
- **Cell 4** – Pursue various combinations of extending or reducing of the customer base and the range of offerings.

We have explained throughout this book that the adaptations made by both supplier and customer are important to demonstrate commitment and to build a relationship. However, we have also shown that adaptations in the content of customer relationships are costly. It is common for suppliers to vary the offerings supplied to customers, often by modularizing the offering, but it is equally common for business customers to request a modified offering that goes beyond the supplier's intended range of variation. The amount of resources available to a company for these adaptations is always limited and not all customers' requests can be met. Business companies have to balance the pressure to adapt and the requirements of relationships against cost-efficiency in operation and focus on resource and technological development. This means that suppliers have to decide which customers to prioritize and to manage their relationship portfolio, as follows.

Relationship portfolio

This book has emphasized that a company's relationships are its prime assets but the strategic management of a portfolio of relationships must cope with varying types and rates of return on the company's investment in different relationships as well as with considerable uncertainty about how each relationship will develop.

The strategic intent of a company involves maximizing the overall return from the portfolio *as a whole*. This means that even if a company denies it, different customers will get different treatment as it is impossible to satisfy the requests of all of them. Giving priority to some customers is part of the process of "investing" in those relationships rather than in others. However, the reasons for giving some customers priority are often hard to see because the various concessions and adaptations are arrived at through interaction with customers. These adaptations are even harder to monitor and keep track of. The problem for management is to monitor how the customer base and customer relationships develop and to make explicit the criteria for attributing priorities to some and not other customer relationships. Assessment of the structure and change of a relationship portfolio offers a base for developing a consistent and effective market strategy and provides guidance on how to allocate efforts, investments and adaptations.

The customer relationships of a company will vary in the volume of business, profitability, rate of growth, strength of the relationship and also in how they can be leveraged for other purposes such as technical development, or more general business development. Asked about which of the above should be taken as a criterion by which to prioritize relationships, the first reaction of a manager is to claim that it should be profitability. Yet research shows that profitability always varies greatly across customer relationships of a company. One of the ways to gauge this aspect is to check customer relationships for relative cost to serve and relative revenue, by constructing a matrix such as that in Figure 10.7.

A snap-shot picture of the different relationships in a portfolio plotted as in Figure 10.7 provides only one of the elements needed in order to make choices regarding the future customer scope of a company, but it can be used both to asses the current portfolio situation and to track changes over time. This can provide a useful starting point for formulating strategy with respect to the customer base. An analysis of the customer portfolio will always show differences in profitability of single relationships. Persistence of some "unprofitable" customers in the portfolio is common and not a bad sign in itself. Some of the less profitable, or non-profitable, customers may be valuable for other reasons. They may be the growing customers with future potential or customers critical as source of technical or commercial know-how, as discussed in Chapter 5.

A single customer relationship cannot be evaluated in isolation and the impact on the company of existing inter-dependencies between relationships has to be taken into account, for example, an offering developed in one relationship may subsequently be profitably employed in others. Just as in financial portfolio management, the principle is to manage the customer base for overall profitability at company-wide level, to which different relationships contribute in different ways.

Another element in deciding on options with respect to the customer base is to monitor relationship development over time. Figure 10.8 brings together changes in the sales volume in particular relationships and the share of a customer's requirements supplied by the company. It has to be kept in mind, however, that analysis of the customer portfolio with respect to profitability and change in the content of relationships

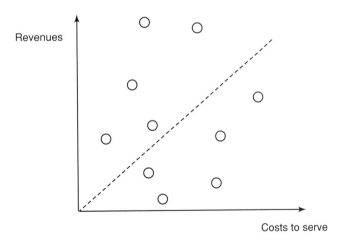

Figure 10.7 Customer portfolio matrix – revenues vs. costs to serve.

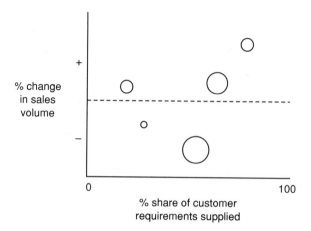

Figure 10.8 Customer portfolio change matrix.

cannot substitute for the need for single account analysis and the individual management of the company's main customer relationships. In Chapter 5 we presented the Relationship Audit as a tool for single relationship assessment and management.

When it comes to evaluating options with respect to their customer base, most companies have the ambition to develop new customer relationships. This is a viable option when there are potential customers that have never been approached. It involves developing new relationships and, as a rule, breaking into the active, existing supplier relationships of a customer. In many mature, global businesses this is an option that may not be easy to pursue. In many of these cases there is a tendency for companies to concentrate instead on trying to more fully exploit their existing customer relationships by broadening their offerings. This was the strategy followed by Jack Walsh at General Electric when he added a wide range of service-based offerings to increase revenue in his existing relationships. The rationale for focusing on existing relationships lies in the typical pattern of profitability of customer relationships over time. Customer relationships are costly to develop, especially in the initial phase because of the costs of developing offerings and of mutual learning. Relationships tend to become more profitable at a later stage, as these initial investments in offerings and management efforts bear fruit. This depends of course on the company being able to control its costs of managing relationships.

Differential of the offering – *what*

This dimension of a company's strategy is difficult to assess or to manage. Yet the differential of its offering is at the core of a company's strategy. It is likely to be a main reason for a customer to use a supplier. It is essential to take the customer's point of view when assessing an offering differential, so as to explore what is *bought* and the value that is received, rather than simply what is *sold*. Customers choose and patronize suppliers for a wide range of reasons, depending on the nature of their problems and uncertainties. They will vary in the importance they attach to different elements of the offering as well as to the supplier's performance in fulfilling it and to their assessment of its trustworthiness, its resources and organization and the kind of relationship they have with it. Some will emphasize short-term financial issues, others will be more concerned with long-term consequences. It is not surprising that customers themselves often find it difficult to spell out their reasons for using one supplier rather than another.

The value that a particular customer receives from a supplier will depend on the following:

- The content of the offering received: product, service, logistics, advice, adaptation and its price. This offering depends on the supplier's problem-solving ability and in turn, on its skills and resources.
- The supplier's ability to fulfil this offering. This depends on its transfer ability.
- How the offering is used by the customer and how it relates to the customer's own offering and its wider operations.
- The nature of the relationship between the supplier and customer. This affects the design of the offering, its fulfilment and its use.
- The customer's wider context: its problems, uncertainties and its position in the network.

Customer perceptions are individual, subjective and, invariably subject to change over time as the circumstances change under which it operates. A supplier company can control the content of the offering to some extent, but it is often developed and adapted interactively between the companies. The context of the customer company is largely out of the supplier's control. This is why the assessment of the actual offering differential is complex and the identification of generic options is uncertain.

Figure 10.9 draws on the ideas on price, costs and value that we developed in Chapter 8 to provide a framework for reviewing the main options for developing offering-differential. Figure 10.9 makes the important separation between the value to the customer of the supplier's offering and the value to the customer of its relationship with the supplier. It also separates the customer's costs into "fixed" and "variable". Variable costs comprise the price paid for an offering and the costs of receiving and using it. The customer's fixed costs are also in two parts: the costs of managing and sustaining its relationship with the supplier and the general costs of its operations that will be allocated to this particular relationship.[9]

Assessing the value and costs of relationship, from a customer's perspective, is a useful analytical exercise even if it cannot be precisely quantified. For example, it may highlight that the supplier's dealings with a customer are currently very dependent on the value to that customer of its relationship with the supplier. Perhaps the current offering is actually providing little value when set against the price and other variable costs of the customer. In this sense the supplier could be "milking" the relationship and this poses obvious danger for its future. Alternatively, the supplier may find that the customer has high costs

---

[9] This breakdown of the elements of cost for the customer is the same as that which we used for the costs of the supplier in Chapter 8.

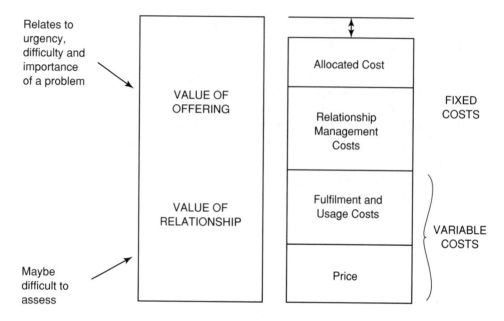

Figure 10.9 Value and costs of a customer's supplier relationship.

of managing the relationship, such as those of making adaptations and coping with problems caused by inefficient fulfilment by the supplier. This may mean that the gap between the combined value of the relationship and the offering and the customer's costs is narrowing.

Assessing offering differential requires knowledge and understanding of the business system of customers, of how the offering is used and how it is valued by the customers and the position of customers in the network. It can be useful in three ways:

- It can help to uncover problems in the supplier's current offerings and fulfilment and the customer's costs and point to options for improving these.
- It can highlight current problems in the supplier's relationship management and the effects of these on customers' valuation of their relationships. It can then point to options for improving these.
- It can point to appropriate action for the supplier in important individual relationships.

Formulating alternative strategies of differential offering is a problem that does not have an easy solution, because valuations of offering and relationship are always individual, subjective and changing. A supplier must continuously review its situation when compared to others and act, often by trial and error. However, in business markets suppliers can always count on some degree of initiative and involvement from their customers and both companies and the offering in their relationship are interactively developed. Customers often ask for, push for and even come with new designs for offerings themselves.

Customer variety and adaptation

Throughout this book we have emphasized that business marketers must cope with variations in customers and adapt to their requirements, but at the same time we have also emphasized how the pressure of costs makes it important for marketers to control and limit these adaptations. The framework in Figure 10.10 helps us to assess the variety in customer requirements and to explore the options available to a company at the strategic level. Figure 10.10 illustrates that in business markets the requirements that customers have of their suppliers typically vary on two dimensions: the problem-solving and transfer abilities of the supplier and the customer-specific adaptations that they require.

We saw in Chapter 6 that some customers require levels of problem-solving ability that are standard and common to most suppliers. Others may need problem-solving ability that is much higher and not mastered by all suppliers. Similarly, the requirements of customers for the transfer ability of suppliers can vary from the simple to the complex.

On the other dimension, some customers are satisfied with a standardized offering or fulfilment, or one that is within the supplier's normal range. Others require specific solutions adapted to their particular requirements. These differences are linked to features of a customer's business. They follow from differences in customers' use of an offering and in their strategic posture. Striving to be the "ideal" supplier for every kind of customer is likely to strain the costs of the company and require quite different organizational and technological resources. On the one hand, this means that suppliers must resist the temptation to offer more in all dimensions to all customers. On the other hand, it also means that many of a supplier's apparent competitors are not real ones for specific customers because their different positions in the matrix do not relate to those customers' *specific* requirements.

The framework illustrated in Figure 10.10 suggests four different avenues for developing the offering differential of a company:

- **Cell 1 Operational efficiency:** A supplier in this cell does not have strength in either or both of problem-solving ability and transfer ability nor does it have skills in adaptation. In this situation its strategy must be based on achieving efficiency in what it does. This may give it a competitive position based on low price with customers whose requirements are low on both dimensions.
- **Cell 2 Relationship development:** A supplier operating in this cell is following a strategy based on skills in adapting to the specific requirements of customers. This is likely to depend on its strong relationship-management skills, but also its flexibility in operations will be important. This strategy will be important to customers that place emphasis on the value of their relationships and suppliers' adaptations within them.
- **Cell 3 Offering/fulfilment excellence:** These suppliers are strong in problem-solving ability and transfer ability, but do not have a strong adaptation capability. This strategy of providing excellence in a standardized offering or fulfilment will be appropriate for customers who do not require adaptation in a relationship, but who place value on a supplier's offering.

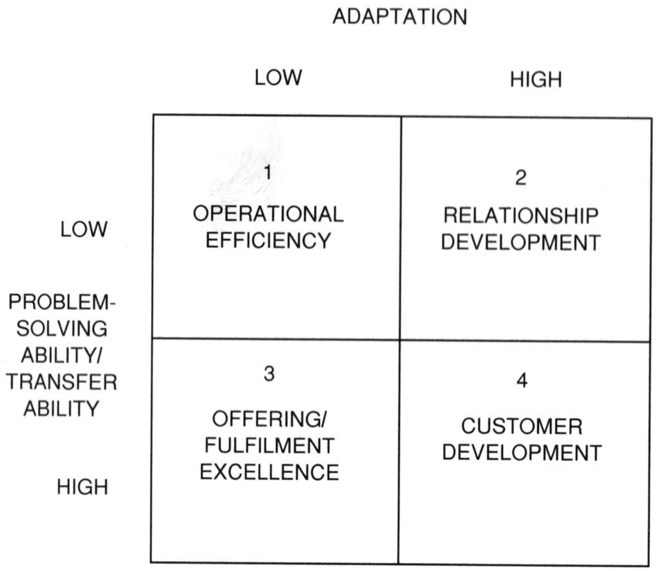

ADAPTATION

LOW   HIGH

	1 OPERATIONAL EFFICIENCY	2 RELATIONSHIP DEVELOPMENT
	3 OFFERING/ FULFILMENT EXCELLENCE	4 CUSTOMER DEVELOPMENT

LOW

PROBLEM-
SOLVING
ABILITY/
TRANSFER
ABILITY

HIGH

Figure 10.10   Customer requirements and supplier strategies.

- **Cell 4 Customer development:** Suppliers in this cell have the resources to be excellent in both problem-solving and transfer ability and also are able to adapt strongly. This strategy is likely to involve the supplier in high costs. It is appropriate for those customers with the most demanding and particular requirements.

Of course a supplier's position in this matrix is not fixed. A supplier can analyse its position on the matrix and relate this to available customers, the changes in their requirements and to the current and emerging position of its competitors. Following this, it can seek to invest resources to change position to one that relates more closely to target customers and/or that separates it from unwelcome competitors.

Technical and organizational arrangements – *how*

Most, if not all companies, struggle continuously with technical and organizational issues. Companies update their product and process technologies, commercial arrangements, organizational structure and support systems. This continuous process of organizing shapes the third dimension that characterizes the market strategy of a company, that we have termed "technological and organizational arrangements".

In Chapter 7 we explored some of the operational issues in fulfilling an offering. Any market strategy along the dimensions of customer scope and offering-differential requires investment in operational resources, product and process technology. Decisions to extend the current customer base, for example, by entering a new foreign market, or to give priority to adaptation or to excellence in offering or fulfilment will entail a series of other operational decisions and changes such as we have discussed. Any change or investment will have important cost considerations and will affect the financial performance of the company.

As with the two previous dimensions, there is no one right organizational and technical solution. But there are at least three criteria on which to assess the impact on economic performance of various organizational and technical solutions underlying a market strategy, as follows:

- **The cost criterion:** This is a rather obvious criterion, but it must not be limited to a concern for short-term cost efficiency. The same offering may be produced by different technologies, the same fulfilment achieved by a variety of operations. These will involve different cost levels and also different cost structures. Some approaches may incur high fixed costs, others will have high variable costs, but perhaps greater flexibility.
- **The commitment criterion:** Some technical or organizational approaches may tie the company into a particular set of relationships, operations, technologies or offerings for a long time. Others may allow much greater strategic flexibility.
- **The development criterion:** Different organizational and technical solutions, once adopted, tend to lead the attention of management in a certain direction and thereby limit the range of alternative options that will be identified. It is common to think that the organizational and technological solutions should match and follow the thrust of market strategy. The reality is more complex. Market strategy often "follows the structure", or as we have suggested in Chapter 3, market strategy often follows the technological strengths of the company.

Conclusion: Strategy Content and Process

The characteristics of business networks that we have explored throughout this book bring to the foreground the inter-dependence of the process and content of strategy. In such a context opportunities do not exist independently of ideas and the capabilities to construct and exploit new possibilities. Ready-made opportunities in business networks do not exist. Consequently, the content of a company's strategy and its competitive effects originate in the capacity of the company to understand the network in which it operates and to handle the process of strategy development.

An effective market strategy involves the capacity to find and enact new, more effective ways to organize activities and deploy resources *and work with others* whether they are customers, suppliers or development partners. The content of a strategy will be effective if it represents a novel or improved solution to customers' problems. But no successful strategy content remains a novel solution for long. This is not necessarily because of competitive action, but because no solution is ever the ultimate one and also because the problem for which it was developed will change or disappear. Thus an effective strategy content is a moving target. It requires the relentless search for further development, which is linked to the effectiveness of the strategy process itself. In this way, the content of strategy follows the process of its development.

Market strategies in business markets will always be a consequence of how the company organizes itself to monitor and induce change in relation to its customers. Nowhere is this more evident than in the company's approach to its strategic management and planning. This must involve those who take the decisions that shape the strategy content of the company, rather than be the province of a headquarters staff department. This is why we have emphasized in this chapter that the primary purpose of strategic management is not to outline a blueprint for strategy but to ensure continuous monitoring of possibilities and formulations of ideas to be developed.

Marketers must manage the processes of individual and collective learning, beyond simply that of gathering and distributing information. The models suggested in this chapter are one way for a company to read its market. Management must make this process of reading systematic and involve everyone in its interpretation.

Further Reading

Henry Mintzberg (1996) Five P's for Strategy, in Henry Mintzberg and James Brian Quinn, *The Strategy Process*, 3rd edition, New York, Prentice-Hall.

Henry Mintzberg (1998) Generic Strategies: Toward a Comprehensive Framework, *Advances in Strategic Management*, vol. 5, Greenwich CT, JAI Press, pp. 1–67.

Kenichi Ohmae (1989) The Global Logic of Strategic Alliances, *Harvard Business Review*, March–April, pp. 143–54.

RT Pascale, Perspectives on Strategy: The Real Story behind Honda's Success, *California Management Review*, vol. XXVI, 1994, pp. 47–72.

Michael Porter (1996) What is Strategy?, *Harvard Business Review*, November–December. pp. 61–78.

James Brian Quinn (1980) *Strategies for Change: Logical Incrementalism*, New York, Irwin.

Index

NEW
WELSHREADER

Finding a Place

New Welsh Reader
New Welsh Review Ltd
PO Box 170, Aberystwyth, SY23 1WZ
Telephone: 01970 628410
www.newwelshreview.com

Editor: Gwen Davies
editor@newwelshreview.com

Administration & Finance Officer:
Bronwen Williams
admin@newwelshreview.com

Marketing & Publicity Officer: Megan Farr
marketing@newwelshreview.com

Management Board: Ali Anwar, Gwen
Davies (Dir), Andrew Green (Dir, Ch),
Richard Gwyn, Ruth Killick, David Michael
(Dir, Treasurer), Richard Marggraf Turley,
Amy McCauley (Poetry Subs Editor,
V-Ch), Claire Flay-Petty.

Design: Ingleby Davies Design
Poetry Subs Filter: Gwen Davies
Cover photo: Odua Images, Shutterstock

Multimedia Assistants: Aled John &
Tomos Radford
Creative Industry Work Placement:
Meher Shiblee
Online Arts Editor: Daniel Leeman
(all Aberystwyth University)

Principal Sponsor & Host:
Aberystwyth University

New Welsh Review Ltd publishes with
the financial support of the Welsh Books
Council and Aberystwyth University (the
latter on an exclusive basis until April 2017).
New Welsh Review Ltd was established in
1988 by Academi (now Literature Wales)
and the Association for Welsh Writing in
English. *New Welsh Reader* is New Welsh
Review's magazine for creative work; we
also publish 8 e-editions annually of reviews
& comment.

Mae croeso ichi ohebu â'r golygydd
yn Gymraeg.

Patrons: Belinda Humfrey, Owen Sheers

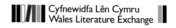

PEOPLE OF SHITPLACE
DUG OUR OWN HOLE

GWEN DAVIES

THE WIDER WORLD MUST HAVE A STRONG IMPRESSION OF BRITISH PEOPLE who now have turned away from change and difference, in work, culture and, perhaps especially, in language. It is dangerous to tell people what they should and shouldn't be afraid of, but really, there are greater threats out there than EU migrants. To environmental diversity, to vulnerable and minority cultures, to the Welsh language. Harm to the latter, however, comes not from globalisation, since it has readily adapted to technology, first with television, now on the twittersphere. Two delightful points were made in *Parch*, Fflur Dafydd's drama on S4C (series 2 reviewed in our November e-edition, subscriber package), through Oksana, a Russian migrant to the Carmarthenshire village of its setting. One is her disarming assumption that Welsh will be the medium of her UK 'citizenship test'; the second, that the Welsh-speaking family and community she marries into accepts and absorbs her differences of language and culture. Apparently Anglophone communities (including those in Welsh-speaking areas of Wales), despite being dominant in most scenarios, struggle to accept in this way. (This is the point that Mike Parker was trying to make in his 2001 *Planet* article whose distortion of which by the local paper lost him a Westminster seat, according to his recent book for Y Lolfa, T*he Greasy Poll: Diary of a Controversial Election*.)

The uninitiated may not easily class Ceredigion farmers as belonging to a threatened cultural and linguistic minority (and here I unashamedly point my finger at certain English environmentalists and nature writers). But, as Caryl Lewis' speech this summer as winner of the

Welsh-language category of Wales Book of the Year (with her novel, *Y Bwthyn*) made clear, that is what they are. Protectors of language and dialects, food culture, flora and fauna, of landscape and a way of life, who in turn should be championed. Lewis' speech, and indeed her fiction, deals with conservation. The subtleties of her speech, given in Welsh, must have been lost on the English category's judge Caroline Sanderson (of *The Bookseller*), who in her own address noted the cosmopolitanism of the English entries, and the winner, Thomas Morris' *We Don't Know What We're Doing*, in particular. This is *not* a situation in which WBOY's Welsh category winner is a 'Leave' novel bemoaning change and fearing loss, while the English winning novel takes us on Remain-worthy Dublin stag parties and alternative worlds. But the EU referendum result, announced only a few weeks previously, coloured my reception of the prize. It colours everything.

Including this issue. In spirit post-Brexit pieces abound, especially Liz Jones' memoir of how Merthyr Tudful waned in her affections amid tales of two-faced bullying of immigrants. While Kirsty Sedgman's essay analysing audience responses to National Theatre Wales productions *The Persians* and *For Mountain, Sand & Sea* shows how issues of universality and national or local relevance contrasted wildly across Wales, with Barmouth audiences scoring high on relevance while those within the theatre-going catchment area of Sennybridge put more weight on artistic quality. I judge these arguments to make a Brexit-voter type distinction, with 'universal' standing in for 'cosmopolitan' and 'artistic quality' for 'educated', while 'local relevance' represents a tentative or even latent patriotism. Finally, surely the inspiration for Jane Houston's biting, satirical '"Heartland"' must be Leave-land, Swansea or Lincoln variety? 'In this once-proud-now-shit / place no-one speaks a real language and people / live in dog years, girls popping out kids, / kids dripping off us all our lives. // People of shitplace dug our own hole, / revel in the muck of it and ready for worse. / If we vote it is with eyes on the sky, / spotting flotillas passing like dark clouds.'

www.newwelshwritingawards.com
#NewWelshAwards

NEW
WELSH WRITING
AWARDS
2017

ABERYSTWYTH UNIVERSITY
PRIZE FOR MEMOIR
* * *
AMERICYMRU PRIZE
FOR THE NOVELLA

* * * PRIZES FOR EACH CATEGORY * * *

First Prize: £1000 Cash, e-publishing deal and
critique with a top literary agent
Second Prize: Week residential writing course at
Tŷ Newydd Writing Centre
Third Prize: Weekend writing retreat at Gladstone's Library

Judges: Gwen Davies and David Lloyd
Closing date: 1 March 2017

Full terms and conditions at www.newwelshwritingawards.com

 PRIFYSGOL ABERYSTWYTH UNIVERSITY

 americymru

 CURTIS BROWN

 Canolfan Ysgrifennu Tŷ Newydd Writing Centre

 GLADSTONE'S LIBRARY

THE ACCIDENTAL THREAD

ELUNED GRAMICH

In writing, as with any creative activity, there will always be a gap between what you intended to produce and the final result. The finished piece is not necessarily any worse or better than what was originally planned, just different. Often this difference adds something new, an element of the unexpected. Jonathan Franzen's *The Corrections* was originally the story of Andy Aberant: a character who 'twice failed to make the cut'. Hundreds of pages about Andy were put to one side in favour of his family, the Lamberts, who 'kept getting larger and larger'. Was it Franzen's intention to write about the Lamberts? No. In some ways, *The Corrections* was not what he intended at all; and yet by writing about Andy, Franzen found his subject, following the narrative like Theseus follows the thread out of the labyrinth.

For me, the most pleasurable stage of writing is the 'thinking time'. This is the best part, because in my mind the novel is, needless to say, brilliant. When I start writing, I quickly realise that thoughts are not the same as words; dreams are not chapters, and sentences are never as obedient as I would have liked. Most unruly and finicky of all are the characters. Like Franzen's Andy, the characters do what they want.

I've noticed that one of the common tics writers have is to talk about their characters as if they are real people. You might hear them say, 'She

> There is nothing good about being shut up within your own designs, as there is nothing good about being locked inside a room.

just popped into my head and started talking to me!' for instance. Before *Notes from the Other Room*, the only novel I've ever finished, I'd always regarded this spiel as a little fake, a bit of put-on eccentricity. Characters don't speak, they're not real, I thought. In any case, I never believed in this mystical side of writing. Writing is hard work.

But then came Catrin and Toru: characters I have been dreaming about for years, who have become as real to me as anyone. Just as with real people, my intentions – that pure, indulgent thought-world – had to be compromised to make way for their will and motives. I learnt that you can't make a character do anything they wouldn't (usually?) do, so no matter how strong your vision might be, you are still subject to those inhabiting your fictional world. It is not possible, in other words, to plan a novel from beginning to end if you want your characters to have a life of their own.

A life of their own is at the heart of the story I decided to write. It began in Japan, the Shinjuku Gyoen Gardens to be exact, a secluded park in Tokyo. It was July. The blossoms were long gone, replaced by a slowly intensifying humidity. I was walking with a Japanese friend – let's call him S – an interesting, very private person. So when S mentioned his family (just this once, briefly), I listened. 'My parents don't speak to me any more,' he said. 'They want me to look after my older brother who has social problems. But I can't.' The brother had dropped out of school, was jobless, friendless; refused to have anything to do with the outside world. His parents were desperate for a solution and tried to make S shoulder responsibility. I didn't think much about it at the time, but I must have stored the comments away because even though S and I lost contact, the figure of the brother kept coming back to me. He's probably still living with his parents now while his younger sibling is carving out a life for himself as best he can.

Hikikomori is the name for young people (typically men aged 16–25) who lock themselves away in their rooms and eschew human contact. The story of S was not the only one I heard in Japan where hikikomorism is a widespread problem. When I returned to Wales, the shadow of the hikkomori followed me, the faint outline of a character. My original intention was to write about south Wales, yet this figure would always be there, standing outside the door of my study, waiting to be let in. I tried to appease him by putting him in a story under the name Toru ['Pulling Out', published in the collection *New Welsh Short Stories*, Seren], but he came back and walked straight into my book and, like the Lamberts, 'grew larger and larger' until he took centre stage, my original plans abandoned.

Writing is as much about chance as it is about restriction and discipline. It is as much about the characters' freedom to move and develop as it is about the perfect chapter. There is nothing good about being shut up within your own designs, as there is nothing good about being locked inside a room. One day you have to leave it. You have to follow the character, the accidental thread, and be strong enough to put the carefully planned plot aside in favour of the unexpected. For your characters' sake, and for your own.

This summer **Eluned Gramich**'s debut nonfiction title, *Woman Who Brings the Rain: A Memoir of Hokkaido, Japan*, was published by New Welsh Rarebyte in print format, when its epub version was shortlisted for the 2016 Wales Book of the Year.

THE PLANNERS' VISION OF RHIWBINA, C1912 (ALL EFFORTS WERE MADE TO SECURE COPYRIGHT)

LOOKING FOR
DOROTHY EDWARDS

STEVEN LOVATT VISITS RHIWBINA IN AN ATTEMPT
TO EXPLAIN THEMES OF DETACHMENT AND
UNREALITY IN THE AUTHOR'S WORK.

It's essential to the narrative microclimates of Dorothy Edwards' stories that nothing very much seems to take place in them, but if the phrase 'to take place' were interpreted literally, then it might also signify – in the horticultural sense of 'take' – the idea of becoming rooted or established somewhere in particular. And in this sense too, her stories give the impression of never quite taking place. Tony Brown notes their 'curiously non-specific locations', while Christopher Meredith refers simply to 'Edwardsland', a moniker which humorously figures her story collection, *Rhapsody*, as a theme park, where the 'theme', presumably, is human misery.

But care is needed. The title of Edwards' unpublished poem, 'Sunday in Ilkley', suggests that she had no aversion to using and naming real places. Certainly it would be unwise to assume that the stories' locations are entirely fantastic. If that were true, it would contradict the well-founded critical consensus that there is much more of Edwards' life in her fictions than first appears; but enough is known about her movements to encourage occasionally rewarding detective work about the locations that inspired her. So, for example, the clifftop ruin in 'A Garland of Earth' is certainly Dunskey Castle in Wigtownshire, which Edwards visited in the mid 1920s. Any attempt to account for the peculiar detachment of the *Rhapsody* locations, and the spiritual restlessness of their characters, by reference to Edwards' own life must inevitably be more speculative, but I think that it's possible to venture helpful forays in that direction.

To begin with, the Edwards criticism has perhaps not made enough of the unreality of Rhiwbina, to which Edwards and her mother Vida moved from Ogmore Vale following the death of her father in 1919. Envisioned by a Chepstow architect and established by committee, the village was then less than eight years old, and still damp from the draughtsman's ink. Their own house at 9 Pen y Dre was yet younger. Even the name Pen y Dre was new, the thoroughfare on which it was superimposed having previously been known as Homfray Road, after the family of exploitative English iron magnates. When the planners moved in they changed the

DUNSKEY CASTLE, WIGTOWNSHIRE, 1930s

name to something more benign (and more Welsh). During the construction of Pen y Dre, for fear of winter flooding (but, it is easy to suppose, also out of the same mania for straight lines that is evident in the plans for the village), the planners even canalised the Rhydwaedlyd Brook, which still flows alongside the road. I increasingly think that Dorothy Edwards may have been haunted by blueprints, not only in the narrow sense of the highly technical and stylised experiments that her stories resemble, but also because the unreality of Rhiwbina, grafted on to the side of the plain north of Cardiff, became a formative model for the displacement that is felt so strongly in the stories and in her own life. If we add that Edwards herself was 'grafted' onto Rhiwbina by circumstance, not choice, and that Frederick Stibbs, upon whom Edwards later became transfixed as a father-substitute, was on the committee that founded the village, we

HAFOD BY WILLIAM TURNER

begin to get an idea of how the insecurity of the place may have pursued her throughout her life.

Edwards' stories are full of landscapes but she rarely calls them that, having instead a strong preference for 'scenery'. This word, with its connotations of spectacle and artifice, came into the English language in the 1770s, when it would have often been on the lips of Thomas Johnes, who in that decade first began planning his Gothic country house at Hafod, on his father's Cardiganshire estate. This fantastic building, embellished with planned grounds complete with grottoes and vantage points intended to satisfy the eighteenth-century taste for the Miltonic sublime, became famous among the aesthetic cognoscenti of the day, and in the early 1790s it was visited and committed to canvas by William Turner. Commenting on the painting, Max Schulz has written, in language that could easily be applied to the settings in *Rhapsody*, that the house, 'for all its impressive size... gives off a fragile air of insubstantiality... as if its hold on reality were tenuous.' The story of Hafod, built at around the same time as the Homfrays were establishing their foundries near Merthyr, provides another example of how landscapes formed in the imagination can then be projected onto reality. It is also, of course, a prime example of how English visions have been (super)imposed upon the Welsh countryside. This is something that Edwards, with her keen patriotism, would have been well aware of, and it is easy to believe that something of this awareness informs her stories' almost obsessive concern with aesthetic fabrication and misperception.

In a letter of the early 1930s, Edwards compares the life of her English Bloomsbury acquaintances to 'a beautiful coloured not very meaningful canvas', which upon her return to Wales she is aware of having 'slipp[ed] behind' to an existence in which she was aware of 'great depth of feeling'. In her story, 'Treachery in a Forest', written some years earlier, Edwards consciously plays with the metaphor of a canvas, in a passage in which the characters – all of whom have English-sounding names – vie with one another to impose their visions upon a tract of forest. Mrs Harding sets down her easel to paint the forest, and to the irritated amusement of her husband and within earshot of the 'hero', Mr Wendover, declares that a large tree that should occupy the middle of the canvas will have to be excluded from the picture. Mr Harding demurs, and can't let the matter rest:

> 'In any case, you know, Lizzie, I can't understand you painting a thing like that. Now if I wanted to paint this forest I should put in all the trees at least [!], and a king and some princes going hunting, and heralds, and certainly a princess on a white horse, and a unicorn behind one of the trees. Wouldn't you?' he asked Mr Wendover.
>
> 'Oh no!' said Mr Wendover eagerly. 'I would have a woodland scene by Bach, with Diana, and her attendants in gaiters and bare knees, and feathers in their hats.'

While the staffage of these fantasies might seem absurd, what Harding and Wendover are doing is essentially no different from what Thomas Johnes sought to do at Hafod. If Bloomsbury and Hafod are not real, they can nevertheless be lived in. The question that Edwards raises but leaves unanswered becomes, then, whether it is possible to inhabit a fantasy for very long without risking permanent damage to one's 'depth of feeling'. This question is pertinent not only to one's 'feeling' for places, of course, but also to one's feeling for other people. Throughout her work, Edwards emphasises the correspondence between failures to perceive the reality of places, failures of visual perspective and failures of emotional 'in-sight'; which is as much to say that the stories are preoccupied with follies, of one sort or another.

In 'Sweet Grapes', Hugo Ferris, holidaying for the summer, rents part of a building 'rather like a castle, but quite obviously built in Victoria's time'. His landlady for the duration of the holiday has a cousin staying with her, a 'girl' of nineteen called Elizabeth, who is attracted to Ferris but whose feelings he either disregards or exploits as a temporary means of combatting what we are told is boredom but suspect is a form of emotional paralysis that immures him within his ego as surely as the stone folly confines his movements. Halfway through the story, Elizabeth persuades the reluctant Ferris to accompany her up the staircase to one of the building's castellated towers:

> But, as a matter of fact, there was nothing to be seen from the top of the tower which could not be seen from the ground, because the house was so high up in any case. And since the tower was exactly the same height as the rest of the house, and there was besides, at the other end, another tower exactly like it, there was no sensation of being far above everyone. The only thing was that perhaps that by slowly turning one could see all the views in turn, and this gave one a better impression of the lines of the hills curving into one another. Ferris began to feel a little bored.

This bleakly funny scene, with its ironic take on the genre of historical romance, extracts comedy from the lengths to which Ferris is reported to go in order to obtain perspective from the non-towering tower. When, in the following passage, Ferris reacts only with bored amusement as

Elizabeth kisses him, an implicit parallel is being drawn between the one-dimensionality of the visual perspective and his inability to respond to her emotionally.

In his analysis of the form and structure of fairy tales, the Swiss academic Max Lüthi stressed what he saw as the necessary connection between the 'depthlessness' of their representation of reality and the one-dimensionality of their characters. Lüthi writes of the 'astonishing insensitivity' which in fairy tales characterises the relations between the quotidian, on the one hand, and the events and characters of what he calls the 'otherworld', on the other. In her letters, Edwards – who confessed to a fascination with the formal properties of fairy tales – refers more than once to the transformative potential of love, and to the tragedy of people's tendency to imprison themselves within the 'invisible cages' of their narrowly defined selves. In 'Sweet Grapes', Elizabeth represents just such transformative potential, but as Lüthi points out, it is a condition of the 'everyday' characters in fairy tales that they are oddly isolated both from surrounding reality and from 'otherworldly' beings such as the passionate Elizabeth represents for the emotionally incarcerated Ferris:

> *A depthless depiction of reality implies a need to isolate the figures portrayed.... The characters depicted in folktales have no inner life, no environment, no relationship to past or future generations, no relationship to time.... The dominant characteristic of this abstract style is the element of isolation.... Isolated human beings and isolated otherworld beings meet, associate, and part; there is no sustained relationship between them. They only interact as participants in the plot and are not linked by any real and thereby lasting interest.*

I would suggest that Lüthi's linking, here, of emotional isolation to the absence of a real 'environment', gets close to the heart of Edwards' curious treatments of character and place.

Throughout her stories, then, Edwards explores the ways in which inhabitable ideals of reality are constructed out of a complex interplay between perception and imagination. This theme is treated most thoroughly and subtly in 'Days', which is, among other things, a sustained inquiry into the nature of the relationship between life and art, and of the constitutive role played in both by narrative and visual perception. The first paragraph of the story is worth quoting in full:

> *Mr George Morn, the novelist, began to write about the people and the scenes of the district around his old home only when he was already over forty, and almost as soon as he had begun to be recognised for these novels as a very great artist, it suddenly seemed to him that all he should ever want for the rest of his life would be to live among these old scenes and he immediately bought a house a few miles away from the house where he was born, and since then he has hardly been seen or heard of.*

This paragraph is so exemplary of Edwards' style and interests that it could be made the subject of an essay in itself. It consists of a single, wonderfully balanced one hundred-word sentence, in which the characteristic surface tension of her narratives is generated by the opposition between the prim, deliberate commas and the breathless use of 'and'. It is, moreover, not only both a sentence and a paragraph, but also a complete fairy tale in itself, its final clause employing a conventional fairy-tale ending to be found, for example, in the Grimms' 'Clever Elsie' and 'The Master-Thief'.

For present purposes, though, of most interest is Edwards' thrice-repeated use of the word 'scene' (we should, of course, most definitely include the homophone 'seen') to describe the district around George Morn's new house. The choice of this word foreshadows the story's concern with aesthetics and reality. More particularly, in its destabilising of the boundary between life and art, it prepares the reader for the obsession of Alexander Sorel, one of the story's principal characters, whose chief peculiarity is that he regards the fictional world of Morn's novels as more real than the actual landscape and people in front of him. Sorel goes with Morn's wife to visit a house in the nearby village, explaining to its elderly occupant, Tom Burgess, that "'I wanted to see this house because the heroine of one of [Morn's] novels once lived here,'" to which Burgess replies 'doubtfully' that "'My family has always lived here as far back as anyone remembers.'" It's worth noting that Tom Burgess is perhaps the only one of Dorothy Edwards' characters who is a 'character' also in the colloquial sense of someone whose personality and quirks have been formed 'organically' by his long inhabitation of a particular place. Alone among the uprooted, modern people of the *Rhapsody* stories, Burgess belongs, in a place and a community. It is therefore all the more startling how easily Sorel exploits Burgess' doubt and persuades him to rearrange his bedroom furniture so that its lay-out more closely resembles that of the fictional room in Morn's novel. In this passage and many others in 'Days', Edwards seems to be questioning what it means to be of a place, instead of merely in it. Returning to the story's opening paragraph, it is revealing that Morn returns to live '*among* these old scenes', this choice of word implying the necessary apartness of the artist but also perhaps, and less consciously on Edwards' part, her own experience of being in a place (which might be Rhiwbina, Wales, or the cosmos), without ever being able to fully feel that she belonged there.

Rhiwbina still seems pretty well heeled. There are plenty of independent shops alongside the chains, and by my unscientific reckoning, plaster gnomes and other garden tat is outnumbered three to one by aloof wooden rocking-horses staring down blankly from the large front-bedroom windows. A mood of gentility endures. 'Shorty', the village graffiti tagger, keeps to a lazy radius, and I suppose that his monopoly has made him complacent. I walk through the village and up Rhiwbina Hill, where Edwards also often walked, particularly when she needed to exorcise her depression. Now the M4 slices through its midriff. The hill and those around it are thickly wooded, although in the 1930s they were almost

RHIWBINA HILL, 1930S (ALL EFFORTS WERE MADE TO SECURE COPYRIGHT)

bare. Not even hills stay the same. To the right is the Wenallt, upon which Edwards wished to rent a cottage in the final year of her life. Here, in a farmland gap just before the trees thicken, is something I hadn't expected: turning, there is a view across Cardiff and, beyond, the sea. The sea, and symbolically unimpeded horizons more generally, are rare presences in the close worlds of Edwards' stories, and it is a mild shock to think that Edwards, bound to Pen y Dre by her ill mother, must often have turned around hereabouts to watch the sea. I have to step backwards into the squeaking wild garlic leaves as an electrician's van accelerates into the dark corridor under the trees, and then I continue to the top of the hill, only to find that it isn't the top at all, but that another summit lies beyond, so that I can only imagine the landscape on the other side. By now, in any case, the sun is beginning to set, so I walk back down to

RHIWBINA HILL, 2016, BY THE AUTHOR

the railway station, past 9 Pen y Dre, from within which a light now shines weakly into the dusk. My train is delayed, so I walk back to the village and into a bookshop, where I find a recent book called *Remarkable Rhiwbinans: 18 Lives*. The book is informative and well produced, but Dorothy Edwards isn't to be found among the eighteen. Neither, I discover later (and in contrast to the former home of Kate Roberts) has 9 Pen y Dre been embossed with a blue memorial plaque. Much as I would wish that to change, perhaps after all it is more fitting that Edwards' presence in the village should be best represented by her absence.

Steven Lovatt teaches at the universities of Bristol and Bath.

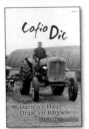

SET OF THE PERSIANS: FARROWS CREATIVE

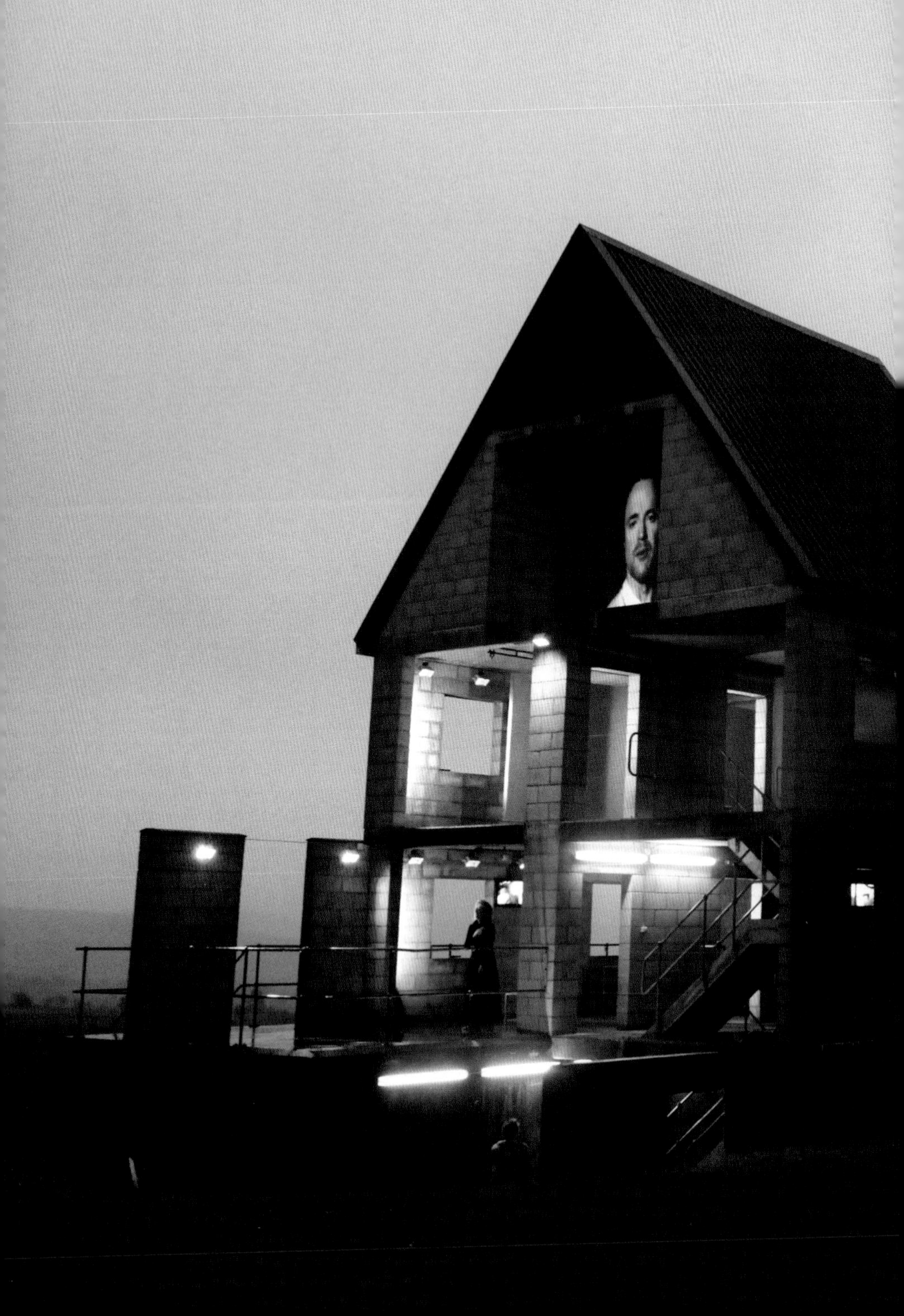

THE APE ON THE ROCK

KIRSTY SEDGMAN REPORTS HOW
UNIVERSALITY & NATIONAL OR LOCAL
RELEVANCE ARE THE CONTRASTING
VALUES SOUGHT BY NATIONAL THEATRE
WALES AUDIENCES IN DIFFERENT PARTS
OF THE COUNTRY

IN TAXIS AND NIGHTCLUBS. ON RAILWAY BRIDGES AND IN LIBRARIES. Walking through a British military range in the Brecon Beacons, or investigating a terraced house near Snowdon. From March 2010 to March the following year, theatre audiences could be spotted throughout the nation exploring the everyday places and extraordinary landscapes of Wales.

That was the inaugural year of National Theatre Wales. Launched in 2009 as an English-language national theatre company, NTW still work out of their base office in Cardiff yet have remained emphatically peripatetic, making performances in unusual spaces and setting out to 'engage communities' by embedding local people within the theatre-making process. Their opening season carried across this mobile playfulness into the audience invitation. Together with NTW we were encouraged to roam: to walk over beaches and up mountains; to journey through urban and rural spaces; to explore place through performance, and performance through place; and, in doing so, to piece together our own ideas about the nation. More specifically: NTW asked us to ask not what Wales *means*, but what it means *to us*.

As a PhD researcher at Aberystwyth University I spent that year studying audiences' responses to NTW's productions. I was interested in how different people reacted to this new company at the moment of its formation. How did they see the role of NTW within the nation? What was its place in their lives? And how did they understand the intricate lines NTW was drawing between people, performance, and place?

The findings from this project later went into my book *Locating the Audience* (Intellect Books), in which I explained how people found value in their experiences of NTW's productions. This was reviewed in *Review 7* (newwelshreview.com/article.php?id=1182, April 2016 e-edition) – and in many ways found wanting. Sophie Baggott's review suggested that interesting insights were swamped by swathes of academic theory, with the focus on statistics and linguistics making it a rather difficult read. Well here's what I say to you, Sophie Baggott: you are right.

For complicated reasons, *Locating the Audience* always had to be an academic book. It's therefore written in a style I like to call 'academicese', unpicking the minutiae of audiences' responses to theatrical events and going deeply into methodology in a way that only 100 people on the planet might enjoy. I'm not proud of it. This was a pragmatic choice: for better or worse it's what universities require, and as an unemployed early-career researcher I needed to play the game. But here's the curious thing. To other academics my writing often seems *too* accessible. This is because it focuses on people's lived experiences of art rather than relying on abstract philosophical theories. For some people it's too dense; for others, not enough.

Why is this significant? Because it's a timely example of precisely what my research set out to show. Our assessments (of books, art, theatre) are totally bound up in our subject positions – who we are, where we come from, the kinds of things we know, and so on. How we judge something depends on the systems of criteria we use to judge it.

This might sound obvious, but actually it's something the study of theatre still hasn't fully understood. In 2009, Helen Freshwater's book *Theatre & Audience* (Palgrave Macmillan) confronted performance scholars for listening only to academics and critics. This means that we tend to talk about theatrical events as if they're essentially 'good', 'bad', or something in between: as if our opinions are unquestionably the right ones. On the contrary, it is pretty clear that actually one person's delight is another's disapproval. People like things in different ways and for different reasons, but only certain judgments are considered worthy of regard. Instead of elevating only the voices of experts, Freshwater called for a research approach that asks 'ordinary' audience members – those with 'no professional stake' in theatre – what they make of a performance.

That's where I come in. As an audience researcher I talk *to* audiences rather than *about* them. Instead of boiling the value of art down to a set of expert commentaries, I draw together a range of reactions from diverse subject positions and identify patterns in how audiences talk. The aim is always to map complexity rather than reducing it, unveiling the connections between people's understandings of cultural institutions, their senses of self-identity, and their ideas about community, location, and nation.

These things come into sharper focus when considered through the lens of Welsh national theatre history. Their 2009 launch made NTW the culmination of decades of debates about the need – or otherwise – for an English-speaking national theatre in Wales. Where should it be located? How and for whom should it operate? A useful summary can be found in Anwen Jones' book, *National Theatres in Context* (UWP), so I won't go into these ideas here. But it's worth understanding the ferocity of these arguments, which tended to question why Wales needed a national theatre in the first place. After all, performance isn't what Wales *does*, it's what it *is* – through eisteddfodau, chapel choristry, *cerdd dant*: activities such as singing and oratory have been embedded in the life of the nation. Wouldn't a central institution risk imposing imperial cultural models on a place with an already rich performance heritage? And how can such a multifaceted nation be represented by a single organisation without belying its complexity?

In *New Welsh Review* 85 (Autumn 2009), founding NTW artistic director John E McGrath's article 'Rapid Response' began to address these concerns. The challenge was to find ways of telling stories about the nation without claiming to 'represent' it: asking what being in Wales means to people without asserting specific notions of national identity, talking *with* people rather than *for* them. This sometimes feels like 'dancing into a minefield', McGrath said. His answer? Perhaps to start with *place*. Through their theatrical map of Wales, NTW's launch year included thirteen productions in thirteen locations, often made in collaboration with local communities and produced by various creative teams. Practitioners from Mike Pearson to Michael Sheen asked what different places mean to different people, and then fed the answers into their productions in ever-questioning ways.

But what about when audiences themselves come into an event with specific ideas about location and how it should be represented? My re-

FOR MOUNTAIN, SAND & SEA, BREAK, JORGE LIZALDE

search explored what happens when people's expectations either con-
curred or conflicted with practitioners' intentions. It did so via around
800 questionnaires and 40 interviews, which together sought to capture
information about both audiences' pre-performance hopes and their
post-show responses. And it found a number of interesting things.

Firstly, people tended to rate NTW's production very highly. My
post-show questionnaire asked people to talk about one of the thirteen
shows that made up NTW's launch year – and of all the responses I received, two-thirds thought the event they'd seen was 'Excellent'. Of the
remaining third, almost everyone rated the production 'Good', with only
a handful choosing the options 'Average' or 'Poor'. Only four people out
of 558 post-show questionnaires rated it 'Very Poor'. However, in and
amongst this overall positivity it was possible to identify some instances
of ambivalence. So what I wanted to know was this. What might make
some people consider a performance an unqualified success where others
found it problematic?

The first task was to identify differences between the thirteen shows

FOR MOUNTAIN, SAND & SEA: CAI TOMOS & JOANIE WILLIAMS, WARREN ORCHARD

themselves. Without getting bogged down in data, it's important to point out here that the majority of responses came from three case-study productions: *For Mountain, Sand & Sea* (June/July 2010), *The Persians* (August 2010), and *Outdoors* (February 2011–12). For that reason *Locating the Audience* doesn't claim to be a comprehensive survey of NTW's theatrical yield. Nonetheless, what the broader scope of my questionnaire offered was a useful chance to read across a range of events and to identify certain differences: both in the *kinds* of audiences they attracted, and the *ways* people reacted to them. Why is this important? Because until recently, we've tended to assume that 'cultural value' is something we can measure. Just think about the words we use: impact, benefit, outcome. These all suggest that value is something audiences carry with them when they leave the theatre, inflexible and fixed, when actually there's evidence to suggest that our experiences change as we continue to think and talk about them. Value, in other words, is not an end-point. It's a process. My

Juanie

FOR MOUNTAIN, SAND & SEA: GIRL WITH LIGHT, WARREN ORCHARD

job is to listen to audiences: to pay attention as they reach for words to describe the ineffable, to hear not just *what* they say but *how* they say it, and to consider how people's reactions are inflected by the subject positions they take up. By doing this, I believe we can get a sense of the meaning-making process in action.

For example, see the varying responses I captured to *For Mountain, Sand & Sea* and *The Persians*. These were very different kinds of experience: the first a walking tour of Barmouth punctuated by snippets of performance art; the second a modern adaptation of Aeschylus' ancient Greek text staged on Sennybridge military range in the Brecon Beacons. I gathered around the same number of questionnaires for each (196 and 211 respectively), and yet the tenor of responses was markedly dissimilar. One of the things I asked audiences to do was to choose up to three 'orientations' from a list of thirteen. Including options like 'Academic Interest', 'Curiosity', and 'Dragged Along!', these asked people to think about how their motivations for attending connected with their senses of self. While over half of *The Persians'* audiences thought of themselves as a 'Theatre Lover', attendees of *For Mountain, Sand & Sea* were more likely to choose 'Welsh Life & Culture' or 'Supporter of Local Events'. What *this* told me was that something interesting might be underpinning audiences' prior expectations. In other words: was *For Mountain, Sand & Sea* expected to be a particularly 'local' or 'Welsh cultural' event, and what might these categories actually mean in practice? And how did *The Persians* stack up as a specific piece of theatre for people who love the artform in general?

The Persians was almost unanimously successful, with 80% rating it 'Excellent' compared to 64% of *For Mountain, Sand & Sea's* respondents. By themselves these numbers are admittedly pretty meaningless: after all, my 'Excellent' may well be someone else's 'Average'. So what's really interesting is *why The Persians* was so popular. How did people articulate the value of this event? It was clear that most people saw *The Persians* as having little national cultural relevance. Comments like 'Good drama should be relevant to people in every country' and 'Relevant is an entirely bogus notion in relation to theatre. Just do good stuff' show how comfortable these audiences were in judging what makes theatre 'good' (or otherwise). Here, NTW's capacity to engage with ideas of local identity was less important than the ability of theatre generally to tap into a kind of essential humanity. Instead, what audiences appreciated was the sense that *The Persians* had looked beyond Wales to the 'universal'.

In comparison, *For Mountain, Sand & Sea's* audiences often attended precisely because they wanted to see local history played out on a national stage. It's important here to remember that in many ways this was a show *about* Barmouth. Its curator, Marc Rees, spent an admirable amount of time in town during the months beforehand, running what he called Story Shops, in which local residents were invited to come and share their memories and images of Barmouth. This information was then used as creative inspiration for the team of international performance artists, who, together with a number of local volunteers, staged aspects of local history in unusual spaces. Audiences were guided up hills, around alley-ways, over bridges and beaches, into a nightclub and through Barmouth's Sailors' Institute, with snatches of performance spilling around them as they walked. Some of these extracts dealt with local stories didactically, as performers thoroughly narrated the history of certain characters or plac-es. Others were summarised in a programme handed out at the end of the show. However, quite a lot of this three-hour journey dealt with Bar-mouth's identity in fragmentary, abbreviated, or abstruse ways. Take, for instance, the moment where a performer in an ape mask climbed a rock, brandishing a bone slow-motion to the *2001: A Space Odyssey* theme. Or another scene in which two performers recited text from the 1946 film, *A Matter of Life and Death*. These deliberately ambiguous nods to moments in Barmouth's history (such as Darwin's walks around town when writing *On the Origin of Species*, or a WWII plane crash) were not always under-stood by audiences. In other words, while *The Persians* was praised for *not* being locally focused or 'inward looking', this was precisely what many audience members anticipated from *For Mountain, Sand & Sea.*

So what? Well, when people expressed disappointment that the 'rel-evance' or 'significance' of scenes to Barmouth had been deliberately under-explained, they tended to be those with little experience of this kind of avant-garde event. A cluster of audience members came precisely to see known stories performed in understandable ways. Meanwhile, *For Mountain, Sand & Sea* invited audiences to play around with fragments of history and create their own picture from the pieces. When places with interesting histories were skirted over, or when they were asked to salute with lilos to the Mawddach Monster, confusion was therefore often co-loured by a sense that maybe they *weren't the right kind of person to judge*. Here's where my focus on audience talk came in handy. In certain inter-views I identified a circling kind of rhetoric, which brought people with significant local knowledge to the brink of criticising *For Mountain, Sand & Sea* – and back again. For example, one person moved from sharing an interesting story about Barmouth to the suggestion that 'perhaps they didn't want to portray that, perhaps they were trying to portray something else, the theatre, I don't know'. What does this tell us? That when local expertise conflicts with NTW's professional theatrical expertise, it often loses the battle.

This is important because of what it says about audiences more generally. People who don't see themselves as 'theatre experts' (to borrow a term from one of my respondents) may be attracted to new experiences through local engagement – but risk alienation when their ideas of place become destabilised. Moreover, my research showed how easy it is for audiences to disconfirm their own responses. This all boils down to a question about legitimacy. Who believes they have the right to speak about theatre and in what ways? So when I closed *Locating the Audience* by urging theatre-makers to 'listen to your audiences', I wanted to stop inadvertently feeding into the sense that certain people's responses do not 'count', or at least count less than others. Because as NTW's work has continued to show us, theatre isn't a one-way street. It's an ongoing conversation with nation, in which everyone is invited to take part.

Kirsty Sedgman's book, *Locating the Audience: How People Found Value in National Theatre Wales,* was published earlier this year by Intellect. As a lecturer and British Academy postdoctoral fellow at the University of Bristol, she is currently undertaking a three-year research project studying regional theatre audiences. kirstysedgman.com

THE PRICE OF BUTTER

LIZ JONES ON LOSING HER
HOME TOWN OF MERTHYR, POST BREXIT

IT WAS THE 1975 REFERENDUM ON EUROPE AND I WAS BARELY OLD ENOUGH to vote. I had landed a job as a polling clerk in Merthyr; a stream of old ladies would come in, shake the rain off their umbrellas (it poured all day) and announce that they had come out to vote against Europe. It was a terrible idea, they'd say, butter would go up to 50 pence a half pound. I smiled and nodded, but inside I was hugging myself. Butter or not, I felt certain that the mood, among young people at least, had shifted. Europe, which seemed almost as big as the world itself, was opening its arms and welcoming us to the party. It almost seemed that once we were there the weather itself would pick up. I'd never heard of the Treaty of Rome, had no idea of what joining Europe actually *meant*. That didn't stop me loving the *idea* of it. I was besotted with all that it represented: youth; freedom; cooperation between nations; culture, along with less noble dreams of cheap wine, cheap holidays and olive-skinned French and Italian boys.

And so I became part of a generation that came of age with Europe; with the casual assumption that it would always be there, always be open to us.

Memory is a shifting, soothing mirage.

Now, when I myself am not so far off from the age of those nice old ladies, I am still a little in love with the idea of Europe. Yet in Merthyr, Middlesbrough, Bradford, Peterborough and all the post-industrial towns across Wales and England, people like me who came of age with the EU have elected to stamp it out. And this time it wasn't about the price of butter.

Returning to Merthyr for the first time in years, I call in at the Red House arts centre (its name a nod to the building's previous life as the red-brick Town Hall.) I remember it in its original incarnation, still glowing with late nineteenth-century municipal pride. Upstairs, its centrepiece stained-glass windows told of workers' struggles and red flags in the breeze. I knew those windows. Every Thursday my gran would take me along and we would queue up together for her home-help's pay packet (working for the council was a dream come true, a huge leap forward from what she called her 'charring' jobs.) The windows' feverish scenes would hold me like a cinema epic; I would lose myself in them up to the moment when she would collect her money and we would go to Zanelli's for an ice cream.

Memory is a soothing tale we whisper to ourselves when we can't sleep at night.

At the Red House 'Heroes and Villains' café (paninis and homemade soups), the wall is covered with a cheerfully random montage of faces and names: a roll call from Merthyr's history (I *think* the 'heroes and villains' tag is tongue-in-cheek). William Crawshay (ironmaster), Harri Webb (poet), Eddie Thomas (boxer and boxing manager), Jack Jones (writer), Joseph Parry (musician and composer), Laura Ashley (clothes designer and entrepreneur), SO Davies (rebel Labour MP, deselected and re-elected as an independent socialist) and others are all jumbled non-judgementally together.

With its theatre and workshops, dance studios, gallery and café, the Red House is a picture-perfect regeneration story. Downstairs, a project room, filled with artwork by children from local schools and Merthyr FE College, alongside a permanent local history exhibition. Its theme? Solidarity and the ever-improving lives of working people; a tale repeated for now how many years? Sixty? Seventy? At what point in its telling did it become a platitude, blunted by repetition?

When I was a teenager, my friend Deborah lived behind the town hall. I envied her, living in town. Just think of all the attractions: the shops, the market, the cafes and of course the pubs (many with staff that weren't too bothered about checking the age of their clientele.) As Deborah's mother would answer the front door, the newly installed central heating would wrap its blanket of warmth around me, even from the doorstep. The other thing I remember is her mother's sandwiches, appearing just minutes after I arrived (refusal was pointless), each slice of bread topped with a shimmering half inch of butter (that golden signifier of post-war peace and prosperity). Later, as we reached legal drinking age, Deborah and I would pop round the corner to the Brunswick, where – in laughable attempts at sophistication – we would eat chicken in the basket with tall, ice-cold glasses of draft Stella.

Today, like other houses in the street, Deborah's old home is a house in multiple occupation. There are few families living there now. And Deborah? She's moved on to a leafy eighties development in Gwaelod-y-garth, the crachach end of town. Semi-retired from her job at the building society (preferential rates on mortgages – Deborah was always the more sensible one), she's married to Keith, her childhood sweetheart. For her children and grandchildren, it's a different story – zero hours contracts, precarious self-employment. The council apprenticeship that her husband had served (as a plumber), the foundation on which they built their secure, comfortable life, is a history as distant to her children as the 1930s hunger marches had been to Deborah and me.

Memory jolts you with a cold, hard slap.

Back at Heroes and Villains, the flyer on my table advertises Mario's Luxury Welsh Dairy Ice Cream and its 'story of a third generation ice cream maker'. So ice cream has a story too.

Merthyr has a story, a story and a half: a powerful, Manichean epic of hardship and solidarity, one it can be proud of. It goes something like this: *We are a town of immigrants. Our ancestors came from rural Wales, the west of England, Spain, even from as far as Russia or Poland, to work in the mines and the steelworks.* It's a story populated by a succession of Welsh industrial archetypes. Firebrand politicians, unscrupulous (yet psychologically complex) ironmasters, along with characters from Welsh valleys central casting: poets and preachers, musicians and actors, writers and artists, entrepreneurs and even a self-made newspaper baron thrown in. (The Merthyr Tydfil Heritage Trust plaque reads, 'Viscount Camrose/ William Ewart Berry, proprietor of the *Daily Telegraph*, born in Merthyr Tydfil 1879.' Well I never.)

The story continues: *In Merthyr we are all proud of our origins, our family history, our Irish or Spanish heritage, proud of the poverty and adversity our ancestors overcame.* Each story is different, but the theme is the same: *The past is the grit that shapes us, makes us shine.* And as we gaze at the past, the present unfolds, its heroes and villains still to be made.

There are other stories too, the ones we choose not to tell; the tension in 1930s Dowlais as locals wanted to ban the Spanish community's annual fiesta. And even the revered Keir Hardy (Merthyr's first Labour MP), back in his native Scotland, railing against the 'Russian Poles' for driving down the wages of Scottish workers, accusing them of bringing in the Black Death and other diseases.

Memory is a liar, a soothing deceiver.

After lunch, I visit Lesley Hodgkinson at Focal Point, a project that supports migrant workers and 'encourages inclusion and social awareness'. Lesley is calm, unflappable, warm. She has worked in the community for decades, she must have seen the referendum result coming? No, she hadn't. She was as shocked by the result as I was. We talk of a kind of grieving process, of having the stuffing knocked out of us, of feeling helpless.

I ask Lesley why she thinks people had voted the way they did. I have to ask it, have to keep an open mind, although I already know the answer.

'Immigration featured highly', she says.

And after the result? 'The fear that went through the immigrant community was potent.'

The 'backlash' when it came could have been worse. It emerged – subtle, muted, slyly cruel – like the techniques of the practised school bully who knows just how far to twist the knife without getting caught. These are some of the typical stories that Lesley has heard: the Polish factory worker whose 'friends' walked straight past him to shake hands with other, Welsh colleagues ('We've got our country back at last!'); the Portuguese woman whose neighbours laughed as they said that now she'd have to pack up her bags and go home ('What you looking like that for? I was only joking.') Oh yes, people know just how far they can go.

So where to from here? 'Stories,' says Lesley, 'There's no use arguing statistics. People follow their emotions. We all do.'

In 1975, those elderly women who came in from the rain to vote against Europe had a point. But I couldn't see it, didn't want to see it. This was the time of the wasteful, shameful Common Agricultural Policy, keeping up prices with its butter mountains and wine lakes. After we joined, the price of butter *did* rise, almost overnight, to fifty pence, just as they had predicted. No, the EEC (nor the EU) was never perfect. Yet now, as we are leaving it behind, it's hard to see beyond it to anything other than a darker, meaner place.

So now it's time – for what? Reflection? Soul-searching? Are we Remainers just middle-class do-gooders, so out of touch with reality that we couldn't see it coming? The accusations have hit hard and some have hit their mark.

On Merthyr high street, I play that bittersweet game enjoyed by someone returning to the scene of their childhood after a long gap – marking what has changed, what has gone. Oh look, my old school, the County Grammar, long demolished and never replaced, the green-lawned entrance still there as if to emphasise its nothingness; the old St Tydfil's hospital, boarded up and decayed; the Miners' Hall, a forest of buddleia; the Gothic-style synagogue-turned-carpet-warehouse up for sale again ('Superb opportunity to purchase a prominent building in the centre of Merthyr.') I am an archaeologist, examining the fragments of my past; or an anthropologist, deconstructing the culture that made me. A sign in the window of the Olde Express (once a disreputable scrumpy den where women were banned), 'A night of clairvoyance and psychometry with Sue Macquade.' At least someone is looking to the future.

Merthyr is a pick-and-mix, an assortment of dereliction and regrowth, gradual decay and bright optimism. Which would you like today? Take your pick – both are available. If it's upbeat you're after, there is the Red House, of course, or that other dazzling showcase funded by lottery/Arts Council monies (as well as those of the EU), Theatr Soar (in a converted eighteenth-century Congregationalist chapel).

If enterprise is more your thing, take a look at Portugales Bar, serene in cream, lime-green and geometric terra cotta (one of three tapas bars in town, run by Portuguese immigrants). Merthyr has always been good at keeping up appearances; scrubbing its own front doorstep, hanging out its rows of starched white sheets. Look closely at those pictures of the 1930s depression, those unemployed men loitering on the corner; each one, to a man, dressed up in his Sunday best.

If it's textbook Valleys council estate you want, then there's the Gurnos, where media reports come with labels like 'infamous' and 'deprived'; where my old youth club, the community centre and the social club are all kitted out with high, horizontal, prison-style strips of glass (vandal-proof by design). The Community Learning Centre (where BBC Wales once filmed a moving documentary on its pioneering access courses for women) is shut down and boarded up; the circle of yellow stars against blue, still above the entrance, had been faded and weather-beaten long before the referendum. EU funding for projects was not to be sneezed at, but it didn't last forever. The Learning Centre was making progress, but changing lifetimes of zero confidence, zero expectations is a knotty one-step-forward, two-steps-backward affair that doesn't easily fit with objectives like 'sustainability' or 'self-generated income'. Of course, the funding was taken up gladly. After three years, when the money was due to be cut off, it would all somehow come alright, wouldn't it?

Outside Pen y Dre High, a banner proclaims 'Aspire, Achieve, Believe'. The building has aged well; it looks cleaner, perkier than when it opened and I had been uprooted from my cosy, decrepit grammar school (four schools were transferred in all). Then, it felt like I'd been exiled to the far reaches of the moon. But we all muddled through it; got lost in featureless corridors, told off by teachers for trailing builders' mud on the vinyl tiles, the 'Lend us one pence love' bullies profiting from our bewilderment.

Past Alder Grove, on the way to the Gurnos shopping centre (where I went mitching with the bad girls, until boredom and driving rain sent me back to school), there are no children's bikes or toys, no sign of the sand-pits and paddling pools that, on a hot summer's day like today, would have been strewn around the grass. Most of the windows are striped with beige vertical blinds; the kind usually chosen by buy-to-let landlords. Past Fir Tree Grove and Palm Road (the name-givers must have really warmed to this tree theme), a row of houses with fresh paintwork and uPVC porches defy the estate's reputation. There is a 'Sold' sign on the house with the gold and black Gothic-style fencing (a nod to the nearby ironmaster's folly of Cyfarthfa Castle?). I wonder where the owners are going, and if the buyer will be measuring up for vertical blinds.

A few miles down the valley, the cavernous Hoover building rattles its emptiness. Opened in 1948 by JW Hoover himself, the factory offered clean, skilled, well-paid jobs for women as well as men. And with it came the swagger of American corporate plenty (subsidised staff canteen, free washing machines for all staff, and, for me, best of all, the two hours of barely contained anarchy that was the annual Hoover Children's Christmas party.) The steel had gone, the coal had long gone, but we had (whisper it) something better. And it came with an American drawl.

Now I'm back in the Red House, climbing the swirling staircase. They're still there, those stained-glass windows. The colours, though – luminescent mint greens and pale mauves – are different, softer than I remember them. A side window reads '1837' and another, '1897'. I don't remember those. In the centrepiece, a framed image of an elderly woman with drooping earrings and a long veil, jewels and ermine on her ill-fitting crown. The image is unmistakable, iconic: Queen Victoria. Where have the scenes of uprising gone? The red flags? And where are all those angry workers demanding justice? So they were a mirage, a delusion I'd built on what? Stories of Merthyr? Etchings in history books, embellished with idealism and downright wishful thinking? Memory again, that unreliable narrator; I wonder what it will make of today. Out on the Heads of the Valleys road, a sign, 'EU Funds; Investing in Wales' peeps out shyly from an overgrown bush. Prematurely rusted, it looks as strange and familiar as a half-remembered artefact.

Liz Jones teaches at the Department of Theatre, Film and Television Studies at Aberystwyth University and is working on a memoir.

THE PALESTINIAN

STORY BY **ROBERT MINHINNICK**

THE WHITE ARSE?

Three words on a piece of paper. That's what the old man called the bird. So I did too. The only time I saw it was in the Gwter Gryn with cliffs on three sides. Not a good place for the tide to catch you.

They're here from April, those white arses. Till they go back to wherever they come from. Grey with that white flash. Close up there's a line on the face like a lightning bolt. Kind of David Bowie cosmetic stripe, the old man said. Made it unmistakable, he thought.

I can't remember the bird's real name. I can't remember David Bowie. But that's what the old man called it.

*

That's a sheet torn from a diary, said Ffrez. April 20th, and his scrawl in pencil. On its own so far, without context. These pages show he wrote constantly about the Gwter Gryn. He was always a beachcomber.

The woman had gathered all the material she could carry, notebooks and magazines. Some of it was dated yet might be unintelligible. It would be a life's work going through those boxes. She had put plastic sheeting over the bale of manuscripts, reading fragments in the evening. But more papers kept turning up.

Most important to her were the old man's letters. Those to her personally she'd added to the hoard. All his correspondence from Festival Island she kept in a plastic wallet.

By doing this she suspected she was joining a game long organised. Was she becoming the old man's archivist? She felt resentful but picked out the first letter.

Dear Ffrez

It was your mother insisted on Ffresni. She was working as a nursing assistant in one of the care homes. There was a sign on a door, 'Ffresni's Room', and she commented on the name. Better than Freshness, she thought. So from way back it was a name your mother wanted. That's how it goes, kid. You end up living someone else's idea....

No, don't blame my mother, she said to herself.
You planned all this.
After skipping a few lines she continued reading:

Took an Abu Dhabi flight. Seven hours, first elated then numbed by gin. Sour Etihad stuff but worked fine. Not a trace of the old problem. Noted there was a library in the terminal so left some books in Arabic translation. I know, I know, but that's what people like me do. Self-publicists till we die. Then the helicopter arrived and the two of us waiting were taken away.... No, we didn't speak, we were well past that.

But I wanted the view. The desert below was the colour of a buzzard's breast.... Kind of frothy coffee. Bird I never liked, by the way. Think I understand why the crows always gang up. Then, a red sun in the Empty Quarter.

And finally the ocean. In the evening light it was indigo. No other word allowed. Some white fringes where the waves broke. I asked the pilot how many islands in the Gulf and he said they're not sure. New islands are being made as we speak. Volcanic activity.

'It's unstable round here,' he said.

I liked that. More than wry.

Then he pointed out Yas Island, which holds Ferrari World. Yes, I drove fast as a young man but most of the writers I know never learned. I think their brains are wired differently. As I get older the more dubious about speed I've become. Ferraris leave me cold. Next door was Warner Brothers. I didn't even glance.

But the last word the pilot spoke was 'there'. When we looked we saw what we'd been promised, 'a dhow-shaped island in a solar sea'. Some marketing type had written that but I was hooked. And green too, our island. Some of the rarest palms transplanted, including those that died out in Baghdad after the Gulf Wars and UN sanctions.

We landed in a compound. I counted three drones and a fleet of Mercedes 4x4s. The island is all dunes and beaches. Remind you of anywhere? But the house is astonishing. They've spelled my name wrong on my stationery, but it's in gold, so fair enough. Bowls of fruit, Portobello gin. Yes, they've done their homework on me. But a quote from Manley Hopkins in a biodegradable tube?... 'In the life I lead now, which is one of a continually jaded and harassed mind, if in any leisure I try to do anything I make no way....' What the...? There'll be another tube very soon....

'Festival Island' we call it. Can't remember its real name. (I know how you love irony, Ffrez.) The only inhabitants had been pearl fishers. Maybe a few remain....

It might be someone's idea of paradise. A real desert island. But the emir who inherited it had once been to the Hay and Toronto Harbourfront festivals, and with oil money he can do anything he wishes. So, Festival Island has become a big ticket invitation.

You've never been on a writing course, Ffrez, but it's along those lines. Science and peace Nobel laureates. An Albanian poet like Trotsky in a Steffano Ricci tie. Then talkshow philosophers from the States, Maharishi economists. With their PAs and personal chefs, their pissed off children and English rose nannies. A festival that lasts six months....

And the punters? Some will park their yachts in Qatar, buying into the next big thing. Namely this. They don't believe they can get it in Marbella.

But why are they here? To breathe the same air as all us geniuses. I kid you not, kiddo. And why me? Friend of a friend's recommendation. Sick joke, maybe. Anyway, I'm one of several writers-in-rez, so I've promised to hand over every gorgeous sentence. But I'm writing about another world. The past. Because I'll always be old school. I'll never catch up with myself.

The girl scowled and turned a page.

The emir even has his own currency. The 'solar dirham' is how we're paid.... No, I haven't met him yet. Maybe he doesn't exist. Pictures are of a tall man with a hawk's nose. Appropriate. These people, how they quarter the world!

The only person I've spoken to is the transport coordinator, Omar Abudeeb. Stepped out of the darkness last night from behind my Mashrabiya wall. I was on my patio, sitting with coffee. A woman in black had brought it. All I have to do is nod and more coffee arrives. Sweetmeats too. That's my latest favourite word. Next, I'll try the cocktails. Just another nod. All beck no call.

Already I'm used to Omar's cigarettes. I know nobody's allowed to smoke here, which is strict for the Gulf, but he ignores the rule. I like that.

Maybe one hundred a day, he said when I asked him.

Don't believe you, I said.

One hundred and ten sometimes, he repeated. And wrote it on the air.

It'll kill you, I said.

I am Palestinian, he said. Should I care?

In the twilight I couldn't tell if he was smiling.

You have a job.

Oh yes.

You speak English....

But not like you.

He might have smiled then. My children are not here, he said. They never can be....

In the dark I could see only the cigarette's glow, the shape of his face. His eyes were invisible but I recalled how they looked in their hollows. Colour of smoke. Hunted, maybe. No, haunted. The other worker I've spoken to is a Ukrainian behind the bar. Yes, bar. Rules are fluid here, it seems. He spoke English too and I imagine his Arabic is non-existent. Part of the tide, Ffrez. As are all of us.

Don't ask how these people arrived on the island. I've stopped trying to make sense of it. Survival of the fittest, kid, or the luckiest, and here's me pretending I have something new to say. And I'll go on pretending till the contract is up....

But solar dirhams, Ffrez! The new currency of sunlight. Getting paid this way feels... honourable. The money is somehow clean. Last evening I watched the solar panels make their final adjustment before nightfall. Black sunflowers counting the steps of the sun....

[Later]

It's morning now. I've been sitting and wondering what I'm really doing. In my garden (yes!) the heat feels like cast iron over my head, but indoors is the drench of aircon. The coffee might not come with cardamom as it did in Baghdad but just one gesture and the woman who hovers like a hummingbird will appear from somewhere.... But all in black. Impossibly modest....

Omar says the women's salons are the best gigs. My first is due in three weeks so no pressure. An interview and reading of the work I begin here. Surely not a big audience. But it's women who feed this culture. Who keep it going with their curiosity. Oil in its barrels, gas in cubic whatever and an obscene amount of money have made the world dull, Ffrez. That's why the emira is ambitious for her island. Maybe it's her mistake I'm here....

I'm looking at her programme now. Zero carbon house building, farming on Mars. The landscape I saw yesterday looked pretty Martian. It seemed to spell out the atrocity of thirst. Worthy stuff, yes, but too late for me. Oh, and a talk titled 'The Promise of Cryonics'. There will be someone explaining how she can freeze memory....

Better start with me, then. I can't recall yesterday without my notebook.

But no need for Omar yet. He's obsessed with his children. Hasn't seen them for a year. I pointed out those children don't exist any more. That they're different people now. I don't think he understood me, which is just as well.

But he's so thin. Skin the colour of olive oil. White shirt, grey slacks but that yellow tinge to him.

I think today counts as my second morning, Ffrez. So another tube has arrived. This one holds a translation: 'The world has not enough to satisfy ambition.' Then a last line: 'Shame won't win the smallest thing.'

Fifteen hundred years old, Ffrez, this poem. I wonder if the emir chooses the quotes himself. Or the emira? Maybe it's done by algorithm? I'm beginning to think they're all personalised. After all, they knew about the gin. So I'm trying to work out what they say about me and what tomorrow's tube will bring.

Record heat here once again, apparently. I thought my highest was 125 °F. But this island beats everything. Perhaps it's the world's first heliocracy....

Ffresni turned another page. At last she'd grown used to the handwriting.

I'd asked Omar to come back when he had time. Got a whiff of those Hollywood Premiums before I saw him. And he looked even thinner to me. Sweat in his armpits. My diminutive Shadrach, smelling of the fire....

Okay, he's missing his children. But I'm missing all of you. I told him I once stood on the Golan Heights and the borders were explained to me. Impossibly complicated. But growing on the hillsides were olive trees. Twisted like Hebrew characters or awkward as the Arabic alphabet. Languages I can't read. But I eat the olives.

She turned a page.

So you've been there? asked Omar.

A mirror smashed by a tank track, I said. That's Palestine. Yeah, I've been. Omar blew smoke.

Well…? he asked.

Look, I said, where I come from there are black plastic bags hanging in the bushes. Bags full of dogshit. Would you rather your dogshit on the ground or hanging in the trees?

Omar laughed at that.

You know what those bags remind me of? I asked. Something I saw in your Palestine.

What?

Pears, I'd thought at first. Hard little pears. Green pears hanging in the trees. But bomblets. Yes, strange word, that. Sounds like something gentle. Something that swings over a cradle. But full of seeds, those pears. Go straight through you. Hard little pears. Hanging in the trees of Palestine….

How typical of the old man, she thought, putting down the page. One thing reminding him of another. They never knew what he was thinking. Flakey or what?

*

Yes, a white arse in the Gwter Gryn. But he couldn't swim, you know. I suppose he was afraid of the water, mangy old lion, though what bothered us was the riptide in his blood.

But the best thing, Ffrez, he used to say, is sand.

Once in the Gwter he told us the sand there felt like hot silk. I remember him saying, 'When people examine the grains they're white and purple and… nothing like sand at all….'

And I wonder whether migrants will ever wash up here. Anything's possible now. But limestone's like razorblades in the Gwter; it would rip a dinghy to shreds. Even if there are coldwater pearls.

Don't think he ever filmed there. But who knows what's in the boxes…? And at least he had the chance to leave something behind….

Notes

THE PALESTINIAN

Whitearse – Wheatear, Tinwen y Garn

From a letter by Gerard Manley Hopkins to Robert Bridges, 1 September 1885.

Lines taken from Gwyn Thomas' translation of 'Gorchan Maeldderw' in *Gododdin: The Earliest British Literature* (Gomer, 2012). Attributable to Taliesin.

Robert Minhinnick is a multi-prizewinning author, and an environmental campaigner. His latest book, the novel, *Limestone Man*, was published by Seren in the summer of last year.

THEORY AND DESIGN IN THE AGE OF INNOCENCE

PREVIEW STORY BY **ALEX BARR**

WE WALKED TO A TREE. THE SUN THROUGH ITS LEAVES AND BRANCHES was warm on my skin. We looked at one of the things hanging on it.

'Right,' he said, 'find a name for that.'

'The pehehehargorribololum.'

Daddy sighed. 'Isn't that a bit of a mouthful?'

I laughed. 'A bit of a mouthful' was a good joke, because the thing hanging there was tasty. I'd tried one and it was sweet and juicy with a small end you could bite to get started.

He said, 'You don't want to say all that each time you refer to it.'

'Why not? Who would I refer to it *to*?'

He smiled – at least I think he did, because I could only look with my eyes half shut.

'To me of course. Or to yourself, to help you think about it.'

'Well how about just the pehehehar?'

'I might think you were laughing.'

'Just pehar, then,' I grumbled. 'Or even pear.'

'Pear sounds fine.'

Daddy moved away and I followed, protesting.

'Where are we going? We haven't finished that tree yet. There are lots of things on it.'

'Yes, and they're all pehars. Pears rather. The one we've just looked at isn't *the* pear, it's *a* pear.'

I pulled a face. I was getting a headache.

'What if I want to refer to that one?'

I pointed to the fruit at the very top.

'You say, "The pear at the top of the tree."'

'You've just said "*the* pear." You said we had to say "*a* pear".' I looked longingly at the treetop. 'Can't I call that one the phlegorog?'

Daddy sighed again. The leaves all around us stirred.

'It's not worth giving them individual names. They don't last long enough. If you don't pick that one soon it'll fall off and rot, and those stripy things you haven't named yet will eat it.' He looked at me with a frown – I think it was a frown. 'Look, talking of stripy things, why don't we leave fruit and name an insect?'

'Fine by me.'

We walked – I walked, he sort of glided – to a clearing, past trees loaded with the things that only yesterday I decided to call mangoes, bananas, and figs. On the grass under the fig tree was a creature with big back legs, the knees back to front.

I said, 'Spregglygoggorus.'

'Sheer cacophony, pathetic,' he spat, showering me with a tropical storm of saliva. 'Find something euphonious.'

I pretended to understand. 'All right, cackledeflumius.'

'Please! Look, an arbitrary relationship between signifier and signified doesn't work well. Just name things for what they *do*.'

'But I want to be original.'

'Originality is overrated,' he said, with some bitterness, I thought.

The thing jumped.

'All right, grassleaper.'

He grunted. 'I don't like that *s* to *l* transition.'

'Not euphonious,' I sneered.

'Just bloody awkward.'

'All right, grass*hopper*. Even though it doesn't hop.'

He nodded. 'Sometimes sound takes precedence over sense.'

We walked on into a clearing. There were two big beasts with clumsy-looking feet, sarcastic expressions and humps.

'Did you design these, Daddy?' (I didn't say I thought they were a disaster.)

'Who else? You think I had help from a committee?'

He sounded so cross I didn't dare ask what a 'committee' was.

I said, 'I suppose it's one name for both.'

'Far more convenient. And please, think expressiveness. Think euphony.'

'Camelammmalamma.'

He raised a huge eyebrow. 'Expressive, yes. Euphonious to a degree. But a sign of the true artist is what he chooses to leave out.'

I could tell which way the wind was blowing. 'All right, camel.'

'Good.'

I studied the beasts. 'They *aren't* the same,' I objected. 'One's got something hanging off its belly.'

'Yes. That's a he-camel. The other's a she-camel.'

Just then the thing on the he-camel started to grow. It stretched and stretched until I thought it might burst. Suddenly the he-camel put his front legs on the back of the other camel and made the thing disappear. He made very strange movements. My skin began to feel hot, and my willy very heavy. I looked down and saw I was stretched to bursting just like the camel.

'What are we to do with you?' Daddy asked.

'I don't know,' I moaned.

'Hmm. It occurs to me that you're the only creature without a mate.' He sighed. 'I'll see what I can do.'

Next morning I was eating a pear – still annoyed because I preferred pehehehar – when Daddy called me. I found him looking at a heap of wool and bone, the remains of a sheep. They seem to die easily.

He said, 'Adam, I'm going to make you a mate.'

'Out of that lot? I thought you made me out of clay?'

He looked around as if someone else might be listening, glowing red like he does when he's cross. Or embarrassed.

'That's as may be. Do you want a mate or not?'

'Well it's not "not",' I grumbled.

'Then watch.'

He took some of the leg bones and stretched them. He squeezed the skull so it was nearly round; I'm not sure how. He did things to the other bones, then laid them all out in the dust, in a shape which I had to admit (feeling my own bones with my fingers) was pretty similar to mine. But I still wasn't optimistic about how she'd turn out.

Sensing my doubts, Daddy said, 'This is *pragmatic* design. Using readily available materials as a starting point.'

'Oh.'

'Or you could call it *elementarist*.'

I began to feel more confident. He obviously knew what he was doing.

'What's elementarist?'

'An element is a structural part that clearly registers in the composition. Preferably of simple geometric form.'

'Great.'

He pulled down some creeper, cleared the tough stems of leaves, and strung them along the bones.

'Now we have an armature. Right. You can help.'

We went to a stream, where he told me to dig handfuls of soft mud from the bottom and put it into his cupped hands. As his hands are very much bigger than mine it took a long time.

'I'm tired,' I said.

'Is that what you'll say to your mate when she asks you to you-know-what?'

'No.'

'No, so keep at it.'

When we had enough we went back to the bones and he moulded the clay around them. I was so excited! It was beginning to look like a real creature. I wasn't sure whether it looked like me, so I went to a still pool to check my reflection. I nearly fell in.

When I got back she was standing up. He was just giving her hair, from the wool from the dead sheep. He put plenty on her head, and quite a lot on her lower belly. I wasn't sure about the body hair.

'What's that for?'

'Ornament. You've got hair there, haven't you?'

'Not as much as that.'

He looked offended. 'Ornament isn't a crime.'

'It's all right, Daddy. I'm sure she'll be great.'

I went close. She had eyes, a nose, and lips like mine, but – maybe my imagination – her face reminded me of a sheep. One of her eyes was bigger than the other.

'I know what you're thinking, Adam. You don't want too much symmetry. It has a deadening effect.'

'Right.'

She was unlike me in having two big lumps on her chest. They were different sizes – to match her eyes, I supposed. Daddy smiled, at least I think he did; when he's glowing I can never tell.

'I made those with implants of that fruit.' (What I later called melon.) 'Do you like them, Adam? When you get to know her you can fondle them. Right, take her away. Oh – you might like to name her first.'

'Unaroonakaboona,' I offered.

Daddy raised a sardonic eyebrow.

'All right, just Una.' To her I said, 'Hello Una.'

'Uechch.'

She sounded like one of those jumping things in ponds. (Must remember – I still haven't named those.)

'Shall we go for a walk?'

'Uh-eech.'

I took her hand and off we went, Daddy watching us proudly.

The sun was going down when we got back. Daddy was lying in the clearing dozing, glowing deep purple. He heard the rustle of leaves as we approached, sat up, and smiled down on us.

'I was tired after all that effort. Well son, how did it go?'

'It didn't. For one thing she doesn't walk right. She keeps falling over.'

'Too much asymmetry, perhaps.'

'And she just makes noises unrelated to any meaning.'

He looked thoughtful. 'Too much reliance on language can lead one astray, you know.'

'Maybe, but also she smells like rotting vegetation. I fondled her – she didn't seem to mind; at least all she said was, "Wer wer" – but her skin feels like tree bark.' Daddy gave another deep sigh, which shook the forest.

'I'm sure the concept is right. The fault must be in the execution. Oh well, back to the drawing-board.'

'What's a drawing-board?'

'Never mind. Your descendants will find out. If you ever have any,' he added darkly.

And off he went, crashing through the bushes. Descendants? What are they? As for Una, I haven't seen her around.

Daddy decided that because I'm such a good 'specimen', whatever that means, he'd try again using what he called *iconic* design.

'I'm going to model her directly onto you. Actually, this may be canonic rather than iconic. Either way, here goes.'

He told me to stand still and started fiddling around behind me.

'Ow, you're hurting.'

He tut-tutted, told me to wait, and went into the bushes. He came back with a length of creeper dripping with sap and held it for me to drink from. Whatever it was, it made me feel good and I couldn't feel what he was up to at my back. All I was aware of was his shadow in the dust ahead of me, his hand busy with a knife and lumps of something – clay perhaps.

I must have dozed off standing up, because the next thing I knew Daddy was tapping me on the shoulder.

'Feel behind you,' he said.

I put my hands behind my back. My back had gone further away! In fact my lower back felt more like a belly. It *was* a belly. A very smooth belly, not hairy like mine. I moved my hands further up. There was something sticking out which I could just about reach – *two* things sticking out. They felt very pleasant, soft but firm, but my shoulders hurt trying to get my arms up to them. I bent forward to see if that made it easier.

'Ow,' said a voice. 'My back.' A musical voice, not gruff and booming like Daddy's, more like a bird singing.

'Who are you?' I asked.

'I haven't got a name.'

Daddy came round and looked down at me, glowing gold, with a huge grin. He spread his hands as if to say 'sorted'. I wanted to call my new companion Deedledeedledurdur but thought better of it.

'I'd like to give you a long name,' I said, 'but Daddy only likes them short. So I'll call you Dee.'

Dee and I spent quite a few days together. She was nice to talk to. When she wanted my attention she bumped the back of my head with hers. She noticed things around the place that I hadn't. 'Look at those birds gorging themselves on berries,' for example. Or after it had rained and the big leaves of the gunnera (as I later called it) were dripping, 'Listen. You can pick out a rhythm.'

When we walked around we had to agree who was going to walk

backwards. We took turns watching camels, sheep, and other beasts mating. 'I'd like to do that,' she said. 'Wouldn't you?'

'Yes.'

But we couldn't. She could just about reach my willy, which was nice, especially as her hands were softer than mine, but it was harder for me to reach what she had instead. I tried bending and putting my hand between our legs, but she complained again about her back.

In the end we fell out. If she said, 'You say such interesting things, Adam,' I wasn't sure she wasn't being sarcastic because I couldn't see her face. When I did a poo she complained about the smell, and when she peed I got annoyed because she couldn't do it properly.

'It's no good,' I said to Daddy one day. 'I need to get her off my back.'

'And him off mine,' Dee added.

'Oh dear.'

'What is iconic design anyway?' I asked.

'You use an existing artefact as a pattern and change one aspect. That's why I built her onto you.'

'We can't watch the moon rise with our arms around each other,' Dee complained. 'I'm tired of taking turns to look at things. And we can't you-know-what like the camels.'

Daddy sighed. 'I'll do what I can.'

One morning I woke with a start. My back and bottom seemed to be on fire. I felt behind me. My bottom had no cheeks! It was horribly flat.

Daddy turned up, glowing amber.

'Where's Dee?' I asked.

'Gone off. You wouldn't like the look of her, Adam. Her back's raw and she's got no bottom.'

'Won't it grow back?'

Daddy looked embarrassed. 'To be honest she doesn't like the look of you either, bottom or no bottom.'

I later learned that, not believing we were the only couple on earth, she'd gone to search for another mate.

Weeks went by. My bum grew back. I kept asking Daddy when he was going to try again, but he just changed the subject, pointing out more plants
and animals for me to name. He quibbled all the time, so it took ages. I
wasn't getting any job satisfaction, or willy satisfaction for that matter.
I kept remembering the feel of Dee's hands, and my hands on her belly,
and feeling sad. Watching animals mate didn't excite me any more. Also, I
didn't see much of Daddy, and began to feel really lonely.

One evening, sitting by a waterfall watching the sunset through the
banana leaves, I heard an unfamiliar voice, powerful and melodious. It
scared me so much I hid among some rocks.

'Run along, dear,' it said. 'Say hello. He won't bite. You-know-who
tried to make him but couldn't get him up and running. I had to sort him
out. Good luck.'

None of it made sense. Whose was the voice? Who was it talking to?
Had to sort me out– how? I sat hunched, waiting for whoever spoke to
go away. After a minute or so there was a rustling in the undergrowth
behind me, and then, amazingly, soft hands on my shoulders.

'Hello Adam,' said a voice – a small voice, not the one I'd just heard,
but just as melodious. More amazingly still, what felt like a warm belly
was pressed against the back of my head.

'I'm supposed to introduce myself.'

I was too scared to turn and look.

'What design are you? Pragmatic? Iconic?'

She laughed, which made her belly tickle my neck.

'So it's true about your upbringing. Oh well, Mummy told me to hu-
mour you.'

'Who's Mummy?'

'Your granny, actually. Which technically makes me your auntie, but
let's leave consanguinity issues aside for now. I've heard you're good at
names. Want to give me one?'

She sounded a bit clever for my liking so I thought I'd impress her with a long one, especially since Daddy wasn't around.

'We don't want too arbitrary a relationship between signified and sig-nifier, do we? As it's evening, I'll call you Eveningdescendsineden.'

'Ridiculous. Find something shorter.'

I thought, Got a mind of her own. Could be trouble. But I didn't care, because she leaned over me, long hair spilling over my shoulder. She smelt like blossom, with an undertone of something rich and exciting.

'What's that thing?' she asked. 'A mushroom growing on you?'

She was right, it *was* growing.

Alex Barr's latest book is *Take a Look At Me-e-e!* from Gomer, a set of stories for children based on life on a smallholding. He recently moved to Fishguard in order to spend less time cutting back brambles. His stories have appeared in leading magazines and have been read on Radio 4. He won first prize in this year's Doolin Writers Competition. This is a preview story from Alex's debut collection, 'My Life with Eva', published by Parthian in the spring.

PENCIL CASE

STORY BY **MARY-ANN CONSTANTINE**

How did it go, love? she says, and he nods and shrugs the way he does and goes upstairs to his room and takes the pencil case out of his bag and puts it in its place on his desk. He puts the other things in their places too, and then sits hunched over on the bed with his tablet and disappears into another world, absorbed and invisible, only shifting position when he becomes aware of his aching arm.

How did it go? she says again, carefully spooning peas and mashed potato so that they do not touch on his plate, and he shrugs and eats, and they let the telly do the talking.

Afterwards he takes the plates and dishes and cutlery over to the dishwasher, which he loads carefully, everything by size and rank, the knives and forks and spoons in separate sections of the basket. His job for the last five years. She drags the ironing board across the room and sets it up so she can see the screen properly, and changes the channel to the programme she has been waiting for, and starts on a pile of school shirts. The chemical smell of clean laundry is so thick it catches in the throat. He sits at the cleared kitchen table and turns his laptop on.

Friday, she says. Bet you're glad, love. You can give it a break tonight.

He nods, makes an effort.

Yes, he says. Having a break; I'll do my city.

She's watching by now, watching the people on the screen, nurses and doctors and people in tears, but she hears him, smiles at him without turning her head. You do that, she says.

And as she watches and irons his stuff he goes in through the gates, unlocking passwords, passing through invisible walls, into the place he has created from nothing. Or from numbers, which are not nothing.

The city is made of glass. Everything in it is transparent. Escalators. Kitchen tables. Trees and flowers of intricate growing crystals, all mineral, all shining, generated by fractals. Tall buildings with light pouring through them. Vehicles, their complex internal engines, levers and cogs and filaments, all perfectly transparent, moving slowly down glassy streets. Water is allowed, he thinks, purified water will be fine, flowing in channels, in clear glass pipes, looping the loop, down the glass streets and in and out of buildings. He decides to work on the water pipes, to focus on getting them to branch out usefully across the city. And it is while he is concentrating on these that he sees briefly, like something flashing across his line of vision, the possible future development of thin, flexible sheet-glass for paper, with sharp crystal implements that etch into it, if anything ever needs writing; though he thinks the people, when they come, will probably communicate in other ways.

She makes tea during the advert break and fetches him a glass of milk. The noise of the kettle masks a new noise, rain on the skylight, getting harder and harder, pushing through the other noises in the room, the bursts of brash music and the voiceovers, the crescendo and click of the kettle. And then there is a crack and a flash, and when it has passed the only sound left is drumming rain, harder and harder, and the room is suddenly, bizarrely, darkened.

She makes a surprised noise in her throat like a cat.

Powercut!

It'll come back in a minute, he says.

It doesn't. Carefully, not wanting to waste it, she pours the not quite boiling water onto her teabag, and fetches the milk out of the fridge again; its hum is silenced and the light fails to come on.

There must be someone to phone, she says. A number.

He goes back to his city. His laptop has three hours and twenty-seven minutes of battery time to run, and he doesn't need to be online. His screen is now the lightest part of the room.

She hunts for the phone in her handbag and then feels her way upstairs to the bedroom in the gathering dark, hunts around by the bedside table. Then she remembers it is downstairs, in her coat pocket; she treads carefully, coming down. The number she rings is her sister, the other side of town. They are also in the dark. Everywhere is out, she says. There's no point ringing, they just say *they're aware of the situation and are working to restore power as quickly as possible.*

Well I'm sure they are, she says, but how long is that? I'm ironing. Well, I was.

Candles, says her sister. Like when we were little, you remember, the storm at Granny Jay's? You got candles?

Maybe, she says, thinking of tiny blue birthday candles in their white holders in a neat ring round his most recent cake. I'll have a look.

They wish each other luck. She remembers her phone has a torch built in. Remembers there are more sensible candles stashed somewhere under the sink. No holders though.

Here, she says, help me put these in bottles, and they get half a dozen white candles set up around the room and light them with one of his dad's old lighters. She is entranced by the way the room moves, by their separate dancing shadows. She sits on the sofa with her cooling tea and sends a couple of texts, but then sees her charge is running low and turns the phone off altogether. The rain drums hard.

Were the questions like what Mr Aikin…?

He shrugs, and makes a quiet noise that could mean anything. But he sees for a moment the paper on the desk in front of him, set perfectly straight, the black explanatory rubric and the words NOW TURN OVER. The questions, he thinks, would be on the other side.

She gives up and goes hunting in a kitchen drawer for a pack of cards, and then moves a couple of candles and settles to playing patience on the coffee table in front of the dead television. The flick and snap of the cards on the wood disturbs him faintly, but not enough to want to move. The city *will* have people, he thinks, he just isn't ready for them yet. They will be all in white, in close-fitting costumes. No pockets, nowhere to hide things. They will move slowly, calmly; they will know what they are about. He starts to fit a room up for the first inhabitants. Perhaps if they could manage on pills, he thinks, it would be easier than food. They would have lots of time for other activities.

After an hour of patience and pottering about she turns on the phone and talks to her sister again. Nothing has changed. Opening the front door she looks out into the street and is amazed by the difference the dark makes, but also rather overwhelmed. She retreats, and decides that the best thing now is just to go to bed, and see where they are at in the morning.

You coming up now? she asks. You must be worn out after today.

He considers this and then agrees with her. They carry the candles up into the bathroom and the two bedrooms and she makes him promise to blow his out the moment he is in bed. Housefires. A split-second's inattention. Candles are the worst, they say. Goodnight now, love.

Lying in the dark with the scent of the extinguished candle lingering and the ghost-ache in his arm making him uncomfortable, he tries to keep himself in the city, but it shimmers and disappears, and now he is waiting outside the sports hall in a queue, with the girls in front whispering and laughing and the boys behind pushing each other surreptitiously, though they leave him alone. Just as they are about to file in they are told that pencil cases are forbidden in the hall, that they are to leave their pencil cases on the trestle-table by the door. He leaves his with the others and finds his seat at a desk far back in the rows and rows and rows of desks that fill the altered hall.

You may begin.

They begin all around him, heads bent, writing hard. He looks at the desk and the paper, and sees that he has nothing to write with, he has left his pen in the pencil case. There are no rules about what to do under such circumstances, none he can remember. It is like a cold skin, the fear of not knowing what to do next. It clings to him. Eventually he raises his hand.

The invigilator is a long way away, at the front of the room, a man he has never seen before, he does not think he is a teacher, perhaps a class-room assistant, someone he has never met. He holds his arm in the air patiently and waits.

The girl beside him has long blonde hair which keeps falling across her exam paper. She pushes it back, keeps writing. He stares straight ahead. His arm is held up high. By now the invigilator has done a preliminary walk round the far part of the room and gone back to sit down.

He feels them all writing fast around him. With his arm in the air he looks directly across the rows and rows of bent heads at the man who sits at the far end of the room, but the man does not look up. Perhaps he is marking or reading. The cold skin tightens. There are no rules about what to do, except the exam rules, which require you to sit and to be silent. He does both. His arm begins to hurt.

The windows to the left have huge slatted blinds to hide outside dis-tractions, but there are glass panes along the top where he can see the sky, the thick heavy warm sky. It is bad weather for thinking. Weather that stifles you. He looks at the sky, at the man who is miles away at the end of the hall, at the paper lying neatly on his desk. Time fills the hall.

His arm aches badly, but he keeps it in the air. The cold skin of panic has warmed to his body now; the situation has ceased to be one he can do anything about. He sits, and is silent, and holds his arm in the air, and waits for the end of the exam, or for the man to see him, whichever hap-pens soonest. Either way he knows it is too late.

Mary-Ann Constantine is the author of two short story collections: *The Breathing* (Planet) and *All the Souls* (Seren). Her debut novel, *Star-shot*, was published late last year by Seren.

LLANMASSIV

Bursts a woman from her door
belting out laughter so hard the paving slabs
shatter under foot, the castle walls crumble
and bells in every belfry clang the type of din
that makes bank-clerks and magistrates
kick chairs away, moon buses, swing shirts
above their heads and chuck them off the bridge,
where the river burbles through culverts,
chases down the weir like some shouty tune
to spiral and eddy as the town rings and families,
giggling, assemble into small dance troupes,
dab glitter on their cheeks in bathroom mirrors,
hotfoot it down staircases so that the door
of every terrace opens in canon along the road
and the children leap, bright as explosions
into the street, set fires in skips, climb lamp-posts,
watch drovers drive their cows in, past lovers,
once estranged, now carousing down the lanes,
and promising always, everything!

'HEARTLAND'

This shit place is forgotten to everyone,
even us people here, nudging each other
in poke-holes, the women laughing loudly
until the men swear.

       In this once-proud-now-shit
place no-one speaks a real language and people
live in dog years, girls popping out kids,
kids dripping off us all our lives.

People of shitplace dug our own hole,
revel in the muck of it and ready for worse.
If we vote it is with eyes on the sky,
spotting flotillas passing like dark clouds.

Bow down, listen a minute now, *clart*,
this here's the heartland that lost its heart.

LAURELS

When Cathy got *Employee of the Month*
the whole team heard by word-of-mouth
and sent themselves by post, to burst
from paper parcels in her porch,
Congratulations Cathy!
                     And the postman
kept yelling, *Cathy, I got another one!*
And delivered Auntie Ally in a Jiffy;
the Finneys in a tube; a woman called Kate;
the old lady who gave Cathy a Smint in a lift;
the woman who lent Cathy *Empowered Choices*
by Lauren D'Lainey on the bus to Tonypandy;
Lauren D'Lainey herself, singing Carly Simon,
resonant, real confident, 'Baby, you're the best'...
(You gotta love Carly, Cathy! Like... hell, yes!)

And those dear, dear cats, Leroy, unlost,
Tuppence, unsquashed, and Dr Strangelove,
with his gifts of pretty, warm wrens.

Jane Houston is originally from Cardiff and now lives near Swansea. She has completed a Literature Wales mentoring course and has published poetry in magazines including *Ambit* and *The Rialto*. She works with children and young people.

MANY TREMORS

do not a woman make. To rectify this, think: radio caverns.
I'd like to sit in my radio cavern and say:
'Could we axe that diver-eared song of muffle-head?'
Let that echo around a little.

Say: 'Let's get ready for your rumble.'
Then put on clothes to make me less of a tremor.
Peter Rabbit fluff socks, cotton pants.
Krasznahorkai's name inside me as an incantation.

Vortex-style overcoat, wellington boots.
Sasquatch hand gear. Pre-heated pill box hat.
Then I'd leave the cavern for a cigarette break.
Take to saying umph 'French Style',

counting my blessings etc,
snowballing myself. Come back in
and play holy moly mother of dogs:
the one you love. Play 'Six Feet Under' by The Unchainables.

Do my disk jockey whirl. Channel the dead
saxophonists of this world
and the last. Say:
'Thank fuck for the voice of the dog.'

As a DJ I'd be styled on hot tamales,
I'd do lashings of sauerkraut.
I'd be Mountain Number 1.
In the mouth of a whale-shaped rock,

I'd indulge my spidery friends, have a yellowed
snacking selection to hand.
I'd be a good icon. Long rid of tremolo.

Nia Davies' *All Fours* is forthcoming from Bloodaxe next year. This is a preview poem from that, her first full-length collection. Hafan/Boiled String published her pamphlet, *Çe koslovakyalılaştıramadıklarımızdanmısınız or Long Words*, earlier this year, and her debut pamphlet, *Then Spree*, was published by Salt in 2012. .

Christopher Cornwell is a poet, originally hailing from Cambridgeshire, who now
lives and studies in Swansea. His work has been featured in *The Lonely Crowd* and
Wales Arts Review for whom he has also contributed criticism and commentary. He
has edited *The Lampeter Review* and is the current editor of newly founded online
magazine, *The Gull*. His work is rooted in verbal experimentation, blending avant-garde
aesthetics with striking Imagism. His first collection, *Ergasy* will be published by the
Lonely Press this spring.

>

CLAY POETRY

6

00:00
The mourning moon is out

In a ditch
A grimoire struck
in the gutter water
gilded with moonstrike.
Fragments like
sherd, potsherd
base and rim,
messages from bottles
pots tops or bases.

Words
skirt like a shine
round enamelled rim
in ancient hand
asleep in the grog,
between times,
unready to be spoken yet again.

Read from the malleable mineral
from which we draw shape
dug-up when dried,
burnt, redried,
reburned and buried yet again.

Pipes, clay pipes of past landworkers,
ploughed into furrows
seven feet deep,
blades scraping the peat,
where ancestors
search in the strata,
layered beneath the striated land,
combing for artefacts in the wake of machines
ploughed edges drawn up,
mounted like cairns,
asleep.

Fragment shapes
buried in the heat of the land,
amongst
the steam-damp
crumbs of freshly churned earth,
interred in the neat,
finished field, tilled and dibbed,
and slick-combed hard back to the scalp
like Sunday-school hair.

Dug up
by now
by scrap glasspaper hands.
Spade clinking stones like
a brace of knocked gault
bricks scraped from the scarps of marl-pits,
deeply grooved and lined with clay
like open legs.

THE FIRE PLACE

No one's in except the sea.
Geta's on the Aber bus
to fix her teeth again, Catrin's
too far out to see her fin.
Is that you, Brown Helen?
I'll make a fire, shall I?

Penllain's out of season,
a vitrine of embers.
I come here when it's empty,
to listen out for you,
your laughter in the walls

to press the shingly bell
before I turn the key and push
into the sandy vestibule.

What is it in you, Helen,
rakes me back to this ingle –
its firedogs and clock
anchored in '69,
its bellows' dusty gills....

And my teeth went CRACK!

A vacant shell still hears.
Come closer to the chimney,
its song to our ears

or is it our mothers
mistaken for the sea?

The bunker's wood is dry.
Helen, it's almost late.
Geta's smile returns
to a kitchen knocked through.
Catrin moors *Gwyneth Blue*
on a new skylight window.

I'll draw these flames to heel.
Your chair is too far away.
The bay is rising now.
Warm your hands on its light.

Tell me you can feel
all our summers in this grate.

Paul Henry's *Boy Running* was shortlisted for Wales Book of the Year 2016.
A Writing Fellow at the University of South Wales, he has presented programmes
for BBC Radio Wales, Radio 3 and Radio 4. paulhenrywales.co.uk

CANALCHEMY

I

Bone 5 lbs	}	Mixed and made into bricks and calcined in the
Lynn Sand 5 lbs		biscuit kiln. The resulting frit is then ground and
Potash 5 lbs		mixed with Cornish clay to suit your mind.

Lucent porcine. Osseous fusion of glue-gun mucilage. We are again in our native country. Nigredo blackening prima materia, primal particles of feldspar flint silica quartz. Winter mornings when frost grips the ropes and makes lock margins treacherous. Up at 4:30 and off by 5. Pupils in varying stages of uniform backpacking into Premier stores. Pebbledashed semidetacheds. Recycling bag lawn-shavings. Half a morning hand-loading paving stone and sacks of flour into the canal boat. Doily netted window bays. Stacked roofs of Rhydyfelin beyond. Grind raw partial. Crushed in water mill. Granular fractions dissolve.

MAIN AVENUE
C01/02 Screwfix
C5.1 City Plumbing Supplies Ltd
C5.2 TO LET
C5.3 TO LET
C6.1 Dougfield Plumbers Supplies
C6.2 HSS Hire
C6.3 Artificial Floral Supplies
C7.2 Birkemp

Frit mix. Silk bisque. Stipple of the neophyte. I dare not name the place we are at fear of my letter being opened. This liquid phase binds the grains of the body together. Water element of emotions letting go of earthly attachments. Leaving Dynea Lock, Land Rover rust drum log pile shed garden, we enter Three Mile Pond. House-plink car stereos. Tiny white petals spot dirt track along the lower slopes of Mynydd Meio's long-abandoned inclines. We were a good deal surprised after the kind and liberal treatment yourself and Mr Billingsley experienced from us, that you both so suddenly left our works. Mallard paddles down shallow channel of moss-rugged walls. Small speckled spider scuttles on rail towards my leaning arm.

> C7.3 Rycon Tool Hire
> C7.B Pirtek (Cardiff)
> C8.1 Tile & Bath Co (UK) Ltd
> C8.2 Costain
> C9 DEVELOPMENT SITE
> C10 Inter-Haul
> C11 Control Gear (Hydraulics) Ltd
> C11a Control Gear (Hydraulics) Ltd

Vertebrae wafers. Tissue-paper slices of pearlish porcellana. My friend informs me that two persons named Walker and Beeley have sent to Government from a small manufactory at Nantgarw a specimen of beautiful china. Corduroy jacket slung on cabin roof, where I keep the lock windlass. Rent-a-car forecourt roof floats past on pillars. Wave of tarmac as I cross road in collarless shirt waistcoat red kerchief. Baggy moleskin trousers tied at bottoms with string. Pinks of honesty and herb robert, bluebells behind palisades. Ferns flourish their spined coils. Garlicky whiffs of lushness. Tincture transmutes alchemical union. Horse bones enamelled. Calcium delicacies.

Steven Hitchins' books include *Bitch Dust* (Hafan, 2012), *Real Radio* (CAD, 2014), *The White City* (Aquifer, 2015) and *Translating the Coal Forests* (Singing Apple Press, 2015). He runs the Literary Pocket Book press, publishing contemporary innovative poetry in miniature origami editions: literarypocketblog.wordpress.com

DESPERATE DAN'S RETIREMENT PLAN

Aunt Aggie's tombstone, black granite
is a hot coal in desert sunset.
It speaks to Dan, his cactus stubble
dusted with grey.

Your bones are rotting,
your muscles fatty
from decades of cow pies,
empty dishes, horns set aside.

The one horse you could ride
is long snapped, a thistle
sucked dry in the arid air.
The sheriff you knew retired,
replaced by a younger man
who put a stop to your danger.
No more blowtorch shaving,
twisting steel girders
into climbing frames
for your niece and nephew
(who never write now anyway).

You're out of time, Desperate Dan:
better work out your retirement plan.

Poet and performer **George Sandifer-Smith**'s children's book, *Cholloo's Birthday*, was published by Lily Publications in 2014.

TIDAL FLATS

26

Am I the dead bull-seal's dream?

And I was suddenly born – right there,
at that moment –
on the sand flats, among sea wrack,
clouds skipping flat across the grey horizon, snake-waves
of sand side-winding east, repetitive crack
of plastic against plastic in the wind; ribs and stones, opening

a tiny perceptual hole....

I gathered twigs, rags, bits of anything I could find
that was dry, tore
paper from my notebook, lit it all on fire, whispered
over the feeble flames the names the seal whispered to me:

Yangtze River Dolphin Caribbean Monk Seal Canarian Oystercatcher
Florida Black Wolf Pyrenean Ibex Japanese Sea Lion
Kona Giant Looper Moth Ivory Billed Woodpecker
Golden Frog Aloatra Grebe
California Grizzly St Helena Earwig

Language, language, rising from the body
of the Aeduella fish shooting through the All Sea, eyes formed
from water to give water sight; water inside muscle
inside water; water
the bone the bone swims through; water's desire
tracking shadows, playing chase with itself: word
that speaks both sides of the skin, reveals skin's illusion, lack
of a precise beginning/end....

And I put a stone in my mouth. I put a stone in my mouth,
let stone speak to stone, found
the fish imprint at the back of the skull, found
the sound of a grey wave sifting through cockles.

Air flushed from fissures between broken shells.
One thousand minute sighs.

Messages from below.

Christien Gholson is the author of the novel, *A Fish Trapped Inside the Wind* (Parthian, 2011), and two books of poetry: *On the Side of the Crow* (Parthian, 2011) and *All the Beautiful Dead* (Bitter Oleander Press, 2016), which was a finalist in the poetry category of the New Mexico–Arizona book award. The poem above is a section towards the end of a series centred around Swansea Bay and Gower. christiengholson.blogspot.co.uk/

Don't miss

CREATIVE & ESSAYS, #114:
A lost memoir and letter of Dylan Thomas:
John Goodby
Stories by Anita Mir & Tony Curtis
Profile of Graham Robb: Ben Skelton

REVIEWS, OPINION & MULTIMEDIA:
Chris Moss on literary festivals
Robert Minhinnick interviews John Barnie
Poetry showcase videos: 'Force of Nature' & 'Models of Behaviour'
My Falling Down House: Jane Joso, reviewed by Ashley Owen
Three Symphonies: Tony Conran, reviewed by Jane Aaron
Y Gwyll & Parch (TV), reviewed by Huw Owen

A memoir of Hokkaido, Japan

Eluned Gramich

Woman Who Brings the Rain

WALES BOOK OF THE YEAR 2016 SHORTLIST

SHORTLISTED FOR WALES
BOOK OF THE YEAR 2016

At 80 pages the perfect stocking filler!
Christmas gift offer on p21

*'Quite beautiful. [The author encounters a culture
that is completely alien] and she does it with a
poet's eye... precisely and vitally. She reads this
unfamiliarity with all her imaginative nerve-
endings open: the effect is quite remarkable...
[reminiscent of] a netsuke [in its] precision.'*

Prof Tony Brown (WBOY adjudication)